ULTIMATE
WORDLE
REFERENCE BOOK

OVER 6,000 FIVE LETTER WORDS, ALPHABETICALLY ARRANGED BY EACH LETTER & TEN WINNING STRATEGIES

D1709506

ISBN: 9798831904765

Cover design by: Adelaide Reed

This book belongs to.....................................

4

CONTENTS

See the table below for the **page numbers** containing the five letter words alphabetically arranged by each of the five letters:

Letter	First	Second	Third	Fourth	Fifth
A	9	56	103	150	197
B	12	63	107	152	198
C	14	63	108	153	199
D	18	64	110	155	199
E	21	65	112	157	202
F	23	70	115	166	208
G	24	70	115	166	209
H	26	71	117	168	209
I	27	73	117	169	211
J	27	78	121	172	-
K	28	78	121	172	211
L	29	78	122	173	213
M	30	81	125	176	215

Letter	First	Second	Third	Fourth	Fifth
N	33	82	127	178	215
O	34	83	130	181	217
P	35	90	134	184	219
Q	39	91	136	185	219
R	39	91	136	185	219
S	42	95	140	188	223
T	49	95	142	190	233
U	52	97	144	193	236
V	53	100	147	195	-
W	53	101	147	195	237
X	55	101	148	196	237
Y	55	102	149	196	237
Z	55	102	149	196	243

THE KEY STRATEGIES FOR WINNING WORDLE

The initial guesses should be the words containing the most common letters,...

According to the Concise Oxford Dictionary, the list of the English letters, ranked from the most common to the least common, is: E, A, R, I, O, T, N, S, L, C, U, D, P, M, H, G, B, F, Y, W, K, V, X, Z, J, Q.

...particularly the vowels.

There are only five vowels in the alphabet and, as noted above, all of them are common in the English language. Checking which vowels are used in the secret word early, gives you much better chances.

Use the words you can rely on.

Find and use the words that combine the most commonly used consonants with as many vowels as possible. For example, SOARE, STARE, ADIEU, CRANE, RAISE, ORATE, ARIEL, PAREO, OATEN, TERAI etc.

Statistically, secret words rarely end with an "S",...

According to an online community Art of Problem Solving, Wordle words rarely end in the letter "S". To increase your chances, you should generally avoid using plurals or other words ending in the letter "S".

...while the following letters appear the most (in order of frequency):

As a first letter: S, C, B, T, P, A, F
As a second letter: A, O, R, E, I, L, U, H
As a third letter: A, I, O, E, U, R, N
As a forth letter: E, N, S, A, L, I, R, C, T, O
As a fifth letter: E, Y, T, R, L, H, N, D

Try using the words that you have not heard of.

You can use a combination of five letters on the off chance that this is a real word, even if you are not sure whether it is. The worst that can happen is that Wordle will not accept it.

Stick to the following principles...

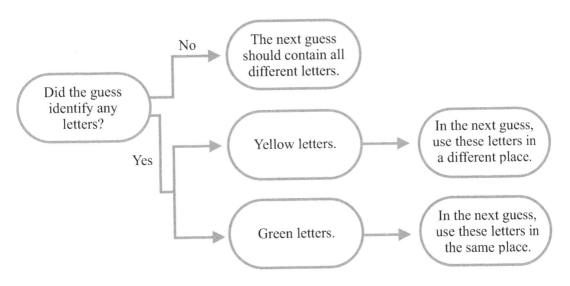

…or not: try skipping the letters you have already guessed in your next guess.

Doing this gives you a higher chance of guessing the remaining letters, without wasting space on the letters you have already guessed.

Pay attention to the alphabet, including the grey letters.

To start with, ignore the grey letters (i.e. those that you have already used, and that are not present in the secret word). If you have guessed any letters, mentally place these letters in various positions, while thinking of the words containing non-grey letters in the remaining positions.

If nothing else works, use the following foolproof strategy:

According to the strategy inventor Greg McKeown, it is all about using as many different letters as possible within your first five guesses. To make the secret word easy to figure out, simply use the following five guess words every time you play: "GLENT", "BRICK", "JUMPY", "VOZHD", "WAQFS" (yes, this is a real word).

Finally, whether you decide to use these strategies or prefer to just guess at random, if you need some help choosing the words, just look in the following sections of this book. Over 6,000 words are arranged alphabetically by each of the five letters, so you can easily find a suitable word and win Wordle every time!

AALII	ABOIL	ACNES	ADOBO	AGERS
AARTI	ABORD	ACORN	ADOPT	AGGIE
ABACA	ABORE	ACRED	ADORE	AGGRO
ABACI	ABORN	ACRES	ADORN	AGILE
ABACK	ABORT	ACRID	ADULT	AGING
ABAFT	ABOUT	ACTED	ADUST	AGIST
ABASE	ABOVE	ACTER	AEGER	AGITA
ABASH	ABUSE	ACTIN	AEGIS	AGLET
ABASK	ABUTS	ACTOR	AEONS	AGLOW
ABATE	ABUTT	ACUTE	AERIE	AGONE
ABAYA	ABUZZ	ACYLS	AFFIX	AGONS
ABBAT	ABYSM	ADAGE	AFIRE	AGONY
ABBEY	ABYSS	ADAPT	AFOOT	AGORA
ABBOT	ACCEL	ADDAX	AFORE	AGREE
ABEAM	ACCUS	ADDED	AFOUL	AGUED
ABEAR	ACERB	ADDER	AFROS	AGUES
ABELE	ACHED	ADDLE	AFTER	AHEAD
ABEND	ACHES	ADEPT	AGAIN	AHING
ABETS	ACHOO	ADIEU	AGAMA	AHOLD
ABHOR	ACIDS	ADIOS	AGAPE	AIDED
ABIDE	ACIDY	ADMAN	AGARS	AIDER
ABLED	ACING	ADMIN	AGATE	AIDES
ABLER	ACINI	ADMIT	AGAVE	AILED
ABLES	ACMES	ADMIX	AGEND	AIMED
ABODE	ACNED	ADOBE	AGENT	AIMER

AIOLI	ALIAS	ALTER	AMISS	ANGRY
AIRED	ALIBI	ALTOS	AMITY	ANGST
AIRES	ALIEN	ALUMN	AMNIA	ANILE
AISLE	ALIGN	ALUMS	AMNIO	ANIMA
AITCH	ALIKE	ALWAY	AMOKS	ANIME
AJUGA	ALIVE	AMAIN	AMOLE	ANION
AKENS	ALKIE	AMASS	AMONG	ANISE
AKITA	ALKYD	AMAZE	AMOUR	ANKLE
ALACK	ALKYL	AMBER	AMPED	ANNAL
ALAMO	ALLAY	AMBIT	AMPLE	ANNAS
ALARM	ALLEY	AMBLE	AMPLY	ANNEX
ALARY	ALLOT	AMBON	AMPUL	ANNOY
ALATE	ALLOW	AMBOS	AMRIT	ANNUL
ALBUM	ALLOY	AMBRY	AMUCK	ANODE
ALCID	ALLYL	AMEBA	AMUSE	ANOLE
ALCOS	ALOED	AMEND	ANALS	ANOMY
ALDER	ALOES	AMENS	ANCHO	ANTED
ALDOL	ALOFT	AMENT	ANCON	ANTES
ALEPH	ALOHA	AMICE	ANDED	ANTIC
ALERT	ALONE	AMICI	ANDRO	ANTRA
ALGAE	ALONG	AMIDE	ANELE	ANTRE
ALGAL	ALOOF	AMIGA	ANENT	ANTSY
ALGID	ALOUD	AMIGO	ANGEL	ANURY
ALGIN	ALPHA	AMINE	ANGER	ANVIL
ALGOR	ALTAR	AMINO	ANGLE	AORTA

APACE	ARDOR	ARROW	ASSAI	AUGHT
APART	AREAL	ARROZ	ASSAY	AUGUR
APERS	AREAS	ARSED	ASSES	AUNTS
APERY	ARECA	ARSES	ASSET	AUNTY
APHID	ARENA	ARSIS	ASTER	AURAE
APHIS	AREPA	ARSON	ASTIR	AURAL
APIAN	ARETE	ARTEL	ASYLA	AURAS
APING	ARGIL	ARTSY	ASYNC	AURIC
APISH	ARGON	ASANA	ATAXY	AUTOS
APNEA	ARGOT	ASCOT	ATILT	AUXIN
APOLS	ARGUE	ASCUS	ATLAS	AVAIL
APPAL	ARHAT	ASDIC	ATMAN	AVANT
APPAR	ARIAS	ASHED	ATMOS	AVAST
APPEL	ARILS	ASHEN	ATOLL	AVENS
APPLE	ARISE	ASHER	ATOMS	AVERS
APPLY	ARMED	ASHES	ATOMY	AVERT
APRON	ARMIE	ASIDE	ATONE	AVGAS
APSIS	ARMOR	ASKED	ATOPY	AVIAN
APTER	AROHA	ASKER	ATRIA	AVION
APTLY	AROID	ASKES	ATTAR	AVISO
AQUAE	AROMA	ASKEW	ATTIC	AVOID
AQUAS	AROSE	ASPEN	AUDAX	AVOWS
ARBOR	ARRAS	ASPER	AUDIO	AWAIT
ARCED	ARRAY	ASPIC	AUDIT	AWAKE
ARCHY	ARRIS	ASPIE	AUGER	AWARD

AWARE	AZURN	BARON	BEANS	BELOW
AWARN	AZURY	BASAL	BEARD	BENCH
AWASH	BABEL	BASED	BEARS	BENDY
AWFUL	BACON	BASES	BEAST	BERET
AWING	BADGE	BASIC	BEATS	BERRY
AWNED	BADLY	BASIL	BEAUT	BERTH
AWNER	BAGEL	BASIN	BEDEW	BERYL
AWOKE	BAGGY	BASIS	BEDIM	BESET
AWORK	BAIRN	BASTE	BEECH	BETTY
AXELS	BAKED	BATCH	BEEFY	BEVEL
AXIAL	BAKER	BATHE	BEFIT	BEVVY
AXILE	BALDY	BATHS	BEFOG	BHUMI
AXING	BALKY	BATIK	BEGAN	BIBLE
AXIOM	BALLS	BATON	BEGET	BIDDY
AXION	BALLY	BATTY	BEGIN	BIDET
AXLED	BALMY	BAULK	BEGOT	BIGHT
AXLES	BANAL	BAWDY	BEGUN	BIGOT
AXMAN	BANDO	BAYOU	BEIGE	BIJOU
AXMEN	BANDY	BEACH	BEING	BIKER
AXONE	BANGS	BEADS	BELAY	BILBY
AXONS	BANNS	BEADY	BELCH	BILGE
AZIDE	BARBS	BEAKY	BELIE	BILLS
AZINE	BARED	BEAMS	BELLE	BILLY
AZOIC	BARGE	BEAMY	BELLS	BIMBO
AZURE	BARMY	BEANO	BELLY	BINDI

BINDS	BLECH	BLURB	BOOBS	BOWED
BINGE	BLEED	BLURT	BOOBY	BOWEL
BINGO	BLEEP	BLUSH	BOOKS	BOWER
BIOME	BLEND	BOARD	BOOMY	BOXED
BIOTA	BLESS	BOAST	BOONG	BOXER
BIRCH	BLEST	BOBBY	BOOST	BOXES
BIRDS	BLIMP	BOCHE	BOOTH	BOYAR
BIRSE	BLIND	BODGE	BOOTS	BRACE
BIRTH	BLING	BOFFO	BOOTY	BRAID
BISON	BLINK	BOGAN	BOOZE	BRAIN
BITCH	BLISS	BOGEY	BOOZY	BRAKE
BITES	BLITZ	BOGGY	BORAX	BRAND
BITSY	BLOAT	BOGLE	BORED	BRASH
BITTY	BLOCK	BOGUS	BORNE	BRASS
BLACK	BLOGS	BOILS	BOSOM	BRAVE
BLADE	BLOKE	BOING	BOSSY	BRAVO
BLAME	BLOND	BOKEH	BOTCH	BRAWL
BLAND	BLOOD	BONCE	BOTHY	BRAWN
BLANK	BLOOM	BONDS	BOTOX	BREAD
BLARE	BLOWN	BONER	BOTTY	BREAK
BLAST	BLOWS	BONES	BOUGH	BREED
BLAZE	BLOWY	BONEY	BOUND	BRIBE
BLEAK	BLUES	BONGO	BOURG	BRICK
BLEAR	BLUFF	BONNY	BOURN	BRIDE
BLEAT	BLUNT	BONUS	BOUTS	BRIEF

BRIER	BUGGY	BUTTE	CAHOW	CANAL
BRILL	BUGLE	BUTTY	CAIRN	CANDY
BRINE	BUILD	BUXOM	CAJUN	CANED
BRING	BUILT	BUYER	CAKED	CANES
BRINK	BULGE	BUZZY	CAKES	CANID
BRINY	BULKY	BYLAW	CAKEY	CANNA
BRISK	BULLS	BYWAY	CALFS	CANNY
BROAD	BULLY	CABAL	CALIF	CANOE
BROIL	BUMPS	CABBY	CALIX	CANON
BROKE	BUMPY	CABER	CALKS	CANTO
BROOD	BUNCH	CABIN	CALLA	CANTS
BROOK	BUNCO	CABLE	CALLI	CANTY
BROOM	BUNNY	CACAO	CALLS	CAPED
BROTH	BURKA	CACAS	CALMS	CAPER
BROWN	BURKE	CACHE	CALMY	CAPES
BRUIT	BURLY	CACTI	CALYX	CAPON
BRUME	BURNS	CADDY	CAMAS	CAPUT
BRUNT	BURNT	CADET	CAMEL	CARAT
BRUSH	BURRO	CADGE	CAMEO	CARDI
BRUTE	BURRY	CADRE	CAMES	CARDS
BUBBA	BURST	CAFES	CAMOS	CARED
BUCKS	BUSBY	CAFFS	CAMPI	CARER
BUDDY	BUSHY	CAGED	CAMPO	CARES
BUDGE	BUSTY	CAGES	CAMPS	CARET
BUFFO	BUTCH	CAGEY	CAMPY	CARGO

CARLE	CAVER	CHAIN	CHEEP	CHINO
CARNY	CAVES	CHAIR	CHEER	CHINS
CAROB	CAVIL	CHAIS	CHEEZ	CHIPS
CAROL	CEASE	CHALK	CHEFS	CHIRO
CAROM	CECAL	CHAMP	CHELA	CHIRP
CARPI	CECUM	CHAMS	CHEMO	CHIRR
CARPS	CEDAR	CHANT	CHERT	CHITS
CARRS	CEDED	CHAOS	CHESS	CHIVE
CARRY	CEDER	CHAPE	CHEST	CHIVY
CARTE	CEIBA	CHAPS	CHEWS	CHOCK
CARTS	CELEB	CHARD	CHEWY	CHOCS
CARUS	CELLA	CHARE	CHIBI	CHODE
CARVE	CELLI	CHARM	CHICA	CHOIR
CASAS	CELLO	CHARS	CHICK	CHOKE
CASED	CELLS	CHART	CHICS	CHOKY
CASES	CELTS	CHARY	CHIDE	CHOLO
CASKS	CENSE	CHASE	CHIEF	CHOMP
CASTE	CENTO	CHASM	CHILD	CHOPS
CASTS	CENTS	CHAST	CHILE	CHORD
CATCH	CERIC	CHATS	CHILI	CHORE
CATER	CERTS	CHAYS	CHILL	CHOSE
CATES	CESTA	CHEAP	CHIME	CHOWS
CATTY	CHADS	CHEAT	CHINA	CHRON
CAULK	CHAFE	CHECK	CHINE	CHUBS
CAUSE	CHAFF	CHEEK	CHINK	CHUCK

CHUFA	CITIE	CLEAT	CLOTS	COCCI
CHUFF	CIVET	CLEEK	CLOUD	COCKS
CHUGS	CIVIC	CLEFT	CLOUT	COCKY
CHUMP	CIVIL	CLEPE	CLOVE	COCOA
CHUMS	CIVVY	CLERK	CLOWN	COCOS
CHUNK	CLACK	CLEVE	CLUBS	CODAS
CHURL	CLADE	CLEWS	CLUCK	CODEC
CHURN	CLAIM	CLICK	CLUES	CODED
CHURR	CLAMP	CLIFF	CLUEY	CODER
CHUTE	CLAMS	CLIFT	CLUMP	CODES
CHYLE	CLANG	CLIMB	CLUNG	CODEX
CHYME	CLANK	CLIME	CLUNK	CODON
CIDER	CLANS	CLINE	COACH	COEDS
CIGAR	CLAPS	CLING	COALS	COHAB
CIGGY	CLARO	CLINK	COALY	COIFS
CILIA	CLARY	CLIPS	COAPT	COIGN
CINCH	CLASH	CLOAK	COAST	COILS
CIRCA	CLASP	CLOCK	COATE	COINE
CIRCS	CLASS	CLODS	COATI	COINS
CISCO	CLAST	CLOGS	COATS	COKED
CISSY	CLAVE	CLOMP	COBBS	COKER
CITAL	CLAWS	CLONE	COBBY	COKES
CITED	CLAYS	CLONK	COBIA	COLAS
CITER	CLEAN	CLOSE	COBRA	COLDS
CITES	CLEAR	CLOTH	COCAS	COLES

COLIC	CONEY	CORAL	COUNT	CRACK
COLON	CONGA	CORDS	COUPE	CRAFT
COLOR	CONIC	CORDY	COUPS	CRAGS
COLTS	CONKS	CORER	COURS	CRAKE
COMAE	CONKY	CORES	COURT	CRAME
COMAS	CONST	COREY	COUTH	CRAMP
COMBE	CONTE	CORGI	COVEN	CRAMS
COMBO	COOED	CORKS	COVER	CRANE
COMBS	COOER	CORKY	COVES	CRANK
COMER	COOKS	CORNS	COVET	CRANS
COMES	COOKY	CORNU	COVEY	CRAPS
COMET	COOLE	CORNY	COVIN	CRASH
COMFY	COOLY	COROL	COWED	CRASS
COMIC	COONS	CORPS	COWER	CRATE
COMIX	COOPS	CORSE	COWLS	CRAVE
COMMA	COOPT	CORVE	COXAE	CRAWL
COMMO	COOTS	COSIE	COXAL	CRAYS
COMMS	COOTY	COSMO	COXED	CRAZE
COMMY	COPAL	COSTA	COXES	CRAZY
COMPO	COPAY	COSTS	COYER	CREAK
COMPS	COPED	COTES	COYLY	CREAM
CONCH	COPES	COTTA	COYPU	CREAT
CONDO	COPRA	COUCH	COZEN	CREDO
CONED	COPSE	COUGH	COZIE	CREDS
CONES	COPSY	COULD	CRABS	CREED

CREEK	CRONE	CRUSH	CURBS	CYANS
CREEL	CRONY	CRUST	CURDS	CYBER
CREEP	CROOK	CRWTH	CURDY	CYCAD
CREMS	CROON	CRYER	CURED	CYCLE
CREPE	CROPS	CRYPT	CURER	CYNIC
CREPT	CRORE	CUBBY	CURES	CYSTS
CREPY	CROSS	CUBEB	CURET	CYTOL
CRESC	CROUP	CUBED	CURIA	CZARS
CRESS	CROWD	CUBER	CURIE	DACHA
CREST	CROWN	CUBES	CURIO	DACKS
CREWS	CROWS	CUBIC	CURLS	DADAS
CRIBS	CROZE	CUBIT	CURLY	DADDY
CRICK	CRUCK	CUDDY	CURRY	DADOS
CRIED	CRUDE	CUFFS	CURSE	DAFFS
CRIER	CRUDS	CULEX	CURST	DAFFY
CRIES	CRUDY	CULLS	CURVE	DAGGA
CRIME	CRUEL	CULLY	CURVY	DAHLS
CRIMP	CRUES	CULTS	CUSHY	DAILY
CRIMS	CRUET	CULTY	CUSPS	DAIRY
CRIPS	CRUMB	CUMIN	CUTER	DAISY
CRISE	CRUMP	CUNTS	CUTES	DALES
CRISP	CRUNK	CUPEL	CUTIE	DALLY
CROAK	CRUOR	CUPID	CUTIN	DAMAR
CROCK	CRURA	CUPPA	CUTIS	DAMES
CROFT	CRUSE	CUPPY	CUTUP	DAMNS

DANCE	DEADS	DEEMS	DEMON	DEVIL
DANDY	DEALE	DEEPS	DEMOS	DEVON
DANIO	DEALS	DEERE	DEMUR	DEWAN
DANKS	DEALT	DEERS	DENAR	DEWAR
DARBY	DEANS	DEETS	DENEB	DHOBI
DARED	DEARN	DEFER	DENES	DHOLE
DARER	DEARS	DEFIB	DENIM	DHOTI
DARES	DEARY	DEFOG	DENSE	DIALS
DARKE	DEATH	DEGUT	DENTS	DIANA
DARKS	DEBAR	DEICE	DEPOT	DIARY
DARKY	DEBIT	DEIFY	DEPTH	DICER
DARTS	DEBTS	DEIGN	DEPTS	DICES
DATED	DEBUG	DEISM	DERBY	DICEY
DATER	DEBUT	DEIST	DERMA	DICKS
DATES	DECAD	DEITY	DERMS	DICKY
DATUM	DECAF	DEKES	DERNS	DICOT
DAUBE	DECAL	DEKKO	DERPY	DICTA
DAUBS	DECAY	DELAY	DESEX	DICTY
DAUNT	DECKS	DELFT	DESIS	DIDDY
DAVID	DECON	DELLS	DESKS	DIDIE
DAVIT	DECOR	DELTA	DETER	DIDOS
DAWNS	DECOY	DELVE	DETOX	DIENE
DAYER	DECRY	DEMIT	DEUCE	DIETS
DAZED	DEEDE	DEMOB	DEVAS	DIFFS
DAZES	DEEDS	DEMOI	DEVEL	DIGIT

DIKER	DIRTY	DOCKS	DOOMY	DOWNS
DIKES	DISAD	DODGE	DOORS	DOWNY
DILDO	DISCO	DODGY	DOOZY	DOWRY
DILLS	DISCS	DOERS	DOPED	DOWSE
DILLY	DISHY	DOGES	DOPER	DOXIE
DIMER	DISIR	DOGGE	DOPES	DOYEN
DIMES	DISKS	DOGGY	DOPEY	DOZEN
DIMLY	DITCH	DOGIE	DORKS	DOZER
DIMPS	DITSY	DOGMA	DORKY	DOZES
DINAR	DITTO	DOILY	DORMS	DRABS
DINER	DITTY	DOING	DORSA	DRAFF
DINGE	DITZY	DOLLS	DOSAS	DRAFT
DINGO	DIVAN	DOLLY	DOSES	DRAGS
DINGS	DIVAS	DOLMA	DOTER	DRAIL
DINGY	DIVER	DOLOR	DOTES	DRAIN
DINKS	DIVES	DOLTS	DOTTY	DRAKE
DINKY	DIVIS	DOMED	DOUBT	DRAMA
DINOS	DIVOT	DOMES	DOUGH	DRAMS
DINTS	DIVVY	DONEE	DOULA	DRANK
DIODE	DIXIE	DONGS	DOUSE	DRAPE
DIPPY	DIZZY	DONNA	DOVES	DRAWL
DIPSO	DJINN	DONOR	DOWDS	DRAWN
DIRGE	DOBBY	DONUT	DOWDY	DRAWS
DIRKE	DOBRA	DOOLY	DOWEL	DRAYS
DIRKS	DOBRO	DOOMS	DOWER	DREAD

DREAM	DRUID	DUNAM	DWEEB	EATEN
DREAR	DRUMS	DUNCE	DWELL	EATER
DRECK	DRUNK	DUNES	DWELT	EAVES
DREGS	DRUPE	DUNGS	DYADS	EBBED
DRESS	DRYAD	DUNKS	DYERS	EBONS
DREYS	DRYER	DUNNY	DYING	EBONY
DRIED	DRYLY	DUOMO	DYKES	ECCHI
DRIER	DUALS	DUPED	DYKEY	ECHOS
DRIES	DUCAT	DUPER	DYNES	EDEMA
DRIFT	DUCES	DUPES	EAGER	EDGED
DRILL	DUCHY	DUPPY	EAGLE	EDGER
DRINK	DUCKS	DURAL	EAGRE	EDGES
DRIPS	DUCKY	DURRA	EARED	EDICT
DRIVE	DUCTS	DURUM	EARLE	EDIFY
DROID	DUDES	DUSKS	EARLS	EDITS
DROIT	DUELS	DUSKY	EARLY	EDUCE
DROLL	DUETS	DUSTS	EARNS	EDUCT
DRONE	DUETT	DUSTY	EARNT	EELED
DROOL	DUKES	DUTCH	EARTH	EELER
DROOP	DULLY	DUTIE	EASED	EERIE
DROPS	DULSE	DUVET	EASEL	EGEST
DROSS	DUMBO	DUXES	EASER	EGGAR
DROVE	DUMMY	DWAAL	EASES	EGGED
DROWN	DUMPS	DWALE	EASTS	EGRET
DRUGS	DUMPY	DWARF	EATED	EIDER

22

EIDOS	EMBED	ENNUI	EQUIP	ETUDE
EIGHT	EMBER	ENOKI	ERASE	ETYMA
EJECT	EMBOG	ENORM	ERECT	EUROS
EJIDO	EMBUS	ENROL	ERGON	EVADE
EKING	EMCEE	ENSKY	ERGOT	EVENS
ELAND	EMEER	ENSUE	ERICA	EVENT
ELANS	EMEND	ENTER	ERMIN	EVERE
ELATE	EMERG	ENTIA	ERNES	EVERT
ELBOW	EMERY	ENTRE	ERODE	EVERY
ELDER	EMIRS	ENTRY	EROSE	EVICT
ELECT	EMITS	ENVOI	ERRED	EVILL
ELEGY	EMMER	ENVOY	ERROR	EVILS
ELEMI	EMMET	ENZYM	ERUCT	EVOKE
ELFIN	EMOJI	EOSIN	ERUPT	EXACT
ELIDE	EMOTE	EPACT	ESKER	EXALT
ELITE	EMPTY	EPHAH	ESPER	EXAMS
ELKES	EMULE	EPHOD	ESSAY	EXCEL
ELMEN	ENACT	EPHOR	ESSES	EXECS
ELOPE	ENATE	EPICK	ESTER	EXERT
ELUDE	ENDED	EPICS	ESTOC	EXILE
ELUTE	ENDOW	EPOCH	ESTOP	EXINE
ELVER	ENDUE	EPODE	ETHER	EXIST
ELVES	ENEMA	EPOXY	ETHIC	EXITS
EMAIL	ENEMY	EQUAL	ETHOS	EXODE
EMBAY	ENJOY	EQUID	ETHYL	EXONS

EXPAT	FAKER	FEATS	FIFTY	FIXES
EXPEL	FAKIR	FECES	FIGHT	FIZZY
EXPOS	FALLS	FEEDS	FILCH	FJORD
EXTOL	FALSE	FEELS	FILED	FLAGS
EXTRA	FAMED	FEIGN	FILES	FLAIL
EXUDE	FANCY	FEINT	FILET	FLAIR
EXULT	FANGS	FEIST	FILLS	FLAKE
EXURB	FANNE	FELLA	FILLY	FLAKY
EYERS	FANNY	FELON	FILMS	FLAME
EYING	FARCE	FEMME	FILMY	FLANK
EYRIE	FARED	FENCE	FILTH	FLAPS
EYRIR	FARES	FERAL	FINAL	FLARE
FABLE	FARSI	FERRY	FINDS	FLASH
FACED	FATAL	FETAL	FINED	FLASK
FACES	FATED	FETCH	FINER	FLAWS
FACET	FATES	FETID	FINES	FLECK
FACTS	FATLY	FETUS	FINIS	FLEEK
FADDY	FATTY	FEVER	FIRED	FLEER
FADED	FAUGH	FEWER	FIREE	FLEET
FADES	FAULT	FIBER	FIRMS	FLESH
FAILS	FAUNA	FIBRE	FIRST	FLICK
FAINT	FAVOR	FIELD	FIRTH	FLIER
FAIRY	FAZED	FIEND	FISHY	FLIES
FAITH	FEARS	FIERY	FIXED	FLING
FAKED	FEAST	FIFTH	FIXER	FLINT

FLIRT	FOCUS	FRANK	FUGGY	GAMIN
FLOAT	FOGEY	FRAUD	FUGUE	GAMMY
FLOCK	FOGGY	FREAK	FULLY	GAMUT
FLOOD	FOIST	FREED	FUMES	GANJA
FLOOR	FOLDS	FREER	FUNDI	GAPED
FLORA	FOLIO	FRESH	FUNDS	GAPER
FLOSS	FOLKS	FRIAR	FUNGI	GARBO
FLOUR	FOLLY	FRICK	FUNKY	GASPS
FLOUT	FOODS	FRIED	FUNNY	GASSY
FLOWS	FOOLS	FRILL	FUROR	GAUDY
FLOWY	FORAY	FRISK	FURRY	GAUGE
FLUFF	FORCE	FRITZ	FURZE	GAUNT
FLUID	FORGE	FRIZZ	FUSED	GAUZE
FLUKE	FORGO	FROCK	FUSSY	GAUZY
FLUKY	FORMS	FROND	FUSTY	GAVEL
FLUME	FORTE	FRONT	FUTON	GAWKY
FLUMP	FORTH	FROST	FUZZY	GAZED
FLUNG	FORTY	FROTH	GABBY	GAZES
FLUNK	FORUM	FROWN	GABLE	GEEKY
FLUSH	FOSSE	FROZE	GAFFE	GEESE
FLUTE	FOUND	FRUIT	GAILY	GELID
FLYBY	FOUNT	FRUMP	GAINS	GENES
FLYER	FOYER	FUBAR	GALAH	GENIC
FOAMY	FRAIL	FUDGE	GAMER	GENIE
FOCAL	FRAME	FUELS	GAMES	GENRE

GENTS	GLEAM	GONAD	GRAPH	GROIN
GENUS	GLEAN	GONER	GRASP	GROOM
GEODE	GLIDE	GONNA	GRASS	GROPE
GERMS	GLINT	GONZO	GRATE	GROSS
GESTE	GLITZ	GOOCH	GRAVE	GROUP
GETUP	GLOAT	GOODS	GRAVY	GROUT
GHOST	GLOBE	GOODY	GRAZE	GROVE
GHOUL	GLOMP	GOOEY	GREAT	GROWL
GIANT	GLOOM	GOOFY	GREED	GROWN
GIDDY	GLOOP	GOOSE	GREEK	GROWS
GIFTS	GLORY	GORGE	GREEN	GRUEL
GILET	GLOSS	GORSE	GREET	GRUFF
GIMPY	GLOVE	GOTTA	GRIEF	GRUMP
GIRLS	GLUED	GOUGE	GRIFT	GRUNT
GIRLY	GLUEY	GOUND	GRIKE	GUANO
GIRTH	GLYPH	GOURD	GRILL	GUARD
GIVEN	GNASH	GRABS	GRIME	GUAVA
GIVER	GNOME	GRACE	GRIMY	GUESS
GIVES	GOALS	GRADE	GRIND	GUEST
GIZMO	GOBBY	GRAFT	GRINS	GUIDE
GLADE	GODLY	GRAIL	GRIOT	GUILD
GLAND	GOFER	GRAIN	GRIPE	GUILE
GLARE	GOING	GRAND	GRITH	GUILT
GLASS	GOLEM	GRANT	GRITS	GUISE
GLAZE	GOLLY	GRAPE	GROAN	GULCH

GULLY	HANDY	HAZEL	HERBS	HOIST
GUMBO	HANGS	HEADS	HERON	HOKEY
GUMMY	HAPPY	HEADY	HERTZ	HOKKU
GUNGE	HARAM	HEAPS	HETRO	HOKUM
GUNGY	HARDS	HEARD	HEXAD	HOLDS
GUNKY	HARDY	HEARS	HIDER	HOLER
GUSHY	HAREM	HEART	HIDES	HOLES
GUSTO	HARMS	HEATH	HIJAB	HOLEY
GUSTY	HARPY	HEAVE	HIJRA	HOLLO
GUTSY	HARRY	HEAVY	HIKER	HOLLY
GUTTY	HARSH	HECKA	HILLS	HOMES
GYOZA	HASTE	HEDGE	HILLY	HOMEY
GYPSY	HASTY	HEDON	HINGE	HOMIE
HABIT	HATCH	HEELS	HINKY	HONED
HACKS	HATED	HEFTY	HINTS	HONEY
HACKY	HATER	HEIRS	HIPPO	HONOR
HADES	HATES	HEIST	HIPPY	HOOCH
HAIKU	HAULM	HELIX	HIRED	HOOEY
HAIRY	HAULT	HELLA	HISSY	HOOKY
HAJJI	HAUNT	HELLO	HITCH	HOOVE
HALAL	HAUTE	HELPS	HIVES	HOPED
HALTS	HAVEN	HELVE	HOARD	HOPES
HALVE	HAVES	HENCE	HOARY	HORDE
HAMMY	HAVOC	HENCH	HOBBY	HORNS
HANDS	HAZED	HENNA	HOICK	HORNY

HORSE	HUSKY	IMMIX	INTRO	JAKES
HORSY	HUSSY	IMPEL	INUIT	JALAP
HOSTS	HUTCH	IMPEX	INURE	JALEO
HOTEL	HYDRA	IMPLY	INURN	JAMBS
HOTLY	HYDRO	INANE	IRATE	JAMMY
HOUND	HYENA	INAPT	IRKED	JANES
HOURS	HYMEN	INCEL	IRONS	JANUS
HOUSE	HYPED	INCUR	IRONY	JAPAN
HOVEL	HYPER	INCUS	ISLAM	JAPED
HOVER	HYRAX	INDEX	ISLET	JAPER
HOWDY	IBLIS	INDIA	ISSUE	JAPES
HUBBY	ICHOR	INDIE	ITCHY	JAUNT
HUFFY	ICILY	INEPT	ITEMS	JAWED
HULKY	ICING	INERT	IVORY	JAZZY
HUMAN	ICONS	INFER	JABOT	JEANS
HUMID	IDEAL	INFIX	JACAL	JEEPS
HUMOR	IDEAS	INGOT	JACKS	JEERS
HUMUS	IDIOM	INLAY	JACKY	JELLY
HUNCH	IDIOT	INLET	JACOB	JEMMY
HUNKS	IDLER	INNER	JADED	JENNY
HUNKY	IDYLL	INPUT	JADES	JERKS
HURLY	IGLOO	INSET	JAGER	JERKY
HURRY	IMAGE	INTEL	JAGGS	JERRY
HURST	IMBED	INTER	JAGGY	JESTS
HURTS	IMBUE	INTRA	JAILS	JESUS

JETTY	JOINS	JUKED	KANJI	KELLS
JEWED	JOINT	JUKES	KAPOK	KELLY
JEWEL	JOIST	JULEP	KAPPA	KEMPT
JEWRY	JOKED	JUMBO	KAPUT	KENAF
JIBBS	JOKER	JUMBY	KAPUT	KENDO
JIBED	JOKES	JUMPS	KARAT	KENTE
JIBES	JOKEY	JUMPY	KARMA	KERFS
JIFFS	JOLLY	JUNCO	KARRI	KERRY
JIFFY	JOLTS	JUNKS	KARST	KETCH
JIGGY	JOLTY	JUNKY	KARTS	KEYED
JIHAD	JONAH	JUNTA	KASHA	KEYER
JILTS	JONES	JUNTO	KAURI	KHAKI
JIMMY	JORUM	JURAL	KAYAK	KHANS
JINGO	JOUAL	JURAT	KAZOO	KHOUM
JINKS	JOULE	JUROR	KEBAB	KIANG
JINNI	JOURS	JUSTS	KECKS	KICKS
JIRGA	JOUST	JUTTY	KEDGE	KICKY
JIVED	JOWLS	JUVIE	KEEKS	KIDDO
JIVER	JOWLY	KAFIR	KEELS	KIDLY
JIVES	JOYED	KAILS	KEENE	KIKES
JIVEY	JUDAH	KAKAS	KEENS	KILIM
JOCKS	JUDGE	KALES	KEEPE	KILLS
JOCKY	JUDGY	KAMAL	KEEPS	KILNS
JOEYS	JUICE	KAMES	KEEVE	KILOS
JOHNS	JUICY	KANAS	KEFIR	KILTS

KINDE	KNOLL	LANDS	LEASE	LIEGE
KINDS	KNOTS	LANKY	LEASH	LIENS
KINDY	KNOUT	LAPSE	LEAST	LIFER
KINGS	KNOWE	LARDY	LEAVE	LIFTS
KININ	KNOWN	LARGE	LEDGE	LIGHT
KINKS	KNOWS	LARKY	LEECH	LIKED
KINKY	KNURL	LARVA	LEERY	LIKEN
KIOSK	KOOKY	LASER	LEFTY	LIKES
KIPED	KUDOS	LASSO	LEGAL	LILAC
KIPES	KVELL	LASTS	LEGIT	LIMBO
KISSY	LABEL	LATCH	LEMAN	LIMBS
KITED	LABIA	LATER	LEMON	LIMEY
KITES	LABOR	LATEX	LENDS	LIMIT
KNACK	LACED	LATIN	LEPER	LINED
KNAPS	LACKS	LATTE	LETCH	LINEN
KNEAD	LADDU	LAUGH	LETUP	LINER
KNEED	LADEN	LAWKS	LEVEE	LINES
KNEEL	LADLE	LAYER	LEVEL	LINGO
KNEES	LAGER	LEACH	LEVER	LINKS
KNELL	LAHAR	LEADS	LEXIS	LIPID
KNELT	LAIRD	LEAFY	LIANG	LISTS
KNIFE	LAITY	LEAKY	LIARS	LITHE
KNITS	LAMIA	LEANS	LIBEL	LIVED
KNIVE	LANAI	LEAPT	LIBRA	LIVEN
KNOCK	LANCE	LEARN	LICIT	LIVER

LIVES	LOOFA	LUCRE	MADAM	MALMS
LIVID	LOOKS	LUDIC	MADLY	MALTA
LLAMA	LOOMS	LUMIC	MAFIA	MALTS
LLANO	LOONY	LUMPY	MAFIC	MALTY
LOADS	LOOPY	LUNAR	MAGES	MAMAS
LOAMY	LOOSE	LUNCH	MAGIC	MAMBA
LOANS	LORDY	LUNGE	MAGMA	MAMBO
LOATH	LORRY	LUNGI	MAGUS	MAMMA
LOBBY	LOSEL	LUNGS	MAHAL	MAMMY
LOCAL	LOSER	LURCH	MAHOE	MANAT
LOCKS	LOSES	LURED	MAIDE	MANED
LOCUM	LOTUS	LURER	MAIDS	MANES
LOCUS	LOUGH	LURES	MAILE	MANGA
LODGE	LOUIS	LURID	MAILS	MANGE
LOFTY	LOUSE	LUSTY	MAINS	MANGO
LOGAN	LOUSY	LYING	MAIRE	MANGY
LOGIC	LOVED	LYMPH	MAIST	MANIA
LOGIN	LOVER	LYNCH	MAIZE	MANIC
LOGON	LOVES	LYRIC	MAJOR	MANIS
LOGOS	LOWER	MACAW	MAKER	MANLY
LOINS	LOWLY	MACES	MAKES	MANNA
LOLLY	LOYAL	MACHO	MALAI	MANNY
LONER	LUBED	MACLE	MALAR	MANOR
LONGS	LUCID	MACON	MALES	MANSE
LOOBY	LUCKY	MACRO	MALLS	MANTA

MANUS	MATER	MEANT	MERGE	MIDGE
MAPLE	MATES	MEANY	MERIT	MIDIS
MARCH	MATEY	MEATS	MERLE	MIDST
MARCS	MATHS	MEATY	MERRY	MIENS
MARDY	MATTE	MECCA	MESAS	MIFFS
MARES	MATTY	MECHA	MESHY	MIGHT
MARGE	MATZO	MEDAL	MESIC	MIKED
MARGO	MAULS	MEDIA	MESNE	MIKES
MARIA	MAUND	MEDIC	MESON	MILCH
MARKE	MAUVE	MEETS	MESSY	MILDS
MARKS	MAVEN	MELEE	METAL	MILER
MARLE	MAVIN	MELON	METER	MILES
MARLY	MAVIS	MELTY	METES	MILKO
MARRY	MAWED	MEMES	METIC	MILKS
MARSH	MAXIM	MEMOS	METRE	MILKY
MARTS	MAXIS	MENDS	METRO	MILLS
MASER	MAYBE	MENSA	METTS	MILOS
MASHY	MAYOR	MENSE	MEWLS	MIMED
MASKS	MAYOS	MENUS	MEZZO	MIMEO
MASON	MAZER	MEOWS	MIASM	MIMER
MASSA	MAZES	MERCH	MIAUL	MIMES
MASSY	MEADS	MERCS	MICAS	MIMIC
MASTS	MEALS	MERCY	MICKS	MINCE
MATCH	MEALY	MERDE	MICRO	MINCY
MATED	MEANS	MERES	MIDDY	MINDE

MINDS	MITRE	MOJOS	MOOLA	MOTES
MINED	MITTS	MOKES	MOONS	MOTET
MINER	MIXED	MOLAL	MOONY	MOTHS
MINES	MIXER	MOLAR	MOORS	MOTHY
MINGY	MIXES	MOLDS	MOORY	MOTIF
MINIM	MIXUP	MOLDY	MOOSE	MOTOR
MINKS	MOANS	MOLES	MOOTS	MOTTE
MINNY	MOANY	MOLLY	MOPED	MOTTO
MINOR	MOATS	MOLTS	MOPER	MOULD
MINTS	MOBES	MOMMA	MOPES	MOULT
MINTY	MOCHA	MOMMY	MOPEY	MOUND
MINUS	MOCHI	MOMSY	MOPPY	MOUNT
MINXY	MOCKS	MONAD	MORAL	MOURN
MIRED	MODAL	MONDO	MORAY	MOUSE
MIREX	MODEL	MONES	MOREL	MOUSY
MIRID	MODEM	MONEY	MORES	MOUTH
MIRTH	MODES	MONGO	MORNS	MOVED
MISER	MODUS	MONGS	MORON	MOVER
MISES	MOGGY	MONKS	MORPH	MOVES
MISSY	MOGUL	MONTE	MORTS	MOVIE
MISTS	MOHEL	MONTH	MOSEY	MOWER
MISTY	MOILE	MOOCH	MOSSY	MOXIE
MITCH	MOILS	MOODS	MOSTS	MUCAL
MITER	MOIRE	MOODY	MOTED	MUCHO
MITES	MOIST	MOOER	MOTEL	MUCID

MUCIN	MURAL	MYNAH	NANAS	NEATH
MUCKY	MUREX	MYOPE	NANCY	NEATO
MUCRO	MURID	MYOPY	NANNY	NEATS
MUCUS	MURKY	MYRRH	NAPPE	NEBBY
MUDAR	MURRE	MYTHS	NAPPY	NECKE
MUDDY	MURUS	MYTHY	NARCO	NECKS
MUDGE	MUSED	NABES	NARES	NECRO
MUDRA	MUSER	NABLA	NARKS	NEDDY
MUFFS	MUSES	NABOB	NARKY	NEEDS
MUFTI	MUSET	NACHO	NASAL	NEEDY
MUGGY	MUSHY	NACRE	NASTY	NEEMB
MULCH	MUSIC	NADIR	NATAL	NEEMS
MULCT	MUSIT	NAGAS	NATCH	NEGRO
MULES	MUSKS	NAGGY	NATES	NEGUS
MULEY	MUSKY	NAIAD	NATTY	NEIGH
MULGA	MUSOS	NAILS	NAVAL	NELLY
MULLA	MUSSY	NAILY	NAVEL	NEONS
MULLS	MUSTS	NAIRA	NAVES	NERDO
MULTI	MUSTY	NAIVE	NAVIE	NERDS
MUMMY	MUTED	NAKED	NAVVY	NERDY
MUMPS	MUTER	NAKER	NAWAB	NERTS
MUMSY	MUTES	NAKFA	NAZES	NERVE
MUNCH	MUTIS	NAMED	NAZIS	NERVY
MUNGO	MUZZY	NAMER	NEARE	NESTS
MUONS	MYLAR	NAMES	NEARS	NETTS

NETTY	NIFTY	NODDY	NORMS	NUDGE
NEUME	NIGGA	NODED	NORTH	NUDIE
NEUMS	NIGHT	NODES	NOSED	NUKER
NEURO	NIHIL	NODUS	NOSER	NUKES
NEVER	NIMBY	NOICE	NOSES	NULLS
NEVES	NINES	NOISE	NOSEY	NUMEN
NEVUS	NINJA	NOISY	NOTAM	NURSE
NEWEL	NINNY	NOMAD	NOTCH	NUTSY
NEWER	NINON	NOMAN	NOTED	NUTTY
NEWES	NINTH	NOMEN	NOTER	NYALA
NEWIE	NIPPY	NOMES	NOTES	NYLON
NEWLY	NIQAB	NONAD	NOTIF	NYMPH
NEWSY	NISEI	NONCE	NOTUM	OAKED
NEWTS	NISSE	NONES	NOUNS	OAKEN
NEXUM	NITES	NONET	NOUNY	OAKUM
NEXUS	NITID	NOOBS	NOVAE	OARED
NGWEE	NITRO	NOOBY	NOVAS	OASES
NICAD	NIVAL	NOOKS	NOVEL	OASIS
NICER	NIXED	NOOKY	NOVUM	OASTS
NICHE	NIXES	NOONE	NOWAY	OATER
NICKS	NIXIE	NOONS	NOWED	OATHS
NIDUS	NOBBY	NOOSE	NOYAU	OAVES
NIECE	NOBLE	NOPAL	NUBBY	OBEAH
NIEVE	NOBLY	NORIA	NUDER	OBELI
NIFFY	NODAL	NORMA	NUDES	OBESE

OBEYS	OGIVE	ONCET	ORATE	OVALS
OBITS	OGLED	ONELY	ORBED	OVARY
OBOES	OGLER	ONERS	ORBIT	OVATE
OCCUR	OGLES	ONERY	ORDER	OVENS
OCEAN	OGRES	ONEST	OREAD	OVERS
OCHER	OHING	ONION	ORGAN	OVERT
OCHRE	OHMIC	ONSET	ORGIC	OVINE
OCREA	OILED	ONTIC	ORIBI	OVOID
OCTAD	OILER	OOMPH	ORIEL	OVOLO
OCTAL	OKAPI	OOTID	ORMER	OVULE
OCTET	OKAYS	OOZED	ORRIS	OWEST
OCULI	OKRAS	OOZES	OSIER	OWING
ODDER	OLDEN	OPALS	OSMOL	OWLER
ODDLY	OLDER	OPENS	OTHER	OWLET
ODEUM	OLDIE	OPERA	OTTER	OWNED
ODIST	OLEUM	OPERS	OUCHE	OWNER
ODIUM	OLIVE	OPINE	OUGHT	OXBOW
ODORS	OLLIE	OPIUM	OUNCE	OXEYE
ODOUR	OLOGY	OPSIN	OUSTS	OXIDE
OFFAL	OMBRE	OPTED	OUTDO	OXLIP
OFFED	OMBUD	OPTER	OUTED	OXTER
OFFER	OMEGA	OPTIC	OUTER	OZONE
OFTEN	OMENS	ORACY	OUTGO	PACED
OFTER	OMITS	ORALS	OUTRE	PACER
OGHAM	ONCER	ORANG	OUZEL	PACES

PACEY	PALMY	PARKA	PATTY	PEATS
PACKS	PALSY	PARKS	PAUCE	PEATY
PACTS	PAMPA	PARKY	PAUSE	PEAVY
PADDY	PANDA	PARLE	PAVED	PECAN
PADRE	PANED	PAROL	PAVER	PECKE
PAEAN	PANEL	PARRY	PAWED	PECKS
PAEDO	PANES	PARSE	PAWER	PEDAL
PAEON	PANGA	PARTS	PAWKY	PEDIS
PAGAN	PANGS	PARTY	PAWNS	PEELS
PAGED	PANIC	PASEO	PAYED	PEENS
PAGER	PANNE	PASHA	PAYEE	PEEPE
PAGES	PANSY	PASSE	PAYER	PEEPS
PAGRI	PANTO	PASTA	PAYOR	PEERS
PAILS	PANTS	PASTE	PEACE	PEEVE
PAINS	PANTY	PASTS	PEACH	PEGGY
PAINT	PAPAL	PASTY	PEAKS	PEKOE
PAIRE	PAPAS	PATCH	PEAKY	PELMA
PAIRS	PAPER	PATED	PEALS	PENAL
PAISA	PAPPY	PATEN	PEANS	PENCE
PALEA	PARCH	PATER	PEARE	PENES
PALED	PARED	PATES	PEARL	PENIS
PALES	PAREN	PATHS	PEARS	PENNA
PALLS	PARER	PATIN	PEART	PENNE
PALLY	PAREU	PATIO	PEARY	PENNI
PALMS	PARGE	PATSY	PEASE	PENNY

PENTS	PETTY	PIETY	PINNA	PIZZE
PEONS	PEWEE	PIGGY	PINNY	PLACE
PEONY	PHAGE	PIGMY	PINOT	PLAGE
PEPLA	PHARM	PIKED	PINTO	PLAID
PEPPY	PHARO	PIKER	PINTS	PLAIN
PERCH	PHASE	PIKES	PINUP	PLAIT
PERDU	PHIAL	PILAF	PIONS	PLANE
PERIL	PHISH	PILED	PIOUS	PLANK
PERKS	PHLOX	PILER	PIPER	PLANS
PERKY	PHONE	PILES	PIPES	PLANT
PERPS	PHONO	PILIS	PIPET	PLASH
PERQS	PHONS	PILLS	PIPIT	PLASM
PERRY	PHONY	PILLY	PIPPY	PLATE
PERSE	PHOTO	PILOT	PIQUE	PLATS
PERVE	PHYLA	PILUS	PISCO	PLATT
PERVS	PIANO	PIMPS	PISSY	PLAYA
PERVY	PICCY	PINAY	PISTE	PLAYS
PESKY	PICKS	PINCH	PITCH	PLAZA
PESOS	PICKY	PINES	PITHY	PLEAD
PESTO	PICOT	PINEY	PITON	PLEAS
PESTS	PICTS	PINGO	PITTA	PLEAT
PESTY	PICUL	PINGS	PIVOT	PLEBE
PETAL	PIECE	PINKO	PIXEL	PLEBS
PETER	PIERS	PINKS	PIXIE	PLICA
PETIT	PIETS	PINKY	PIZZA	PLIER

PLIES	POETE	PONDY	PORNS	PRANA
PLINK	POETS	PONGS	PORNY	PRANG
PLONK	POGEY	PONGY	PORTA	PRANK
PLOTS	POGOS	POOCH	PORTS	PRASE
PLOWS	POILU	POODS	POSED	PRATE
PLOYS	POINT	POOFS	POSER	PRAWN
PLUCK	POISE	POOFY	POSES	PREDS
PLUGS	POKED	POOKA	POSIT	PREEN
PLUMB	POKER	POOLS	POSSE	PREGO
PLUME	POKES	POONS	POSTS	PRESS
PLUMP	POKEY	POOPS	POTCH	PREST
PLUMS	POKIE	POORE	POTOO	PREXY
PLUMY	POLAR	POOTS	POTTO	PRIAL
PLUNK	POLES	POPES	POTTY	PRICE
PLUSH	POLIO	POPPA	POUCH	PRICK
PLUTE	POLIS	POPPY	POUFS	PRICY
PLYER	POLKA	POPSY	POULT	PRIDE
POACH	POLLS	PORCH	POUND	PRIED
POCKS	POLLY	PORED	POUTS	PRIER
PODGE	POLOS	PORER	POUTY	PRIGS
PODGY	POLYP	PORES	POWER	PRILL
PODIA	POMMY	PORGY	POXES	PRIME
POEME	POMPS	PORIN	PRADS	PRIMO
POEMS	PONCE	PORKY	PRAME	PRIMP
POESY	PONDS	PORNO	PRAMS	PRINK

PRINT	PROWL	PULPS	PURSY	QUEER
PRION	PROWS	PULPY	PUSHY	QUELL
PRIOR	PROXY	PULSE	PUSSY	QUERY
PRISE	PRUDE	PUMAS	PUTTO	QUEST
PRISM	PRUNE	PUMPS	PUTTS	QUEUE
PRIVY	PRYER	PUNCH	PUTTY	QUICK
PRIZE	PSALM	PUNIC	PYGMY	QUIET
PROBE	PSEUD	PUNKS	PYLON	QUILL
PROBS	PSHAW	PUNKY	PYRAL	QUILT
PROEM	PSYCH	PUNNY	PYRES	QUIPS
PROFS	PUBES	PUNTS	PYXIS	QUIRK
PROLE	PUBIC	PUNTY	PZAZZ	QUITE
PROMO	PUBIS	PUPAE	QANAT	QUITS
PROMS	PUCES	PUPAL	QILIN	QUOIN
PRONE	PUCKS	PUPAS	QUACK	QUOTA
PRONG	PUDGE	PUPIL	QUAFF	QUOTE
PRONS	PUDGY	PUPPY	QUAIL	RABBI
PROOF	PUFFY	PURED	QUAKE	RABIC
PROPS	PUKER	PUREE	QUAKY	RABID
PROSE	PUKES	PURER	QUALM	RACED
PROSS	PUKKA	PURGE	QUASH	RACER
PROSY	PULER	PURIS	QUASI	RACES
PROTO	PULES	PURRS	QUEAN	RACKS
PROUD	PULLS	PURRY	QUEEF	RACON
PROVE	PULLY	PURSE	QUEEN	RADAR

RADII	RAMPS	RASTA	REALS	REDUX
RADIO	RAMUS	RATCH	REAME	REEDE
RADIX	RANCH	RATED	REAMS	REEDS
RADON	RANDS	RATEL	REARM	REEDY
RAFTS	RANDY	RATER	REARS	REEFS
RAGED	RANEE	RATES	REATA	REEFY
RAGER	RANGA	RATHE	REBAR	REEKS
RAGES	RANGE	RATIO	REBBE	REEKY
RAGGY	RANGI	RATTY	REBEC	REELS
RAIDS	RANGY	RAVEL	REBEL	REENS
RAILE	RANIS	RAVEN	REBUS	REEVE
RAILS	RANKE	RAVER	REBUT	REFER
RAINS	RANKS	RAVES	RECAP	REFIT
RAINY	RANTS	RAVIN	RECCE	REFIX
RAISE	RAPED	RAWER	RECIT	REFUT
RAITA	RAPER	RAYED	RECON	REGAL
RAJAH	RAPES	RAYON	RECTA	REGEN
RAJAS	RAPHE	RAZED	RECTO	REHAB
RAKED	RAPID	RAZER	RECUR	REIFY
RAKER	RAPPA	RAZOR	REDAN	REIGN
RAKES	RARER	REACH	REDDS	REIKI
RALLY	RASES	REACT	REDDY	REINS
RAMED	RASHY	READS	REDID	REJIG
RAMEN	RASPS	READY	REDOS	REKEY
RAMIE	RASPY	REALM	REDOX	RELAX

RELAY	RETRO	RIFFS	RISER	RODEO
RELIC	RETRY	RIFLE	RISES	RODES
RELLY	REUSE	RIFTS	RISHI	ROGER
REMEX	REVEL	RIGHT	RISKS	ROGUE
REMIT	REVER	RIGID	RISKY	ROGUY
REMIX	REVUE	RIGOR	RITES	ROIDS
RENAL	RHEUM	RILED	RITZY	ROILY
RENEW	RHINO	RILEY	RIVAL	ROKES
RENIG	RHOMB	RILLE	RIVEL	ROLES
RENIN	RHUMB	RILLS	RIVEN	ROLLS
RENTS	RHYME	RIMED	RIVER	ROLLY
REORG	RIALS	RIMER	RIVES	ROMAN
REPAY	RIATA	RIMES	RIVET	ROMEO
REPEL	RIBBY	RINDS	RIYAL	ROMPS
REPLY	RICER	RINDY	ROACH	RONDE
REPOS	RICES	RINED	ROADS	RONDO
REPOT	RICHE	RINES	ROARS	RONIN
REPRO	RICIN	RINGS	ROAST	ROODS
RERUN	RICKS	RINKS	ROBED	ROOFS
RESES	RIDER	RINSE	ROBES	ROOFY
RESET	RIDES	RIOTS	ROBIN	ROOKE
RESIN	RIDGE	RIPEN	ROBOT	ROOKS
RESIT	RIDGY	RIPER	ROCHE	ROOKY
RESTS	RIDIC	RIPES	ROCKS	ROOME
RETCH	RIFER	RISEN	ROCKY	ROOMS

ROOMY	ROWEL	RUNNY	SAGAS	SAMEY
ROOST	ROWEN	RUNTS	SAGES	SAMMY
ROOTS	ROWER	RUNTY	SAGGY	SAMPS
ROOTY	ROYAL	RUPEE	SAGUM	SANDO
ROPER	RUBES	RURAL	SAHIB	SANDS
ROPES	RUBLE	RUSES	SAILE	SANDY
ROQUE	RUCHE	RUSHY	SAILS	SANTO
ROSEN	RUDDY	RUSKS	SAINT	SAPID
ROSES	RUDER	RUSTS	SAKER	SAPOR
ROSIN	RUFFE	RUSTY	SAKES	SAPPY
ROTAS	RUFFS	RUTIN	SALAD	SARAH
ROTES	RUGBY	RUTTY	SALAL	SAREE
ROTIS	RUINS	SABER	SALAT	SARGE
ROTOR	RULED	SABLE	SALEP	SARIN
ROUGE	RULER	SABOT	SALES	SARIS
ROUGH	RULES	SABRA	SALLY	SARKS
ROUND	RUMBA	SABRE	SALMI	SARKY
ROUSE	RUMEN	SACKS	SALON	SAROD
ROUST	RUMMY	SACRA	SALSA	SASSE
ROUTE	RUMOR	SADES	SALTS	SASSY
ROUTS	RUMPS	SADHU	SALTY	SATAN
ROVER	RUNED	SADLY	SALVE	SATAY
ROWAN	RUNES	SAFER	SALVO	SATED
ROWDY	RUNGS	SAFES	SAMBA	SATES
ROWED	RUNIC	SAGAR	SAMBO	SATIN

SATYR	SCANT	SCOPA	SCUMS	SEINS
SAUCE	SCAPE	SCOPE	SCURF	SEISM
SAUCY	SCAPI	SCORE	SCUTA	SEITY
SAULT	SCARD	SCORN	SCUTE	SEIZE
SAUNA	SCARE	SCOTS	SCUZZ	SELFS
SAURY	SCARF	SCOUR	SEALS	SELLE
SAUTE	SCARP	SCOUT	SEAMS	SELLS
SAVED	SCARS	SCOWL	SEAMY	SELLY
SAVER	SCARY	SCOWS	SEATS	SELVA
SAVES	SCATH	SCRAG	SEBUM	SEMEN
SAVIN	SCATT	SCRAM	SECCO	SEMIS
SAVOR	SCAUP	SCRAN	SECTS	SENDS
SAVOY	SCENA	SCRAP	SEDAN	SENES
SAVVY	SCEND	SCREE	SEDER	SENNA
SAWER	SCENE	SCREW	SEDGE	SENOR
SAYER	SCENT	SCRIM	SEDUM	SENSE
SCABS	SCHMO	SCRIP	SEEDE	SENTE
SCADS	SCHWA	SCROD	SEEDS	SENTI
SCALD	SCION	SCROW	SEEDY	SENTS
SCALE	SCOBS	SCRUB	SEEKS	SEPAL
SCALP	SCOFF	SCRUM	SEEMS	SEPIA
SCALY	SCOLD	SCUBA	SEEPS	SEPOY
SCAMP	SCONE	SCUDO	SEERS	SEPTA
SCAMS	SCOOP	SCUFF	SEGUE	SEPTS
SCANS	SCOOT	SCULL	SEINE	SERAC

SERAI	SHAHS	SHEER	SHOCK	SHULS
SERES	SHAKA	SHEET	SHOER	SHUNT
SERFS	SHAKE	SHEIK	SHOES	SHUSH
SERGE	SHAKO	SHELF	SHOJI	SHUTS
SERIE	SHAKY	SHELL	SHONE	SHYER
SERIF	SHALE	SHERO	SHOOK	SHYLY
SERIN	SHALL	SHETH	SHOON	SIBYL
SEROW	SHAME	SHIER	SHOOP	SICKO
SERUM	SHAMS	SHIES	SHOOT	SIDES
SERVE	SHANK	SHIFT	SHOPS	SIDLE
SERVO	SHAPE	SHILL	SHORE	SIEGE
SETAE	SHARD	SHINE	SHORT	SIENS
SETTS	SHARE	SHINS	SHOTS	SIENT
SETUP	SHARK	SHINY	SHOUT	SIEVE
SEVEN	SHARP	SHIPS	SHOVE	SIGHS
SEVER	SHART	SHIRE	SHOWN	SIGHT
SEWER	SHAVE	SHIRK	SHOWS	SIGIL
SEXER	SHAWL	SHIRT	SHOWY	SIGMA
SEXES	SHAWM	SHITE	SHRED	SIGNA
SHACK	SHAYS	SHITS	SHREW	SIGNS
SHADE	SHEAF	SHIVA	SHRUB	SILES
SHADS	SHEAR	SHIVE	SHRUG	SILEX
SHADY	SHEDS	SHIVS	SHTIK	SILKS
SHAFT	SHEEN	SHOAL	SHTUP	SILKY
SHAGS	SHEEP	SHOAT	SHUCK	SILLS

SILLY	SITES	SKIPS	SLEDS	SLOSH
SILOS	SITUS	SKIRR	SLEEK	SLOTH
SILVA	SIXER	SKIRT	SLEEP	SLOTS
SIMAS	SIXES	SKITE	SLEET	SLOWS
SIMBA	SIXTH	SKITS	SLEPT	SLUFF
SIMON	SIXTY	SKIVE	SLEYS	SLUGS
SIMPS	SIZER	SKOAL	SLICE	SLUMP
SIMUL	SIZES	SKOSH	SLICK	SLUMS
SINCE	SKALD	SKULK	SLIDE	SLUNK
SINES	SKANK	SKULL	SLIME	SLURP
SINEW	SKARN	SKUNK	SLIMS	SLURS
SINGE	SKATE	SKYEY	SLIMY	SLUSH
SINGS	SKATS	SLABS	SLING	SLUTS
SINKS	SKEAN	SLACK	SLINK	SLYLY
SINUS	SKEET	SLAGS	SLIPS	SLYPE
SIPES	SKEIN	SLAIN	SLITE	SMACK
SIPPY	SKIDS	SLAKE	SLITS	SMAIL
SIREE	SKIER	SLANG	SLIVE	SMALL
SIREN	SKIES	SLANT	SLOBS	SMARM
SIRES	SKIFF	SLAPS	SLOES	SMART
SISAL	SKILL	SLASH	SLOGS	SMASH
SISES	SKILS	SLATE	SLOKA	SMAZE
SISSY	SKIMP	SLATS	SLOOP	SMEAR
SISTA	SKINS	SLATY	SLOPE	SMELL
SITAR	SKINT	SLAVE	SLOPS	SMELT

SMEWS	SNELL	SOARS	SOLOS	SORTS
SMILE	SNICK	SOBBY	SOLUS	SORUS
SMIRK	SNIDE	SOBER	SOLVE	SOUGH
SMITE	SNIFF	SOCKS	SOMAN	SOULE
SMITH	SNIFT	SOCLE	SOMAS	SOULS
SMOCK	SNIPE	SODAS	SONAR	SOUND
SMOKE	SNIPS	SODDY	SONDE	SOUPS
SMOKO	SNOBS	SOFAR	SONES	SOUPY
SMOKY	SNOOD	SOFAS	SONGS	SOURS
SMOLT	SNOOK	SOFTA	SONIC	SOUSE
SMURF	SNOOP	SOFTS	SONNY	SOUTH
SMUTS	SNOOT	SOFTY	SOOKS	SOWED
SNACK	SNORE	SOGGY	SOOKY	SOWER
SNAFU	SNORT	SOILE	SOOTH	SPACE
SNAGS	SNOTS	SOILS	SOOTY	SPACY
SNAIL	SNOUT	SOKEN	SOPHS	SPADE
SNAKE	SNOWS	SOKES	SOPHY	SPAHI
SNAKY	SNOWY	SOKOL	SOPOR	SPAIN
SNAPS	SNUBS	SOLAN	SOPPY	SPALL
SNARE	SNUCK	SOLAR	SORBS	SPAMS
SNARK	SNUFF	SOLDO	SORES	SPANG
SNARL	SNUGS	SOLER	SOROR	SPANK
SNEAK	SOAKS	SOLES	SORRY	SPANS
SNECK	SOAPS	SOLID	SORTA	SPARE
SNEER	SOAPY	SOLON	SORTE	SPARK

SPARS	SPIKE	SPORK	STABS	STAVE
SPASM	SPIKY	SPORT	STACK	STAYS
SPATE	SPILE	SPOTS	STADE	STEAD
SPATS	SPILL	SPOUT	STAFF	STEAK
SPAWN	SPILT	SPRAG	STAGE	STEAL
SPAWS	SPINE	SPRAT	STAGS	STEAM
SPAZZ	SPINS	SPRAY	STAGY	STEAN
SPEAK	SPINY	SPREE	STAID	STEED
SPEAR	SPIRE	SPRIG	STAIN	STEEK
SPECK	SPITE	SPRIT	STAIR	STEEL
SPECS	SPITS	SPROG	STAKE	STEEP
SPEED	SPITZ	SPRUE	STALE	STEER
SPEEL	SPIVS	SPUME	STALK	STEIN
SPELL	SPLAT	SPUMY	STALL	STELA
SPELT	SPLAY	SPUNK	STAMP	STELE
SPEND	SPLIT	SPURN	STAND	STEMS
SPENT	SPLOT	SPURS	STANE	STENO
SPERM	SPOIL	SPURT	STANK	STENT
SPICA	SPOKE	SPYAL	STARE	STEPS
SPICE	SPOOF	SQUAB	STARK	STERN
SPICY	SPOOK	SQUAD	STARS	STEWS
SPIED	SPOOL	SQUAT	START	STICK
SPIEL	SPOON	SQUAW	STASH	STIES
SPIES	SPOOR	SQUIB	STATE	STIFF
SPIFF	SPORE	SQUID	STATS	STIKE

STILB	STONY	STUCK	SUITE	SWAIN
STILE	STOOD	STUDS	SUITS	SWALE
STILL	STOOK	STUDY	SULKS	SWAMI
STILT	STOOL	STUFF	SULKY	SWAMP
STIME	STOOP	STUMP	SULLY	SWANG
STIMY	STOPE	STUMS	SULUS	SWANK
STING	STOPS	STUNG	SUMAC	SWANS
STINK	STORE	STUNT	SUMMA	SWAPE
STINT	STORK	STUPA	SUMPS	SWAPS
STIPE	STORM	STUPE	SUNNA	SWARD
STIRK	STORY	STYLE	SUNNI	SWARM
STIRS	STOTE	STYMY	SUNNY	SWART
STIVE	STOUP	SUAVE	SUNUP	SWASH
STOAT	STOUT	SUCKA	SUPER	SWATH
STOCK	STOVE	SUCKS	SURAH	SWATS
STOEP	STRAP	SUCKY	SURAS	SWAYS
STOGY	STRAW	SUCRE	SURDS	SWEAR
STOIC	STRAY	SUDOR	SURGE	SWEAT
STOKE	STREW	SUDSY	SURLY	SWEDE
STOLE	STRIA	SUEDE	SUSHI	SWEEP
STOMA	STRIP	SUERS	SUSUS	SWEET
STOMP	STROP	SUETY	SUTRA	SWELL
STONE	STRUM	SUFIS	SWABS	SWEPT
STONG	STRUT	SUGAR	SWAGE	SWIFT
STONK	STUBS	SUING	SWAGS	SWIGS

SWILL	SYSOP	TALCS	TANKY	TASTY
SWIMS	TABBY	TALCY	TANSY	TATER
SWINE	TABES	TALED	TANTO	TATHS
SWING	TABLA	TALES	TAPED	TATTS
SWINK	TABLE	TALKE	TAPER	TATTY
SWIPE	TABOO	TALKS	TAPES	TAUNT
SWIRL	TABOR	TALKY	TAPET	TAUPE
SWISH	TABUN	TALLY	TAPIR	TAWNY
SWISS	TACHE	TALMA	TAPIS	TAWSE
SWIZZ	TACHS	TALON	TARDY	TAXED
SWOLE	TACIT	TALUS	TARED	TAXER
SWOON	TACKS	TAMAS	TARES	TAXES
SWOOP	TACKY	TAMED	TARNS	TAXIS
SWOPS	TACOS	TAMER	TAROT	TAXON
SWORD	TACTS	TAMES	TARPS	TAXOR
SWORE	TAFFY	TAMIS	TARRE	TAYRA
SWORN	TAGGY	TAMMY	TARRY	TAZZA
SWOTS	TAIGA	TAMPS	TARSI	TAZZE
SWUNG	TAILS	TANGA	TARTS	TEACH
SYLPH	TAINT	TANGI	TARTY	TEADE
SYNCH	TAKED	TANGO	TASED	TEAED
SYNCS	TAKEN	TANGS	TASER	TEAKS
SYNOD	TAKER	TANGY	TASES	TEALS
SYRAH	TAKES	TANKA	TASKS	TEAMS
SYRUP	TAKIN	TANKS	TASTE	TEARE

TEARS	TENDU	TEXAS	THILL	THYME
TEARY	TENET	TEXTS	THING	THYMI
TEASE	TENGE	THANE	THINK	THYMY
TEATS	TENNO	THANK	THINS	TIARA
TECHS	TENON	THATS	THIOL	TIBIA
TECHY	TENOR	THAWS	THIRD	TICKS
TECTA	TENSE	THAWY	THOLE	TICKY
TEDDY	TENTH	THEBE	THONG	TIDAL
TEEMS	TENTS	THECA	THORN	TIDED
TEENS	TENUE	THEED	THORO	TIDES
TEENY	TEPAL	THEES	THORP	TIERS
TEETH	TEPEE	THEFT	THOUS	TIFFS
TEHEE	TEPID	THEGN	THREE	TIGER
TELCO	TERAI	THEIR	THREW	TIGHT
TELEX	TERCE	THEME	THRID	TIGON
TELIC	TERGA	THERE	THROB	TIGRE
TELLS	TERMS	THERM	THROE	TIKKA
TELLY	TERRA	THESE	THROW	TILDE
TELOS	TERRY	THESP	THRUM	TILED
TEMPI	TERSE	THETA	THUDS	TILER
TEMPO	TESLA	THEWS	THUGS	TILES
TEMPS	TESTA	THEWY	THUJA	TILLS
TEMPT	TESTS	THICK	THUMB	TILLY
TENCH	TESTY	THIEF	THUMP	TILTH
TENDS	TETRA	THIGH	THUNK	TILTS

TIMED	TOADS	TONGS	TORTS	TOYON
TIMER	TOADY	TONIC	TORUS	TRACE
TIMES	TOAST	TONNE	TOSSY	TRACH
TIMID	TODAY	TONUS	TOTAL	TRACK
TINCT	TODDY	TOOKE	TOTED	TRACT
TINED	TOFUS	TOOLS	TOTEM	TRADE
TINES	TOGAE	TOONS	TOTER	TRAIL
TINGE	TOGAS	TOOTH	TOTES	TRAIN
TINGS	TOILE	TOOTS	TOUCH	TRAIT
TINKS	TOILS	TOPAZ	TOUGH	TRAMP
TINNY	TOKED	TOPER	TOURS	TRAMS
TINTS	TOKEN	TOPIC	TOUSY	TRANQ
TIPPY	TOKES	TOPOS	TOUTS	TRANS
TIPSY	TOLAR	TOPPY	TOWED	TRANT
TIRED	TOLED	TOQUE	TOWEE	TRAPS
TIRES	TOLES	TORAN	TOWEL	TRAPT
TIROS	TOLLS	TORCH	TOWER	TRASH
TITAN	TOMBS	TORES	TOWNE	TRASS
TITCH	TOMES	TORIC	TOWNS	TRAVE
TITER	TONAL	TORII	TOWNY	TRAWL
TITHE	TONDO	TORSE	TOWRE	TRAYS
TITLE	TONED	TORSI	TOXIC	TREAD
TITTY	TONER	TORSK	TOXIN	TREAT
TIYIN	TONES	TORSO	TOYED	TREED
TIZZY	TONGA	TORTE	TOYER	TREEN

TREES	TRODS	TRYST	TUPIK	TWINE
TREKS	TROLL	TSARS	TUQUE	TWINS
TREND	TROMP	TUBAL	TURBO	TWINY
TRESS	TRONA	TUBAS	TURFS	TWIRL
TRETS	TROOP	TUBBY	TURFY	TWIST
TREWS	TROPE	TUBED	TURNS	TWITE
TREYS	TROTH	TUBER	TURPS	TWITS
TRIAD	TROTS	TUBES	TUSKS	TYING
TRIAL	TROUT	TUCKS	TUSKY	TYPED
TRIBE	TROVE	TUFAS	TUTEE	TYPES
TRICE	TROWS	TUFFS	TUTOR	TYPIC
TRICK	TRUCE	TUFTS	TUTTI	TYPOS
TRIED	TRUCK	TUFTY	TWAIN	TYRAN
TRIER	TRUED	TULIP	TWANG	TYRED
TRIES	TRUER	TULLE	TWANK	TYRES
TRIGS	TRUES	TUMID	TWEAK	TYROS
TRIKE	TRULL	TUMMY	TWEED	UGALI
TRILL	TRULY	TUMOR	TWEEN	UKASE
TRIMS	TRUMP	TUMPS	TWEET	ULCER
TRINE	TRUNK	TUNAS	TWERK	ULTRA
TRIOS	TRUSS	TUNED	TWERP	UMAMI
TRIPE	TRUST	TUNER	TWICE	UMBER
TRIPS	TRUTH	TUNES	TWICT	UMBRA
TRITE	TRYED	TUNIC	TWIGS	UNAPT
TRODE	TRYER	TUNNY	TWILL	UNBAN

UNBOX	UNWED	VALVE	VICAR	VOILA
UNCLE	UNZIP	VAPID	VICES	VOLAR
UNCOS	UPEND	VAPOR	VIDEO	VOMIT
UNCUT	UPPED	VASTY	VIEWS	VOTED
UNDER	UPPER	VATIC	VIGIL	VOTER
UNDUE	UPSET	VAULT	VIGOR	VOUCH
UNFIT	URBAN	VAUNT	VILLA	VOWED
UNFIX	URGED	VEGAN	VINES	VOWEL
UNFUN	URGES	VEINS	VINYL	VULGO
UNIFY	URINE	VEINY	VIOLA	VULVA
UNION	USAGE	VELUM	VIPER	VYING
UNITE	USERS	VENAL	VIRAL	WACKE
UNITS	USHER	VENGE	VIRGA	WACKO
UNITY	USING	VENOM	VIRUS	WACKY
UNLAY	USUAL	VENUE	VISIT	WADDY
UNLIT	USURP	VENUS	VISOR	WADER
UNMAN	USURY	VERBS	VISTA	WAFER
UNMET	UTILE	VERGE	VITAL	WAGED
UNPEG	UTTER	VERSE	VIVID	WAGER
UNSAY	UVULA	VERSO	VIXEN	WAGES
UNSET	VAGUE	VERVE	VLOGS	WAGON
UNSEX	VALET	VETCH	VOCAL	WAHOO
UNTIE	VALID	VEXED	VODKA	WAIST
UNTIL	VALOR	VIAND	VOGUE	WAITS
UNUSE	VALUE	VIBES	VOICE	WAIVE

WAKEN	WEDGE	WHIMS	WILDS	WOODS
WALES	WEDGY	WHINE	WILES	WOODY
WALKS	WEEDS	WHINY	WILLY	WOOED
WALLS	WEEDY	WHIRL	WIMPY	WOOER
WALTZ	WEENY	WHIRR	WINCE	WOOLY
WANED	WEEPY	WHISH	WINCH	WOOZY
WANNA	WEIGH	WHISK	WINDS	WORDS
WANTS	WEIRD	WHITE	WINDY	WORDY
WARES	WELLY	WHITY	WINGS	WORKS
WARNS	WELSH	WHIZZ	WINZE	WORLD
WARTY	WENCH	WHOLE	WIPED	WORMY
WASHY	WHACK	WHOMP	WIPER	WORRY
WASPY	WHALE	WHOOP	WIPES	WORSE
WASTE	WHANG	WHORE	WIRED	WORST
WATCH	WHARF	WHORL	WIRRA	WORTH
WATER	WHEAL	WHOSE	WISER	WOULD
WAULK	WHEAT	WHUMP	WISPY	WOUND
WAVED	WHEEL	WICCA	WITCH	WOVEN
WAVER	WHELK	WIDEN	WITHY	WOWED
WAVES	WHELM	WIDER	WITTY	WRACK
WAVEY	WHELP	WIDOW	WODGE	WRAPS
WAXEN	WHERE	WIDTH	WOMAN	WRATH
WEARS	WHICH	WIELD	WOMEN	WREAK
WEARY	WHIFF	WIFEY	WONGA	WRECK
WEAVE	WHILE	WIGHT	WONKY	WREST

WRICK	XYSTS	YESES	YUCCA	ZINKY
WRING	XYZZY	YETIS	YUCKS	ZIPPO
WRIST	YACHT	YETTS	YUCKY	ZIPPY
WRITE	YAHOO	YIELD	YUKKY	ZITTY
WRONG	YAKKY	YIPPY	YUMMO	ZLOTY
WROTE	YAKOW	YOBBO	YUMMY	ZOMBI
WROTH	YAMEN	YODEL	YUPPY	ZONAL
WRUNG	YANKS	YOGAS	ZAIRE	ZONED
WRYLY	YAPPS	YOGIC	ZAKAT	ZONER
WURST	YAPPY	YOGIN	ZAMIA	ZONES
XEBEC	YARDS	YOGIS	ZAPPY	ZONKS
XENIA	YARER	YOKED	ZAXES	ZONKY
XENIC	YARNS	YOKEL	ZAYIN	ZOOID
XENON	YAWED	YOKES	ZEALE	ZOOMS
XENYL	YAWNS	YOLKS	ZEALS	ZOOMY
XERIC	YAWNY	YOLKY	ZEBRA	ZOOTY
XEROX	YAWPS	YONIC	ZEROS	
XERUS	YEARE	YONIS	ZESTS	
XOANA	YEARN	YONKS	ZESTY	
XYLAN	YEARS	YORKS	ZILCH	
XYLEM	YEAST	YOUNG	ZINCO	
XYLIC	YEGGS	YOURS	ZINCS	
XYLOL	YELLS	YOUSE	ZINCY	
XYLYL	YELPS	YOUTH	ZINGS	
XYSTI	YENTA	YOWLS	ZINGY	

AALII

AARTI	BASAL	CACTI	CALYX	CAPON
BABEL	BASED	CADDY	CAMAS	CAPUT
BACON	BASES	CADET	CAMEL	CARAT
BADGE	BASIC	CADGE	CAMEO	CARDI
BADLY	BASIL	CADRE	CAMES	CARDS
BAGEL	BASIN	CAFES	CAMOS	CARED
BAGGY	BASIS	CAFFS	CAMPI	CARER
BAIRN	BASTE	CAGED	CAMPO	CARES
BAKED	BATCH	CAGES	CAMPS	CARET
BAKER	BATHE	CAGEY	CAMPY	CARGO
BALDY	BATHS	CAHOW	CANAL	CARLE
BALKY	BATIK	CAIRN	CANDY	CARNY
BALLS	BATON	CAJUN	CANED	CAROB
BALLY	BATTY	CAKED	CANES	CAROL
BALMY	BAULK	CAKES	CANID	CAROM
BANAL	BAWDY	CAKEY	CANNA	CARPI
BANDO	BAYOU	CALFS	CANNY	CARPS
BANDY	CABAL	CALIF	CANOE	CARRS
BANGS	CABBY	CALIX	CANON	CARRY
BANNS	CABER	CALKS	CANTO	CARTE
BARBS	CABIN	CALLA	CANTS	CARTS
BARED	CABLE	CALLI	CANTY	CARUS
BARGE	CACAO	CALLS	CAPED	CARVE
BARMY	CACAS	CALMS	CAPER	CASAS
BARON	CACHE	CALMY	CAPES	CASED

CASES	DALES	DAVIT	FACED	FATAL
CASKS	DALLY	DAWNS	FACES	FATED
CASTE	DAMAR	DAYER	FACET	FATES
CASTS	DAMES	DAZED	FACTS	FATLY
CATCH	DAMNS	DAZES	FADDY	FATTY
CATER	DANCE	EAGER	FADED	FAUGH
CATES	DANDY	EAGLE	FADES	FAULT
CATTY	DANIO	EAGRE	FAILS	FAUNA
CAULK	DANKS	EARED	FAINT	FAVOR
CAUSE	DARBY	EARLE	FAIRY	FAZED
CAVER	DARED	EARLS	FAITH	GABBY
CAVES	DARER	EARLY	FAKED	GABLE
CAVIL	DARES	EARNS	FAKER	GAFFE
DACHA	DARKE	EARNT	FAKIR	GAILY
DACKS	DARKS	EARTH	FALLS	GAINS
DADAS	DARKY	EASED	FALSE	GALAH
DADDY	DARTS	EASEL	FAMED	GAMER
DADOS	DATED	EASER	FANCY	GAMES
DAFFS	DATER	EASES	FANGS	GAMIN
DAFFY	DATES	EASTS	FANNE	GAMMY
DAGGA	DATUM	EATED	FANNY	GAMUT
DAHLS	DAUBE	EATEN	FARCE	GANJA
DAILY	DAUBS	EATER	FARED	GAPED
DAIRY	DAUNT	EAVES	FARES	GAPER
DAISY	DAVID	FABLE	FARSI	GARBO

GASPS	HAPPY	JACAL	KAILS	LADDU
GASSY	HARAM	JACKS	KAKAS	LADEN
GAUDY	HARDS	JACKY	KALES	LADLE
GAUGE	HARDY	JACOB	KAMAL	LAGER
GAUNT	HAREM	JADED	KAMES	LAHAR
GAUZE	HARMS	JADES	KANAS	LAIRD
GAUZY	HARPY	JAGER	KANJI	LAITY
GAVEL	HARRY	JAGGS	KAPOK	LAMIA
GAWKY	HARSH	JAGGY	KAPPA	LANAI
GAZED	HASTE	JAILS	KAPUT	LANCE
GAZES	HASTY	JAKES	KAPUT	LANDS
HABIT	HATCH	JALAP	KARAT	LANKY
HACKS	HATED	JALEO	KARMA	LAPSE
HACKY	HATER	JAMBS	KARRI	LARDY
HADES	HATES	JAMMY	KARST	LARGE
HAIKU	HAULM	JANES	KARTS	LARKY
HAIRY	HAULT	JANUS	KASHA	LARVA
HAJJI	HAUNT	JAPAN	KAURI	LASER
HALAL	HAUTE	JAPED	KAYAK	LASSO
HALTS	HAVEN	JAPER	KAZOO	LASTS
HALVE	HAVES	JAPES	LABEL	LATCH
HAMMY	HAVOC	JAUNT	LABIA	LATER
HANDS	HAZED	JAWED	LABOR	LATEX
HANDY	HAZEL	JAZZY	LACED	LATIN
HANGS	JABOT	KAFIR	LACKS	LATTE

LAUGH	MAIST	MANIA	MASER	MAYBE
LAWKS	MAIZE	MANIC	MASHY	MAYOR
LAYER	MAJOR	MANIS	MASKS	MAYOS
MACAW	MAKER	MANLY	MASON	MAZER
MACES	MAKES	MANNA	MASSA	MAZES
MACHO	MALAI	MANNY	MASSY	NABES
MACLE	MALAR	MANOR	MASTS	NABLA
MACON	MALES	MANSE	MATCH	NABOB
MACRO	MALLS	MANTA	MATED	NACHO
MADAM	MALMS	MANUS	MATER	NACRE
MADLY	MALTA	MAPLE	MATES	NADIR
MAFIA	MALTS	MARCH	MATEY	NAGAS
MAFIC	MALTY	MARCS	MATHS	NAGGY
MAGES	MAMAS	MARDY	MATTE	NAIAD
MAGIC	MAMBA	MARES	MATTY	NAILS
MAGMA	MAMBO	MARGE	MATZO	NAILY
MAGUS	MAMMA	MARGO	MAULS	NAIRA
MAHAL	MAMMY	MARIA	MAUND	NAIVE
MAHOE	MANAT	MARKE	MAUVE	NAKED
MAIDE	MANED	MARKS	MAVEN	NAKER
MAIDS	MANES	MARLE	MAVIN	NAKFA
MAILE	MANGA	MARLY	MAVIS	NAMED
MAILS	MANGE	MARRY	MAWED	NAMER
MAINS	MANGO	MARSH	MAXIM	NAMES
MAIRE	MANGY	MARTS	MAXIS	NANAS

NANCY	OARED	PAINT	PAPAL	PASTY
NANNY	OASES	PAIRE	PAPAS	PATCH
NAPPE	OASIS	PAIRS	PAPER	PATED
NAPPY	OASTS	PAISA	PAPPY	PATEN
NARCO	OATER	PALEA	PARCH	PATER
NARES	OATHS	PALED	PARED	PATES
NARKS	OAVES	PALES	PAREN	PATHS
NARKY	PACED	PALLS	PARER	PATIN
NASAL	PACER	PALLY	PAREU	PATIO
NASTY	PACES	PALMS	PARGE	PATSY
NATAL	PACEY	PALMY	PARKA	PATTY
NATCH	PACKS	PALSY	PARKS	PAUCE
NATES	PACTS	PAMPA	PARKY	PAUSE
NATTY	PADDY	PANDA	PARLE	PAVED
NAVAL	PADRE	PANED	PAROL	PAVER
NAVEL	PAEAN	PANEL	PARRY	PAWED
NAVES	PAEDO	PANES	PARSE	PAWER
NAVIE	PAEON	PANGA	PARTS	PAWKY
NAVVY	PAGAN	PANGS	PARTY	PAWNS
NAWAB	PAGED	PANIC	PASEO	PAYED
NAZES	PAGER	PANNE	PASHA	PAYEE
NAZIS	PAGES	PANSY	PASSE	PAYER
OAKED	PAGRI	PANTO	PASTA	PAYOR
OAKEN	PAILS	PANTS	PASTE	QANAT
OAKUM	PAINS	PANTY	PASTS	RABBI

RABIC	RAJAS	RAPHE	RAZED	SAKES
RABID	RAKED	RAPID	RAZER	SALAD
RACED	RAKER	RAPPA	RAZOR	SALAL
RACER	RAKES	RARER	SABER	SALAT
RACES	RALLY	RASES	SABLE	SALEP
RACKS	RAMED	RASHY	SABOT	SALES
RACON	RAMEN	RASPS	SABRA	SALLY
RADAR	RAMIE	RASPY	SABRE	SALMI
RADII	RAMPS	RASTA	SACKS	SALON
RADIO	RAMUS	RATCH	SACRA	SALSA
RADIX	RANCH	RATED	SADES	SALTS
RADON	RANDS	RATEL	SADHU	SALTY
RAFTS	RANDY	RATER	SADLY	SALVE
RAGED	RANEE	RATES	SAFER	SALVO
RAGER	RANGA	RATHE	SAFES	SAMBA
RAGES	RANGE	RATIO	SAGAR	SAMBO
RAGGY	RANGI	RATTY	SAGAS	SAMEY
RAIDS	RANGY	RAVEL	SAGES	SAMMY
RAILE	RANIS	RAVEN	SAGGY	SAMPS
RAILS	RANKE	RAVER	SAGUM	SANDO
RAINS	RANKS	RAVES	SAHIB	SANDS
RAINY	RANTS	RAVIN	SAILE	SANDY
RAISE	RAPED	RAWER	SAILS	SANTO
RAITA	RAPER	RAYED	SAINT	SAPID
RAJAH	RAPES	RAYON	SAKER	SAPOR

SAPPY	SAVES	TAINT	TANGI	TARTY
SARAH	SAVIN	TAKED	TANGO	TASED
SAREE	SAVOR	TAKEN	TANGS	TASER
SARGE	SAVOY	TAKER	TANGY	TASES
SARIN	SAVVY	TAKES	TANKA	TASKS
SARIS	SAWER	TAKIN	TANKS	TASTE
SARKS	SAYER	TALCS	TANKY	TASTY
SARKY	TABBY	TALCY	TANSY	TATER
SAROD	TABES	TALED	TANTO	TATHS
SASSE	TABLA	TALES	TAPED	TATTS
SASSY	TABLE	TALKE	TAPER	TATTY
SATAN	TABOO	TALKS	TAPES	TAUNT
SATAY	TABOR	TALKY	TAPET	TAUPE
SATED	TABUN	TALLY	TAPIR	TAWNY
SATES	TACHE	TALMA	TAPIS	TAWSE
SATIN	TACHS	TALON	TARDY	TAXED
SATYR	TACIT	TALUS	TARED	TAXER
SAUCE	TACKS	TAMAS	TARES	TAXES
SAUCY	TACKY	TAMED	TARNS	TAXIS
SAULT	TACOS	TAMER	TAROT	TAXON
SAUNA	TACTS	TAMES	TARPS	TAXOR
SAURY	TAFFY	TAMIS	TARRE	TAYRA
SAUTE	TAGGY	TAMMY	TARRY	TAZZA
SAVED	TAIGA	TAMPS	TARSI	TAZZE
SAVER	TAILS	TANGA	TARTS	VAGUE

VALET	WAKEN	YAKOW	ABATE	ABUTT
VALID	WALES	YAMEN	ABAYA	ABUZZ
VALOR	WALKS	YANKS	ABBAT	ABYSM
VALUE	WALLS	YAPPS	ABBEY	ABYSS
VALVE	WALTZ	YAPPY	ABBOT	EBBED
VAPID	WANED	YARDS	ABEAM	EBONS
VAPOR	WANNA	YARER	ABEAR	EBONY
VASTY	WANTS	YARNS	ABELE	IBLIS
VATIC	WARES	YAWED	ABEND	OBEAH
VAULT	WARNS	YAWNS	ABETS	OBELI
VAUNT	WARTY	YAWNY	ABHOR	OBESE
WACKE	WASHY	YAWPS	ABIDE	OBEYS
WACKO	WASPY	ZAIRE	ABLED	OBITS
WACKY	WASTE	ZAKAT	ABLER	OBOES
WADDY	WATCH	ZAMIA	ABLES	ACCEL
WADER	WATER	ZAPPY	ABODE	ACCUS
WAFER	WAULK	ZAXES	ABOIL	ACERB
WAGED	WAVED	ZAYIN	ABORD	ACHED
WAGER	WAVER	ABACA	ABORE	ACHES
WAGES	WAVES	ABACI	ABORN	ACHOO
WAGON	WAVEY	ABACK	ABORT	ACIDS
WAHOO	WAXEN	ABAFT	ABOUT	ACIDY
WAIST	YACHT	ABASE	ABOVE	ACING
WAITS	YAHOO	ABASH	ABUSE	ACINI
WAIVE	YAKKY	ABASK	ABUTS	ACMES

ACNED	OCTET	SCENE	SCREW	ADMAN
ACNES	OCULI	SCENT	SCRIM	ADMIN
ACORN	SCABS	SCHMO	SCRIP	ADMIT
ACRED	SCADS	SCHWA	SCROD	ADMIX
ACRES	SCALD	SCION	SCROW	ADOBE
ACRID	SCALE	SCOBS	SCRUB	ADOBO
ACTED	SCALP	SCOFF	SCRUM	ADOPT
ACTER	SCALY	SCOLD	SCUBA	ADORE
ACTIN	SCAMP	SCONE	SCUDO	ADORN
ACTOR	SCAMS	SCOOP	SCUFF	ADULT
ACUTE	SCANS	SCOOT	SCULL	ADUST
ACYLS	SCANT	SCOPA	SCUMS	EDEMA
ECCHI	SCAPE	SCOPE	SCURF	EDGED
ECHOS	SCAPI	SCORE	SCUTA	EDGER
ICHOR	SCARD	SCORN	SCUTE	EDGES
ICILY	SCARE	SCOTS	SCUZZ	EDICT
ICING	SCARF	SCOUR	ADAGE	EDIFY
ICONS	SCARP	SCOUT	ADAPT	EDITS
OCCUR	SCARS	SCOWL	ADDAX	EDUCE
OCEAN	SCARY	SCOWS	ADDED	EDUCT
OCHER	SCATH	SCRAG	ADDER	IDEAL
OCHRE	SCATT	SCRAM	ADDLE	IDEAS
OCREA	SCAUP	SCRAN	ADEPT	IDIOM
OCTAD	SCENA	SCRAP	ADIEU	IDIOT
OCTAL	SCEND	SCREE	ADIOS	IDLER

IDYLL	BEDEW	BERYL	DEALE	DEEPS
ODDER	BEDIM	BESET	DEALS	DEERE
ODDLY	BEECH	BETTY	DEALT	DEERS
ODEUM	BEEFY	BEVEL	DEANS	DEETS
ODIST	BEFIT	BEVVY	DEARN	DEFER
ODIUM	BEFOG	CEASE	DEARS	DEFIB
ODORS	BEGAN	CECAL	DEARY	DEFOG
ODOUR	BEGET	CECUM	DEATH	DEGUT
AEGER	BEGIN	CEDAR	DEBAR	DEICE
AEGIS	BEGOT	CEDED	DEBIT	DEIFY
AEONS	BEGUN	CEDER	DEBTS	DEIGN
AERIE	BEIGE	CEIBA	DEBUG	DEISM
BEACH	BEING	CELEB	DEBUT	DEIST
BEADS	BELAY	CELLA	DECAD	DEITY
BEADY	BELCH	CELLI	DECAF	DEKES
BEAKY	BELIE	CELLO	DECAL	DEKKO
BEAMS	BELLE	CELLS	DECAY	DELAY
BEAMY	BELLS	CELTS	DECKS	DELFT
BEANO	BELLY	CENSE	DECON	DELLS
BEANS	BELOW	CENTO	DECOR	DELTA
BEARD	BENCH	CENTS	DECOY	DELVE
BEARS	BENDY	CERIC	DECRY	DEMIT
BEAST	BERET	CERTS	DEEDE	DEMOB
BEATS	BERRY	CESTA	DEEDS	DEMOI
BEAUT	BERTH	DEADS	DEEMS	DEMON

DEMOS	DEVON	FEVER	HEDGE	JERKS
DEMUR	DEWAN	FEWER	HEDON	JERKY
DENAR	DEWAR	GEEKY	HEELS	JERRY
DENEB	EELED	GEESE	HEFTY	JESTS
DENES	EELER	GELID	HEIRS	JESUS
DENIM	EERIE	GENES	HEIST	JETTY
DENSE	FEARS	GENIC	HELIX	JEWED
DENTS	FEAST	GENIE	HELLA	JEWEL
DEPOT	FEATS	GENRE	HELLO	JEWRY
DEPTH	FECES	GENTS	HELPS	KEBAB
DEPTS	FEEDS	GENUS	HELVE	KECKS
DERBY	FEELS	GEODE	HENCE	KEDGE
DERMA	FEIGN	GERMS	HENCH	KEEKS
DERMS	FEINT	GESTE	HENNA	KEELS
DERNS	FEIST	GETUP	HERBS	KEENE
DERPY	FELLA	HEADS	HERON	KEENS
DESEX	FELON	HEADY	HERTZ	KEEPE
DESIS	FEMME	HEAPS	HETRO	KEEPS
DESKS	FENCE	HEARD	HEXAD	KEEVE
DETER	FERAL	HEARS	JEANS	KEFIR
DETOX	FERRY	HEART	JEEPS	KELLS
DEUCE	FETAL	HEATH	JEERS	KELLY
DEVAS	FETCH	HEAVE	JELLY	KEMPT
DEVEL	FETID	HEAVY	JEMMY	KENAF
DEVIL	FETUS	HECKA	JENNY	KENDO

KENTE	LENDS	MEMES	METIC	NERDO
KERFS	LEPER	MEMOS	METRE	NERDS
KERRY	LETCH	MENDS	METRO	NERDY
KETCH	LETUP	MENSA	METTS	NERTS
KEYED	LEVEE	MENSE	MEWLS	NERVE
KEYER	LEVEL	MENUS	MEZZO	NERVY
LEACH	LEVER	MEOWS	NEARE	NESTS
LEADS	LEXIS	MERCH	NEARS	NETTS
LEAFY	MEADS	MERCS	NEATH	NETTY
LEAKY	MEALS	MERCY	NEATO	NEUME
LEANS	MEALY	MERDE	NEATS	NEUMS
LEAPT	MEANS	MERES	NEBBY	NEURO
LEARN	MEANT	MERGE	NECKE	NEVER
LEASE	MEANY	MERIT	NECKS	NEVES
LEASH	MEATS	MERLE	NECRO	NEVUS
LEAST	MEATY	MERRY	NEDDY	NEWEL
LEAVE	MECCA	MESAS	NEEDS	NEWER
LEDGE	MECHA	MESHY	NEEDY	NEWES
LEECH	MEDAL	MESIC	NEEMB	NEWIE
LEERY	MEDIA	MESNE	NEEMS	NEWLY
LEFTY	MEDIC	MESON	NEGRO	NEWSY
LEGAL	MEETS	MESSY	NEGUS	NEWTS
LEGIT	MELEE	METAL	NEIGH	NEXUM
LEMAN	MELON	METER	NELLY	NEXUS
LEMON	MELTY	METES	NEONS	PEACE

PEACH	PEGGY	PERVE	REBBE	REEKY
PEAKS	PEKOE	PERVS	REBEC	REELS
PEAKY	PELMA	PERVY	REBEL	REENS
PEALS	PENAL	PESKY	REBUS	REEVE
PEANS	PENCE	PESOS	REBUT	REFER
PEARE	PENES	PESTO	RECAP	REFIT
PEARL	PENIS	PESTS	RECCE	REFIX
PEARS	PENNA	PESTY	RECIT	REFUT
PEART	PENNE	PETAL	RECON	REGAL
PEARY	PENNI	PETER	RECTA	REGEN
PEASE	PENNY	PETIT	RECTO	REHAB
PEATS	PENTS	PETTY	RECUR	REIFY
PEATY	PEONS	PEWEE	REDAN	REIGN
PEAVY	PEONY	REACH	REDDS	REIKI
PECAN	PEPLA	REACT	REDDY	REINS
PECKE	PEPPY	READS	REDID	REJIG
PECKS	PERCH	READY	REDOS	REKEY
PEDAL	PERDU	REALM	REDOX	RELAX
PEDIS	PERIL	REALS	REDUX	RELAY
PEELS	PERKS	REAME	REEDE	RELIC
PEENS	PERKY	REAMS	REEDS	RELLY
PEEPE	PERPS	REARM	REEDY	REMEX
PEEPS	PERQS	REARS	REEFS	REMIT
PEERS	PERRY	REATA	REEFY	REMIX
PEEVE	PERSE	REBAR	REEKS	RENAL

RENEW	SEAMS	SELLS	SERIN	TECHY
RENIG	SEAMY	SELLY	SEROW	TECTA
RENIN	SEATS	SELVA	SERUM	TEDDY
RENTS	SEBUM	SEMEN	SERVE	TEEMS
REORG	SECCO	SEMIS	SERVO	TEENS
REPAY	SECTS	SENDS	SETAE	TEENY
REPEL	SEDAN	SENES	SETTS	TEETH
REPLY	SEDER	SENNA	SETUP	TEHEE
REPOS	SEDGE	SENOR	SEVEN	TELCO
REPOT	SEDUM	SENSE	SEVER	TELEX
REPRO	SEEDE	SENTE	SEWER	TELIC
RERUN	SEEDS	SENTI	SEXER	TELLS
RESES	SEEDY	SENTS	SEXES	TELLY
RESET	SEEKS	SEPAL	TEACH	TELOS
RESIN	SEEMS	SEPIA	TEADE	TEMPI
RESIT	SEEPS	SEPOY	TEAED	TEMPO
RESTS	SEERS	SEPTA	TEAKS	TEMPS
RETCH	SEGUE	SEPTS	TEALS	TEMPT
RETRO	SEINE	SERAC	TEAMS	TENCH
RETRY	SEINS	SERAI	TEARE	TENDS
REUSE	SEISM	SERES	TEARS	TENDU
REVEL	SEITY	SERFS	TEARY	TENET
REVER	SEIZE	SERGE	TEASE	TENGE
REVUE	SELFS	SERIE	TEATS	TENNO
SEALS	SELLE	SERIF	TECHS	TENON

TENOR	VELUM	WELSH	ZESTS	AGILE
TENSE	VENAL	WENCH	ZESTY	AGING
TENTH	VENGE	XEBEC	AFFIX	AGIST
TENTS	VENOM	XENIA	AFIRE	AGITA
TENUE	VENUE	XENIC	AFOOT	AGLET
TEPAL	VENUS	XENON	AFORE	AGLOW
TEPEE	VERBS	XENYL	AFOUL	AGONE
TEPID	VERGE	XERIC	AFROS	AGONS
TERAI	VERSE	XEROX	AFTER	AGONY
TERCE	VERSO	XERUS	OFFAL	AGORA
TERGA	VERVE	YEARE	OFFED	AGREE
TERMS	VETCH	YEARN	OFFER	AGUED
TERRA	VEXED	YEARS	OFTEN	AGUES
TERRY	WEARS	YEAST	OFTER	EGEST
TERSE	WEARY	YEGGS	AGAIN	EGGAR
TESLA	WEAVE	YELLS	AGAMA	EGGED
TESTA	WEDGE	YELPS	AGAPE	EGRET
TESTS	WEDGY	YENTA	AGARS	IGLOO
TESTY	WEEDS	YESES	AGATE	NGWEE
TETRA	WEEDY	YETIS	AGAVE	OGHAM
TEXAS	WEENY	YETTS	AGEND	OGIVE
TEXTS	WEEPY	ZEALE	AGENT	OGLED
VEGAN	WEIGH	ZEALS	AGERS	OGLER
VEINS	WEIRD	ZEBRA	AGGIE	OGLES
VEINY	WELLY	ZEROS	AGGRO	OGRES

UGALI	CHASM	CHILD	CHOPS	KHAKI
AHEAD	CHAST	CHILE	CHORD	KHANS
AHING	CHATS	CHILI	CHORE	KHOUM
AHOLD	CHAYS	CHILL	CHOSE	OHING
BHUMI	CHEAP	CHIME	CHOWS	OHMIC
CHADS	CHEAT	CHINA	CHRON	PHAGE
CHAFE	CHECK	CHINE	CHUBS	PHARM
CHAFF	CHEEK	CHINK	CHUCK	PHARO
CHAIN	CHEEP	CHINO	CHUFA	PHASE
CHAIR	CHEER	CHINS	CHUFF	PHIAL
CHAIS	CHEEZ	CHIPS	CHUGS	PHISH
CHALK	CHEFS	CHIRO	CHUMP	PHLOX
CHAMP	CHELA	CHIRP	CHUMS	PHONE
CHAMS	CHEMO	CHIRR	CHUNK	PHONO
CHANT	CHERT	CHITS	CHURL	PHONS
CHAOS	CHESS	CHIVE	CHURN	PHONY
CHAPE	CHEST	CHIVY	CHURR	PHOTO
CHAPS	CHEWS	CHOCK	CHUTE	PHYLA
CHARD	CHEWY	CHOCS	CHYLE	RHEUM
CHARE	CHIBI	CHODE	CHYME	RHINO
CHARM	CHICA	CHOIR	DHOBI	RHOMB
CHARS	CHICK	CHOKE	DHOLE	RHUMB
CHART	CHICS	CHOKY	DHOTI	RHYME
CHARY	CHIDE	CHOLO	GHOST	SHACK
CHASE	CHIEF	CHOMP	GHOUL	SHADE

SHADS	SHEAR	SHIVE	SHRUG	THESE
SHADY	SHEDS	SHIVS	SHTIK	THESP
SHAFT	SHEEN	SHOAL	SHTUP	THETA
SHAGS	SHEEP	SHOAT	SHUCK	THEWS
SHAHS	SHEER	SHOCK	SHULS	THEWY
SHAKA	SHEET	SHOER	SHUNT	THICK
SHAKE	SHEIK	SHOES	SHUSH	THIEF
SHAKO	SHELF	SHOJI	SHUTS	THIGH
SHAKY	SHELL	SHONE	SHYER	THILL
SHALE	SHERO	SHOOK	SHYLY	THING
SHALL	SHETH	SHOON	THANE	THINK
SHAME	SHIER	SHOOP	THANK	THINS
SHAMS	SHIES	SHOOT	THATS	THIOL
SHANK	SHIFT	SHOPS	THAWS	THIRD
SHAPE	SHILL	SHORE	THAWY	THOLE
SHARD	SHINE	SHORT	THEBE	THONG
SHARE	SHINS	SHOTS	THECA	THORN
SHARK	SHINY	SHOUT	THEED	THORO
SHARP	SHIPS	SHOVE	THEES	THORP
SHART	SHIRE	SHOWN	THEFT	THOUS
SHAVE	SHIRK	SHOWS	THEGN	THREE
SHAWL	SHIRT	SHOWY	THEIR	THREW
SHAWM	SHITE	SHRED	THEME	THRID
SHAYS	SHITS	SHREW	THERE	THROB
SHEAF	SHIVA	SHRUB	THERM	THROE

THROW	WHIMS	AIRES	BISON	DIARY
THRUM	WHINE	AISLE	BITCH	DICER
THUDS	WHINY	AITCH	BITES	DICES
THUGS	WHIRL	BIBLE	BITSY	DICEY
THUJA	WHIRR	BIDDY	BITTY	DICKS
THUMB	WHISH	BIDET	CIDER	DICKY
THUMP	WHISK	BIGHT	CIGAR	DICOT
THUNK	WHITE	BIGOT	CIGGY	DICTA
THYME	WHITY	BIJOU	CILIA	DICTY
THYMI	WHIZZ	BIKER	CINCH	DIDDY
THYMY	WHOLE	BILBY	CIRCA	DIDIE
WHACK	WHOMP	BILGE	CIRCS	DIDOS
WHALE	WHOOP	BILLS	CISCO	DIENE
WHANG	WHORE	BILLY	CISSY	DIETS
WHARF	WHORL	BIMBO	CITAL	DIFFS
WHEAL	WHOSE	BINDI	CITED	DIGIT
WHEAT	WHUMP	BINDS	CITER	DIKER
WHEEL	AIDED	BINGE	CITES	DIKES
WHELK	AIDER	BINGO	CITIE	DILDO
WHELM	AIDES	BIOME	CIVET	DILLS
WHELP	AILED	BIOTA	CIVIC	DILLY
WHERE	AIMED	BIRCH	CIVIL	DIMER
WHICH	AIMER	BIRDS	CIVVY	DIMES
WHIFF	AIOLI	BIRSE	DIALS	DIMLY
WHILE	AIRED	BIRTH	DIANA	DIMPS

DINAR	DITTO	FILES	GIFTS	HIVES
DINER	DITTY	FILET	GILET	JIBBS
DINGE	DITZY	FILLS	GIMPY	JIBED
DINGO	DIVAN	FILLY	GIRLS	JIBES
DINGS	DIVAS	FILMS	GIRLY	JIFFS
DINGY	DIVER	FILMY	GIRTH	JIFFY
DINKS	DIVES	FILTH	GIVEN	JIGGY
DINKY	DIVIS	FINAL	GIVER	JIHAD
DINOS	DIVOT	FINDS	GIVES	JILTS
DINTS	DIVVY	FINED	GIZMO	JIMMY
DIODE	DIXIE	FINER	HIDER	JINGO
DIPPY	DIZZY	FINES	HIDES	JINKS
DIPSO	EIDER	FINIS	HIJAB	JINNI
DIRGE	EIDOS	FIRED	HIJRA	JIRGA
DIRKE	EIGHT	FIREE	HIKER	JIVED
DIRKS	FIBER	FIRMS	HILLS	JIVER
DIRTY	FIBRE	FIRST	HILLY	JIVES
DISAD	FIELD	FIRTH	HINGE	JIVEY
DISCO	FIEND	FISHY	HINKY	KIANG
DISCS	FIERY	FIXED	HINTS	KICKS
DISHY	FIFTH	FIXER	HIPPO	KICKY
DISIR	FIFTY	FIXES	HIPPY	KIDDO
DISKS	FIGHT	FIZZY	HIRED	KIDLY
DITCH	FILCH	GIANT	HISSY	KIKES
DITSY	FILED	GIDDY	HITCH	KILIM

KILLS	LIFTS	MIAUL	MIMES	MISTS
KILNS	LIGHT	MICAS	MIMIC	MISTY
KILOS	LIKED	MICKS	MINCE	MITCH
KILTS	LIKEN	MICRO	MINCY	MITER
KINDE	LIKES	MIDDY	MINDE	MITES
KINDS	LILAC	MIDGE	MINDS	MITRE
KINDY	LIMBO	MIDIS	MINED	MITTS
KINGS	LIMBS	MIDST	MINER	MIXED
KININ	LIMEY	MIENS	MINES	MIXER
KINKS	LIMIT	MIFFS	MINGY	MIXES
KINKY	LINED	MIGHT	MINIM	MIXUP
KIOSK	LINEN	MIKED	MINKS	NICAD
KIPED	LINER	MIKES	MINNY	NICER
KIPES	LINES	MILCH	MINOR	NICHE
KISSY	LINGO	MILDS	MINTS	NICKS
KITED	LINKS	MILER	MINTY	NIDUS
KITES	LIPID	MILES	MINUS	NIECE
LIANG	LISTS	MILKO	MINXY	NIEVE
LIARS	LITHE	MILKS	MIRED	NIFFY
LIBEL	LIVED	MILKY	MIREX	NIFTY
LIBRA	LIVEN	MILLS	MIRID	NIGGA
LICIT	LIVER	MILOS	MIRTH	NIGHT
LIEGE	LIVES	MIMED	MISER	NIHIL
LIENS	LIVID	MIMEO	MISES	NIMBY
LIFER	MIASM	MIMER	MISSY	NINES

NINJA	PIERS	PINKS	PIXIE	RILEY
NINNY	PIETS	PINKY	PIZZA	RILLE
NINON	PIETY	PINNA	PIZZE	RILLS
NINTH	PIGGY	PINNY	QILIN	RIMED
NIPPY	PIGMY	PINOT	RIALS	RIMER
NIQAB	PIKED	PINTO	RIATA	RIMES
NISEI	PIKER	PINTS	RIBBY	RINDS
NISSE	PIKES	PINUP	RICER	RINDY
NITES	PILAF	PIONS	RICES	RINED
NITID	PILED	PIOUS	RICHE	RINES
NITRO	PILER	PIPER	RICIN	RINGS
NIVAL	PILES	PIPES	RICKS	RINKS
NIXED	PILIS	PIPET	RIDER	RINSE
NIXES	PILLS	PIPIT	RIDES	RIOTS
NIXIE	PILLY	PIPPY	RIDGE	RIPEN
OILED	PILOT	PIQUE	RIDGY	RIPER
OILER	PILUS	PISCO	RIDIC	RIPES
PIANO	PIMPS	PISSY	RIFER	RISEN
PICCY	PINAY	PISTE	RIFFS	RISER
PICKS	PINCH	PITCH	RIFLE	RISES
PICKY	PINES	PITHY	RIFTS	RISHI
PICOT	PINEY	PITON	RIGHT	RISKS
PICTS	PINGO	PITTA	RIGID	RISKY
PICUL	PINGS	PIVOT	RIGOR	RITES
PIECE	PINKO	PIXEL	RILED	RITZY

RIVAL	SILLS	SITAR	TILER	TITER
RIVEL	SILLY	SITES	TILES	TITHE
RIVEN	SILOS	SITUS	TILLS	TITLE
RIVER	SILVA	SIXER	TILLY	TITTY
RIVES	SIMAS	SIXES	TILTH	TIYIN
RIVET	SIMBA	SIXTH	TILTS	TIZZY
RIYAL	SIMON	SIXTY	TIMED	VIAND
SIBYL	SIMPS	SIZER	TIMER	VIBES
SICKO	SIMUL	SIZES	TIMES	VICAR
SIDES	SINCE	TIARA	TIMID	VICES
SIDLE	SINES	TIBIA	TINCT	VIDEO
SIEGE	SINEW	TICKS	TINED	VIEWS
SIENS	SINGE	TICKY	TINES	VIGIL
SIENT	SINGS	TIDAL	TINGE	VIGOR
SIEVE	SINKS	TIDED	TINGS	VILLA
SIGHS	SINUS	TIDES	TINKS	VINES
SIGHT	SIPES	TIERS	TINNY	VINYL
SIGIL	SIPPY	TIFFS	TINTS	VIOLA
SIGMA	SIREE	TIGER	TIPPY	VIPER
SIGNA	SIREN	TIGHT	TIPSY	VIRAL
SIGNS	SIRES	TIGON	TIRED	VIRGA
SILES	SISAL	TIGRE	TIRES	VIRUS
SILEX	SISES	TIKKA	TIROS	VISIT
SILKS	SISSY	TILDE	TITAN	VISOR
SILKY	SISTA	TILED	TITCH	VISTA

VITAL	WIRRA	EKING	SKITS	ALGOR
VIVID	WISER	OKAPI	SKIVE	ALIAS
VIXEN	WISPY	OKAYS	SKOAL	ALIBI
WICCA	WITCH	OKRAS	SKOSH	ALIEN
WIDEN	WITHY	SKALD	SKULK	ALIGN
WIDER	WITTY	SKANK	SKULL	ALIKE
WIDOW	YIELD	SKARN	SKUNK	ALIVE
WIDTH	YIPPY	SKATE	SKYEY	ALKIE
WIELD	ZILCH	SKATS	UKASE	ALKYD
WIFEY	ZINCO	SKEAN	ALACK	ALKYL
WIGHT	ZINCS	SKEET	ALAMO	ALLAY
WILDS	ZINCY	SKEIN	ALARM	ALLEY
WILES	ZINGS	SKIDS	ALARY	ALLOT
WILLY	ZINGY	SKIER	ALATE	ALLOW
WIMPY	ZINKY	SKIES	ALBUM	ALLOY
WINCE	ZIPPO	SKIFF	ALCID	ALLYL
WINCH	ZIPPY	SKILL	ALCOS	ALOED
WINDS	ZITTY	SKILS	ALDER	ALOES
WINDY	AJUGA	SKIMP	ALDOL	ALOFT
WINGS	DJINN	SKINS	ALEPH	ALOHA
WINZE	EJECT	SKINT	ALERT	ALONE
WIPED	EJIDO	SKIPS	ALGAE	ALONG
WIPER	FJORD	SKIRR	ALGAL	ALOOF
WIPES	AKENS	SKIRT	ALGID	ALOUD
WIRED	AKITA	SKITE	ALGIN	ALPHA

ALTAR	BLING	CLANG	CLIMB	CLUNG
ALTER	BLINK	CLANK	CLIME	CLUNK
ALTOS	BLISS	CLANS	CLINE	ELAND
ALUMN	BLITZ	CLAPS	CLING	ELANS
ALUMS	BLOAT	CLARO	CLINK	ELATE
ALWAY	BLOCK	CLARY	CLIPS	ELBOW
BLACK	BLOGS	CLASH	CLOAK	ELDER
BLADE	BLOKE	CLASP	CLOCK	ELECT
BLAME	BLOND	CLASS	CLODS	ELEGY
BLAND	BLOOD	CLAST	CLOGS	ELEMI
BLANK	BLOOM	CLAVE	CLOMP	ELFIN
BLARE	BLOWN	CLAWS	CLONE	ELIDE
BLAST	BLOWS	CLAYS	CLONK	ELITE
BLAZE	BLOWY	CLEAN	CLOSE	ELKES
BLEAK	BLUES	CLEAR	CLOTH	ELMEN
BLEAR	BLUFF	CLEAT	CLOTS	ELOPE
BLEAT	BLUNT	CLEEK	CLOUD	ELUDE
BLECH	BLURB	CLEFT	CLOUT	ELUTE
BLEED	BLURT	CLEPE	CLOVE	ELVER
BLEEP	BLUSH	CLERK	CLOWN	ELVES
BLEND	CLACK	CLEVE	CLUBS	FLAGS
BLESS	CLADE	CLEWS	CLUCK	FLAIL
BLEST	CLAIM	CLICK	CLUES	FLAIR
BLIMP	CLAMP	CLIFF	CLUEY	FLAKE
BLIND	CLAMS	CLIFT	CLUMP	FLAKY

FLAME	FLOUT	GLOAT	PLANE	PLUCK
FLANK	FLOWS	GLOBE	PLANK	PLUGS
FLAPS	FLOWY	GLOMP	PLANS	PLUMB
FLARE	FLUFF	GLOOM	PLANT	PLUME
FLASH	FLUID	GLOOP	PLASH	PLUMP
FLASK	FLUKE	GLORY	PLASM	PLUMS
FLAWS	FLUKY	GLOSS	PLATE	PLUMY
FLECK	FLUME	GLOVE	PLATS	PLUNK
FLEEK	FLUMP	GLUED	PLATT	PLUSH
FLEER	FLUNG	GLUEY	PLAYA	PLUTE
FLEET	FLUNK	GLYPH	PLAYS	PLYER
FLESH	FLUSH	LLAMA	PLAZA	SLABS
FLICK	FLUTE	LLANO	PLEAD	SLACK
FLIER	FLYBY	OLDEN	PLEAS	SLAGS
FLIES	FLYER	OLDER	PLEAT	SLAIN
FLING	GLADE	OLDIE	PLEBE	SLAKE
FLINT	GLAND	OLEUM	PLEBS	SLANG
FLIRT	GLARE	OLIVE	PLICA	SLANT
FLOAT	GLASS	OLLIE	PLIER	SLAPS
FLOCK	GLAZE	OLOGY	PLIES	SLASH
FLOOD	GLEAM	PLACE	PLINK	SLATE
FLOOR	GLEAN	PLAGE	PLONK	SLATS
FLORA	GLIDE	PLAID	PLOTS	SLATY
FLOSS	GLINT	PLAIN	PLOWS	SLAVE
FLOUR	GLITZ	PLAIT	PLOYS	SLEDS

SLEEK	SLOTH	AMBOS	AMRIT	IMMIX
SLEEP	SLOTS	AMBRY	AMUCK	IMPEL
SLEET	SLOWS	AMEBA	AMUSE	IMPEX
SLEPT	SLUFF	AMEND	EMAIL	IMPLY
SLEYS	SLUGS	AMENS	EMBAY	OMBRE
SLICE	SLUMP	AMENT	EMBED	OMBUD
SLICK	SLUMS	AMICE	EMBER	OMEGA
SLIDE	SLUNK	AMICI	EMBOG	OMENS
SLIME	SLURP	AMIDE	EMBUS	OMITS
SLIMS	SLURS	AMIGA	EMCEE	SMACK
SLIMY	SLUSH	AMIGO	EMEER	SMAIL
SLING	SLUTS	AMINE	EMEND	SMALL
SLINK	SLYLY	AMINO	EMERG	SMARM
SLIPS	SLYPE	AMISS	EMERY	SMART
SLITE	ULCER	AMITY	EMIRS	SMASH
SLITS	ULTRA	AMNIA	EMITS	SMAZE
SLIVE	VLOGS	AMNIO	EMMER	SMEAR
SLOBS	ZLOTY	AMOKS	EMMET	SMELL
SLOES	AMAIN	AMOLE	EMOJI	SMELT
SLOGS	AMASS	AMONG	EMOTE	SMEWS
SLOKA	AMAZE	AMOUR	EMPTY	SMILE
SLOOP	AMBER	AMPED	EMULE	SMIRK
SLOPE	AMBIT	AMPLE	IMAGE	SMITE
SLOPS	AMBLE	AMPLY	IMBED	SMITH
SLOSH	AMBON	AMPUL	IMBUE	SMOCK

SMOKE	ANISE	ENJOY	INERT	KNITS
SMOKO	ANKLE	ENNUI	INFER	KNIVE
SMOKY	ANNAL	ENOKI	INFIX	KNOCK
SMOLT	ANNAS	ENORM	INGOT	KNOLL
SMURF	ANNEX	ENROL	INLAY	KNOTS
SMUTS	ANNOY	ENSKY	INLET	KNOUT
UMAMI	ANNUL	ENSUE	INNER	KNOWE
UMBER	ANODE	ENTER	INPUT	KNOWN
UMBRA	ANOLE	ENTIA	INSET	KNOWS
ANALS	ANOMY	ENTRE	INTEL	KNURL
ANCHO	ANTED	ENTRY	INTER	ONCER
ANCON	ANTES	ENVOI	INTRA	ONCET
ANDED	ANTIC	ENVOY	INTRO	ONELY
ANDRO	ANTRA	ENZYM	INUIT	ONERS
ANELE	ANTRE	GNASH	INURE	ONERY
ANENT	ANTSY	GNOME	INURN	ONEST
ANGEL	ANURY	INANE	KNACK	ONION
ANGER	ANVIL	INAPT	KNAPS	ONSET
ANGLE	ENACT	INCEL	KNEAD	ONTIC
ANGRY	ENATE	INCUR	KNEED	SNACK
ANGST	ENDED	INCUS	KNEEL	SNAFU
ANILE	ENDOW	INDEX	KNEES	SNAGS
ANIMA	ENDUE	INDIA	KNELL	SNAIL
ANIME	ENEMA	INDIE	KNELT	SNAKE
ANION	ENEMY	INEPT	KNIFE	SNAKY

SNAPS	SNUBS	UNSAY	BONER	BOTTY
SNARE	SNUCK	UNSET	BONES	BOUGH
SNARK	SNUFF	UNSEX	BONEY	BOUND
SNARL	SNUGS	UNTIE	BONGO	BOURG
SNEAK	UNAPT	UNTIL	BONNY	BOURN
SNECK	UNBAN	UNUSE	BONUS	BOUTS
SNEER	UNBOX	UNWED	BOOBS	BOWED
SNELL	UNCLE	UNZIP	BOOBY	BOWEL
SNICK	UNCOS	AORTA	BOOKS	BOWER
SNIDE	UNCUT	BOARD	BOOMY	BOXED
SNIFF	UNDER	BOAST	BOONG	BOXER
SNIFT	UNDUE	BOBBY	BOOST	BOXES
SNIPE	UNFIT	BOCHE	BOOTH	BOYAR
SNIPS	UNFIX	BODGE	BOOTS	COACH
SNOBS	UNFUN	BOFFO	BOOTY	COALS
SNOOD	UNIFY	BOGAN	BOOZE	COALY
SNOOK	UNION	BOGEY	BOOZY	COAPT
SNOOP	UNITE	BOGGY	BORAX	COAST
SNOOT	UNITS	BOGLE	BORED	COATE
SNORE	UNITY	BOGUS	BORNE	COATI
SNORT	UNLAY	BOILS	BOSOM	COATS
SNOTS	UNLIT	BOING	BOSSY	COBBS
SNOUT	UNMAN	BOKEH	BOTCH	COBBY
SNOWS	UNMET	BONCE	BOTHY	COBIA
SNOWY	UNPEG	BONDS	BOTOX	COBRA

COCAS	COLES	CONES	COPSY	COULD
COCCI	COLIC	CONEY	CORAL	COUNT
COCKS	COLON	CONGA	CORDS	COUPE
COCKY	COLOR	CONIC	CORDY	COUPS
COCOA	COLTS	CONKS	CORER	COURS
COCOS	COMAE	CONKY	CORES	COURT
CODAS	COMAS	CONST	COREY	COUTH
CODEC	COMBE	CONTE	CORGI	COVEN
CODED	COMBO	COOED	CORKS	COVER
CODER	COMBS	COOER	CORKY	COVES
CODES	COMER	COOKS	CORNS	COVET
CODEX	COMES	COOKY	CORNU	COVEY
CODON	COMET	COOLE	CORNY	COVIN
COEDS	COMFY	COOLY	COROL	COWED
COHAB	COMIC	COONS	CORPS	COWER
COIFS	COMIX	COOPS	CORSE	COWLS
COIGN	COMMA	COOPT	CORVE	COXAE
COILS	COMMO	COOTS	COSIE	COXAL
COINE	COMMS	COOTY	COSMO	COXED
COINS	COMMY	COPAL	COSTA	COXES
COKED	COMPO	COPAY	COSTS	COYER
COKER	COMPS	COPED	COTES	COYLY
COKES	CONCH	COPES	COTTA	COYPU
COLAS	CONDO	COPRA	COUCH	COZEN
COLDS	CONED	COPSE	COUGH	COZIE

DOBBY	DONUT	DOWDY	FORAY	GOODS
DOBRA	DOOLY	DOWEL	FORCE	GOODY
DOBRO	DOOMS	DOWER	FORGE	GOOEY
DOCKS	DOOMY	DOWNS	FORGO	GOOFY
DODGE	DOORS	DOWNY	FORMS	GOOSE
DODGY	DOOZY	DOWRY	FORTE	GORGE
DOERS	DOPED	DOWSE	FORTH	GORSE
DOGES	DOPER	DOXIE	FORTY	GOTTA
DOGGE	DOPES	DOYEN	FORUM	GOUGE
DOGGY	DOPEY	DOZEN	FOSSE	GOUND
DOGIE	DORKS	DOZER	FOUND	GOURD
DOGMA	DORKY	DOZES	FOUNT	HOARD
DOILY	DORMS	EOSIN	FOYER	HOARY
DOING	DORSA	FOAMY	GOALS	HOBBY
DOLLS	DOSAS	FOCAL	GOBBY	HOICK
DOLLY	DOSES	FOCUS	GODLY	HOIST
DOLMA	DOTER	FOGEY	GOFER	HOKEY
DOLOR	DOTES	FOGGY	GOING	HOKKU
DOLTS	DOTTY	FOIST	GOLEM	HOKUM
DOMED	DOUBT	FOLDS	GOLLY	HOLDS
DOMES	DOUGH	FOLIO	GONAD	HOLER
DONEE	DOULA	FOLKS	GONER	HOLES
DONGS	DOUSE	FOLLY	GONNA	HOLEY
DONNA	DOVES	FOODS	GONZO	HOLLO
DONOR	DOWDS	FOOLS	GOOCH	HOLLY

HOMES	HOWDY	KOOKY	LOONY	MOCKS
HOMEY	JOCKS	LOADS	LOOPY	MODAL
HOMIE	JOCKY	LOAMY	LOOSE	MODEL
HONED	JOEYS	LOANS	LORDY	MODEM
HONEY	JOHNS	LOATH	LORRY	MODES
HONOR	JOINS	LOBBY	LOSEL	MODUS
HOOCH	JOINT	LOCAL	LOSER	MOGGY
HOOEY	JOIST	LOCKS	LOSES	MOGUL
HOOKY	JOKED	LOCUM	LOTUS	MOHEL
HOOVE	JOKER	LOCUS	LOUGH	MOILE
HOPED	JOKES	LODGE	LOUIS	MOILS
HOPES	JOKEY	LOFTY	LOUSE	MOIRE
HORDE	JOLLY	LOGAN	LOUSY	MOIST
HORNS	JOLTS	LOGIC	LOVED	MOJOS
HORNY	JOLTY	LOGIN	LOVER	MOKES
HORSE	JONAH	LOGON	LOVES	MOLAL
HORSY	JONES	LOGOS	LOWER	MOLAR
HOSTS	JORUM	LOINS	LOWLY	MOLDS
HOTEL	JOUAL	LOLLY	LOYAL	MOLDY
HOTLY	JOULE	LONER	MOANS	MOLES
HOUND	JOURS	LONGS	MOANY	MOLLY
HOURS	JOUST	LOOBY	MOATS	MOLTS
HOUSE	JOWLS	LOOFA	MOBES	MOMMA
HOVEL	JOWLY	LOOKS	MOCHA	MOMMY
HOVER	JOYED	LOOMS	MOCHI	MOMSY

MONAD	MORAL	MOURN	NONAD	NOTIF
MONDO	MORAY	MOUSE	NONCE	NOTUM
MONES	MOREL	MOUSY	NONES	NOUNS
MONEY	MORES	MOUTH	NONET	NOUNY
MONGO	MORNS	MOVED	NOOBS	NOVAE
MONGS	MORON	MOVER	NOOBY	NOVAS
MONKS	MORPH	MOVES	NOOKS	NOVEL
MONTE	MORTS	MOVIE	NOOKY	NOVUM
MONTH	MOSEY	MOWER	NOONE	NOWAY
MOOCH	MOSSY	MOXIE	NOONS	NOWED
MOODS	MOSTS	NOBBY	NOOSE	NOYAU
MOODY	MOTED	NOBLE	NOPAL	OOMPH
MOOER	MOTEL	NOBLY	NORIA	OOTID
MOOLA	MOTES	NODAL	NORMA	OOZED
MOONS	MOTET	NODDY	NORMS	OOZES
MOONY	MOTHS	NODED	NORTH	POACH
MOORS	MOTHY	NODES	NOSED	POCKS
MOORY	MOTIF	NODUS	NOSER	PODGE
MOOSE	MOTOR	NOICE	NOSES	PODGY
MOOTS	MOTTE	NOISE	NOSEY	PODIA
MOPED	MOTTO	NOISY	NOTAM	POEME
MOPER	MOULD	NOMAD	NOTCH	POEMS
MOPES	MOULT	NOMAN	NOTED	POESY
MOPEY	MOUND	NOMEN	NOTER	POETE
MOPPY	MOUNT	NOMES	NOTES	POETS

POGEY	PONGY	PORTA	ROBES	ROOFY
POGOS	POOCH	PORTS	ROBIN	ROOKE
POILU	POODS	POSED	ROBOT	ROOKS
POINT	POOFS	POSER	ROCHE	ROOKY
POISE	POOFY	POSES	ROCKS	ROOME
POKED	POOKA	POSIT	ROCKY	ROOMS
POKER	POOLS	POSSE	RODEO	ROOMY
POKES	POONS	POSTS	RODES	ROOST
POKEY	POOPS	POTCH	ROGER	ROOTS
POKIE	POORE	POTOO	ROGUE	ROOTY
POLAR	POOTS	POTTO	ROGUY	ROPER
POLES	POPES	POTTY	ROIDS	ROPES
POLIO	POPPA	POUCH	ROILY	ROQUE
POLIS	POPPY	POUFS	ROKES	ROSEN
POLKA	POPSY	POULT	ROLES	ROSES
POLLS	PORCH	POUND	ROLLS	ROSIN
POLLY	PORED	POUTS	ROLLY	ROTAS
POLOS	PORER	POUTY	ROMAN	ROTES
POLYP	PORES	POWER	ROMEO	ROTIS
POMMY	PORGY	POXES	ROMPS	ROTOR
POMPS	PORIN	ROACH	RONDE	ROUGE
PONCE	PORKY	ROADS	RONDO	ROUGH
PONDS	PORNO	ROARS	RONIN	ROUND
PONDY	PORNS	ROAST	ROODS	ROUSE
PONGS	PORNY	ROBED	ROOFS	ROUST

ROUTE	SOGGY	SOOKY	SOWER	TONGA
ROUTS	SOILE	SOOTH	TOADS	TONGS
ROVER	SOILS	SOOTY	TOADY	TONIC
ROWAN	SOKEN	SOPHS	TOAST	TONNE
ROWDY	SOKES	SOPHY	TODAY	TONUS
ROWED	SOKOL	SOPOR	TODDY	TOOKE
ROWEL	SOLAN	SOPPY	TOFUS	TOOLS
ROWEN	SOLAR	SORBS	TOGAE	TOONS
ROWER	SOLDO	SORES	TOGAS	TOOTH
ROYAL	SOLER	SOROR	TOILE	TOOTS
SOAKS	SOLES	SORRY	TOILS	TOPAZ
SOAPS	SOLID	SORTA	TOKED	TOPER
SOAPY	SOLON	SORTE	TOKEN	TOPIC
SOARS	SOLOS	SORTS	TOKES	TOPOS
SOBBY	SOLUS	SORUS	TOLAR	TOPPY
SOBER	SOLVE	SOUGH	TOLED	TOQUE
SOCKS	SOMAN	SOULE	TOLES	TORAN
SOCLE	SOMAS	SOULS	TOLLS	TORCH
SODAS	SONAR	SOUND	TOMBS	TORES
SODDY	SONDE	SOUPS	TOMES	TORIC
SOFAR	SONES	SOUPY	TONAL	TORII
SOFAS	SONGS	SOURS	TONDO	TORSE
SOFTA	SONIC	SOUSE	TONED	TORSI
SOFTS	SONNY	SOUTH	TONER	TORSK
SOFTY	SOOKS	SOWED	TONES	TORSO

TORTE	TOYER	WORDS	YONIC	APHIS
TORTS	TOYON	WORDY	YONIS	APIAN
TORUS	VOCAL	WORKS	YONKS	APING
TOSSY	VODKA	WORLD	YORKS	APISH
TOTAL	VOGUE	WORMY	YOUNG	APNEA
TOTED	VOICE	WORRY	YOURS	APOLS
TOTEM	VOILA	WORSE	YOUSE	APPAL
TOTER	VOLAR	WORST	YOUTH	APPAR
TOTES	VOMIT	WORTH	YOWLS	APPEL
TOUCH	VOTED	WOULD	ZOMBI	APPLE
TOUGH	VOTER	WOUND	ZONAL	APPLY
TOURS	VOUCH	WOVEN	ZONED	APRON
TOUSY	VOWED	WOWED	ZONER	APSIS
TOUTS	VOWEL	XOANA	ZONES	APTER
TOWED	WODGE	YOBBO	ZONKS	APTLY
TOWEE	WOMAN	YODEL	ZONKY	EPACT
TOWEL	WOMEN	YOGAS	ZOOID	EPHAH
TOWER	WONGA	YOGIC	ZOOMS	EPHOD
TOWNE	WONKY	YOGIN	ZOOMY	EPHOR
TOWNS	WOODS	YOGIS	ZOOTY	EPICK
TOWNY	WOODY	YOKED	APACE	EPICS
TOWRE	WOOED	YOKEL	APART	EPOCH
TOXIC	WOOER	YOKES	APERS	EPODE
TOXIN	WOOLY	YOLKS	APERY	EPOXY
TOYED	WOOZY	YOLKY	APHID	OPALS

OPENS	SPAWN	SPILT	SPRAG	SQUAD
OPERA	SPAWS	SPINE	SPRAT	SQUAT
OPERS	SPAZZ	SPINS	SPRAY	SQUAW
OPINE	SPEAK	SPINY	SPREE	SQUIB
OPIUM	SPEAR	SPIRE	SPRIG	SQUID
OPSIN	SPECK	SPITE	SPRIT	ARBOR
OPTED	SPECS	SPITS	SPROG	ARCED
OPTER	SPEED	SPITZ	SPRUE	ARCHY
OPTIC	SPEEL	SPIVS	SPUME	ARDOR
SPACE	SPELL	SPLAT	SPUMY	AREAL
SPACY	SPELT	SPLAY	SPUNK	AREAS
SPADE	SPEND	SPLIT	SPURN	ARECA
SPAHI	SPENT	SPLOT	SPURS	ARENA
SPAIN	SPERM	SPOIL	SPURT	AREPA
SPALL	SPICA	SPOKE	SPYAL	ARETE
SPAMS	SPICE	SPOOF	UPEND	ARGIL
SPANG	SPICY	SPOOK	UPPED	ARGON
SPANK	SPIED	SPOOL	UPPER	ARGOT
SPANS	SPIEL	SPOON	UPSET	ARGUE
SPARE	SPIES	SPOOR	AQUAE	ARHAT
SPARK	SPIFF	SPORE	AQUAS	ARIAS
SPARS	SPIKE	SPORK	EQUAL	ARILS
SPASM	SPIKY	SPORT	EQUID	ARISE
SPATE	SPILE	SPOTS	EQUIP	ARMED
SPATS	SPILL	SPOUT	SQUAB	ARMIE

ARMOR	BRAWL	BRUME	CREAM	CRISE
AROHA	BRAWN	BRUNT	CREAT	CRISP
AROID	BREAD	BRUSH	CREDO	CROAK
AROMA	BREAK	BRUTE	CREDS	CROCK
AROSE	BREED	CRABS	CREED	CROFT
ARRAS	BRIBE	CRACK	CREEK	CRONE
ARRAY	BRICK	CRAFT	CREEL	CRONY
ARRIS	BRIDE	CRAGS	CREEP	CROOK
ARROW	BRIEF	CRAKE	CREMS	CROON
ARROZ	BRIER	CRAME	CREPE	CROPS
ARSED	BRILL	CRAMP	CREPT	CRORE
ARSES	BRINE	CRAMS	CREPY	CROSS
ARSIS	BRING	CRANE	CRESC	CROUP
ARSON	BRINK	CRANK	CRESS	CROWD
ARTEL	BRINY	CRANS	CREST	CROWN
ARTSY	BRISK	CRAPS	CREWS	CROWS
BRACE	BROAD	CRASH	CRIBS	CROZE
BRAID	BROIL	CRASS	CRICK	CRUCK
BRAIN	BROKE	CRATE	CRIED	CRUDE
BRAKE	BROOD	CRAVE	CRIER	CRUDS
BRAND	BROOK	CRAWL	CRIES	CRUDY
BRASH	BROOM	CRAYS	CRIME	CRUEL
BRASS	BROTH	CRAZE	CRIMP	CRUES
BRAVE	BROWN	CRAZY	CRIMS	CRUET
BRAVO	BRUIT	CREAK	CRIPS	CRUMB

CRUMP	DREAD	DRUGS	FREAK	GRAIN
CRUNK	DREAM	DRUID	FREED	GRAND
CRUOR	DREAR	DRUMS	FREER	GRANT
CRURA	DRECK	DRUNK	FRESH	GRAPE
CRUSE	DREGS	DRUPE	FRIAR	GRAPH
CRUSH	DRESS	DRYAD	FRICK	GRASP
CRUST	DREYS	DRYER	FRIED	GRASS
CRWTH	DRIED	DRYLY	FRILL	GRATE
CRYER	DRIER	ERASE	FRISK	GRAVE
CRYPT	DRIES	ERECT	FRITZ	GRAVY
DRABS	DRIFT	ERGON	FRIZZ	GRAZE
DRAFF	DRILL	ERGOT	FROCK	GREAT
DRAFT	DRINK	ERICA	FROND	GREED
DRAGS	DRIPS	ERMIN	FRONT	GREEK
DRAIL	DRIVE	ERNES	FROST	GREEN
DRAIN	DROID	ERODE	FROTH	GREET
DRAKE	DROIT	EROSE	FROWN	GRIEF
DRAMA	DROLL	ERRED	FROZE	GRIFT
DRAMS	DRONE	ERROR	FRUIT	GRIKE
DRANK	DROOL	ERUCT	FRUMP	GRILL
DRAPE	DROOP	ERUPT	GRABS	GRIME
DRAWL	DROPS	FRAIL	GRACE	GRIMY
DRAWN	DROSS	FRAME	GRADE	GRIND
DRAWS	DROVE	FRANK	GRAFT	GRINS
DRAYS	DROWN	FRAUD	GRAIL	GRIOT

GRIPE	ORATE	PREXY	PROLE	TRAIL
GRITH	ORBED	PRIAL	PROMO	TRAIN
GRITS	ORBIT	PRICE	PROMS	TRAIT
GROAN	ORDER	PRICK	PRONE	TRAMP
GROIN	OREAD	PRICY	PRONG	TRAMS
GROOM	ORGAN	PRIDE	PRONS	TRANQ
GROPE	ORGIC	PRIED	PROOF	TRANS
GROSS	ORIBI	PRIER	PROPS	TRANT
GROUP	ORIEL	PRIGS	PROSE	TRAPS
GROUT	ORMER	PRILL	PROSS	TRAPT
GROVE	ORRIS	PRIME	PROSY	TRASH
GROWL	PRADS	PRIMO	PROTO	TRASS
GROWN	PRAME	PRIMP	PROUD	TRAVE
GROWS	PRAMS	PRINK	PROVE	TRAWL
GRUEL	PRANA	PRINT	PROWL	TRAYS
GRUFF	PRANG	PRION	PROWS	TREAD
GRUMP	PRANK	PRIOR	PROXY	TREAT
GRUNT	PRASE	PRISE	PRUDE	TREED
IRATE	PRATE	PRISM	PRUNE	TREEN
IRKED	PRAWN	PRIVY	PRYER	TREES
IRONS	PREDS	PRIZE	TRACE	TREKS
IRONY	PREEN	PROBE	TRACH	TREND
ORACY	PREGO	PROBS	TRACK	TRESS
ORALS	PRESS	PROEM	TRACT	TRETS
ORANG	PREST	PROFS	TRADE	TREWS

TREYS	TROTH	WRAPS	ASKES	OSMOL
TRIAD	TROTS	WRATH	ASKEW	PSALM
TRIAL	TROUT	WREAK	ASPEN	PSEUD
TRIBE	TROVE	WRECK	ASPER	PSHAW
TRICE	TROWS	WREST	ASPIC	PSYCH
TRICK	TRUCE	WRICK	ASPIE	TSARS
TRIED	TRUCK	WRING	ASSAI	USAGE
TRIER	TRUED	WRIST	ASSAY	USERS
TRIES	TRUER	WRITE	ASSES	USHER
TRIGS	TRUES	WRONG	ASSET	USING
TRIKE	TRULL	WROTE	ASTER	USUAL
TRILL	TRULY	WROTH	ASTIR	USURP
TRIMS	TRUMP	WRUNG	ASYLA	USURY
TRINE	TRUNK	WRYLY	ASYNC	ATAXY
TRIOS	TRUSS	ASANA	ESKER	ATILT
TRIPE	TRUST	ASCOT	ESPER	ATLAS
TRIPS	TRUTH	ASCUS	ESSAY	ATMAN
TRITE	TRYED	ASDIC	ESSES	ATMOS
TRODE	TRYER	ASHED	ESTER	ATOLL
TRODS	TRYST	ASHEN	ESTOC	ATOMS
TROLL	URBAN	ASHER	ESTOP	ATOMY
TROMP	URGED	ASHES	ISLAM	ATONE
TRONA	URGES	ASIDE	ISLET	ATOPY
TROOP	URINE	ASKED	ISSUE	ATRIA
TROPE	WRACK	ASKER	OSIER	ATTAR

ATTIC	STAMP	STELE	STOCK	STOVE
ETHER	STAND	STEMS	STOEP	STRAP
ETHIC	STANE	STENO	STOGY	STRAW
ETHOS	STANK	STENT	STOIC	STRAY
ETHYL	STARE	STEPS	STOKE	STREW
ETUDE	STARK	STERN	STOLE	STRIA
ETYMA	STARS	STEWS	STOMA	STRIP
ITCHY	START	STICK	STOMP	STROP
ITEMS	STASH	STIES	STONE	STRUM
OTHER	STATE	STIFF	STONG	STRUT
OTTER	STATS	STIKE	STONK	STUBS
STABS	STAVE	STILB	STONY	STUCK
STACK	STAYS	STILE	STOOD	STUDS
STADE	STEAD	STILL	STOOK	STUDY
STAFF	STEAK	STILT	STOOL	STUFF
STAGE	STEAL	STIME	STOOP	STUMP
STAGS	STEAM	STIMY	STOPE	STUMS
STAGY	STEAN	STING	STOPS	STUNG
STAID	STEED	STINK	STORE	STUNT
STAIN	STEEK	STINT	STORK	STUPA
STAIR	STEEL	STIPE	STORM	STUPE
STAKE	STEEP	STIRK	STORY	STYLE
STALE	STEER	STIRS	STOTE	STYMY
STALK	STEIN	STIVE	STOUP	UTILE
STALL	STELA	STOAT	STOUT	UTTER

AUDAX	BULLS	CUBEB	CURET	DUCTS
AUDIO	BULLY	CUBED	CURIA	DUDES
AUDIT	BUMPS	CUBER	CURIE	DUELS
AUGER	BUMPY	CUBES	CURIO	DUETS
AUGHT	BUNCH	CUBIC	CURLS	DUETT
AUGUR	BUNCO	CUBIT	CURLY	DUKES
AUNTS	BUNNY	CUDDY	CURRY	DULLY
AUNTY	BURKA	CUFFS	CURSE	DULSE
AURAE	BURKE	CULEX	CURST	DUMBO
AURAL	BURLY	CULLS	CURVE	DUMMY
AURAS	BURNS	CULLY	CURVY	DUMPS
AURIC	BURNT	CULTS	CUSHY	DUMPY
AUTOS	BURRO	CULTY	CUSPS	DUNAM
AUXIN	BURRY	CUMIN	CUTER	DUNCE
BUBBA	BURST	CUNTS	CUTES	DUNES
BUCKS	BUSBY	CUPEL	CUTIE	DUNGS
BUDDY	BUSHY	CUPID	CUTIN	DUNKS
BUDGE	BUSTY	CUPPA	CUTIS	DUNNY
BUFFO	BUTCH	CUPPY	CUTUP	DUOMO
BUGGY	BUTTE	CURBS	DUALS	DUPED
BUGLE	BUTTY	CURDS	DUCAT	DUPER
BUILD	BUXOM	CURDY	DUCES	DUPES
BUILT	BUYER	CURED	DUCHY	DUPPY
BULGE	BUZZY	CURER	DUCKS	DURAL
BULKY	CUBBY	CURES	DUCKY	DURRA

DURUM	FUSED	GUTSY	JUKES	LUNAR
DUSKS	FUSSY	GUTTY	JULEP	LUNCH
DUSKY	FUSTY	HUBBY	JUMBO	LUNGE
DUSTS	FUTON	HUFFY	JUMBY	LUNGI
DUSTY	FUZZY	HULKY	JUMPS	LUNGS
DUTCH	GUANO	HUMAN	JUMPY	LURCH
DUTIE	GUARD	HUMID	JUNCO	LURED
DUVET	GUAVA	HUMOR	JUNKS	LURER
DUXES	GUESS	HUMUS	JUNKY	LURES
EUROS	GUEST	HUNCH	JUNTA	LURID
FUBAR	GUIDE	HUNKS	JUNTO	LUSTY
FUDGE	GUILD	HUNKY	JURAL	MUCAL
FUELS	GUILE	HURLY	JURAT	MUCHO
FUGGY	GUILT	HURRY	JUROR	MUCID
FUGUE	GUISE	HURST	JUSTS	MUCIN
FULLY	GULCH	HURTS	JUTTY	MUCKY
FUMES	GULLY	HUSKY	JUVIE	MUCRO
FUNDI	GUMBO	HUSSY	KUDOS	MUCUS
FUNDS	GUMMY	HUTCH	LUBED	MUDAR
FUNGI	GUNGE	JUDAH	LUCID	MUDDY
FUNKY	GUNGY	JUDGE	LUCKY	MUDGE
FUNNY	GUNKY	JUDGY	LUCRE	MUDRA
FUROR	GUSHY	JUICE	LUDIC	MUFFS
FURRY	GUSTO	JUICY	LUMIC	MUFTI
FURZE	GUSTY	JUKED	LUMPY	MUGGY

MULCH	MUSIC	OUCHE	PULPS	PURSY
MULCT	MUSIT	OUGHT	PULPY	PUSHY
MULES	MUSKS	OUNCE	PULSE	PUSSY
MULEY	MUSKY	OUSTS	PUMAS	PUTTO
MULGA	MUSOS	OUTDO	PUMPS	PUTTS
MULLA	MUSSY	OUTED	PUNCH	PUTTY
MULLS	MUSTS	OUTER	PUNIC	QUACK
MULTI	MUSTY	OUTGO	PUNKS	QUAFF
MUMMY	MUTED	OUTRE	PUNKY	QUAIL
MUMPS	MUTER	OUZEL	PUNNY	QUAKE
MUMSY	MUTES	PUBES	PUNTS	QUAKY
MUNCH	MUTIS	PUBIC	PUNTY	QUALM
MUNGO	MUZZY	PUBIS	PUPAE	QUASH
MUONS	NUBBY	PUCES	PUPAL	QUASI
MURAL	NUDER	PUCKS	PUPAS	QUEAN
MUREX	NUDES	PUDGE	PUPIL	QUEEF
MURID	NUDGE	PUDGY	PUPPY	QUEEN
MURKY	NUDIE	PUFFY	PURED	QUEER
MURRE	NUKER	PUKER	PUREE	QUELL
MURUS	NUKES	PUKES	PURER	QUERY
MUSED	NULLS	PUKKA	PURGE	QUEST
MUSER	NUMEN	PULER	PURIS	QUEUE
MUSES	NURSE	PULES	PURRS	QUICK
MUSET	NUTSY	PULLS	PURRY	QUIET
MUSHY	NUTTY	PULLY	PURSE	QUILL

QUILT	RUNED	SUETY	SUTRA	TUQUE
QUIPS	RUNES	SUFIS	TUBAL	TURBO
QUIRK	RUNGS	SUGAR	TUBAS	TURFS
QUITE	RUNIC	SUING	TUBBY	TURFY
QUITS	RUNNY	SUITE	TUBED	TURNS
QUOIN	RUNTS	SUITS	TUBER	TURPS
QUOTA	RUNTY	SULKS	TUBES	TUSKS
QUOTE	RUPEE	SULKY	TUCKS	TUSKY
RUBES	RURAL	SULLY	TUFAS	TUTEE
RUBLE	RUSES	SULUS	TUFFS	TUTOR
RUCHE	RUSHY	SUMAC	TUFTS	TUTTI
RUDDY	RUSKS	SUMMA	TUFTY	VULGO
RUDER	RUSTS	SUMPS	TULIP	VULVA
RUFFE	RUSTY	SUNNA	TULLE	WURST
RUFFS	RUTIN	SUNNI	TUMID	YUCCA
RUGBY	RUTTY	SUNNY	TUMMY	YUCKS
RUINS	SUAVE	SUNUP	TUMOR	YUCKY
RULED	SUCKA	SUPER	TUMPS	YUKKY
RULER	SUCKS	SURAH	TUNAS	YUMMO
RULES	SUCKY	SURAS	TUNED	YUMMY
RUMBA	SUCRE	SURDS	TUNER	YUPPY
RUMEN	SUDOR	SURGE	TUNES	AVAIL
RUMMY	SUDSY	SURLY	TUNIC	AVANT
RUMOR	SUEDE	SUSHI	TUNNY	AVAST
RUMPS	SUERS	SUSUS	TUPIK	AVENS

AVERS	OVERT	OWING	SWEAT	SWOTS
AVERT	OVINE	OWLER	SWEDE	SWUNG
AVGAS	OVOID	OWLET	SWEEP	TWAIN
AVIAN	OVOLO	OWNED	SWEET	TWANG
AVION	OVULE	OWNER	SWELL	TWANK
AVISO	UVULA	SWABS	SWEPT	TWEAK
AVOID	AWAIT	SWAGE	SWIFT	TWEED
AVOWS	AWAKE	SWAGS	SWIGS	TWEEN
EVADE	AWARD	SWAIN	SWILL	TWEET
EVENS	AWARE	SWALE	SWIMS	TWERK
EVENT	AWARN	SWAMI	SWINE	TWERP
EVERE	AWASH	SWAMP	SWING	TWICE
EVERT	AWFUL	SWANG	SWINK	TWICT
EVERY	AWING	SWANK	SWIPE	TWIGS
EVICT	AWNED	SWANS	SWIRL	TWILL
EVILL	AWNER	SWAPE	SWISH	TWINE
EVILS	AWOKE	SWAPS	SWISS	TWINS
EVOKE	AWORK	SWARD	SWIZZ	TWINY
IVORY	DWAAL	SWARM	SWOLE	TWIRL
KVELL	DWALE	SWART	SWOON	TWIST
OVALS	DWARF	SWASH	SWOOP	TWITE
OVARY	DWEEB	SWATH	SWOPS	TWITS
OVATE	DWELL	SWATS	SWORD	AXELS
OVENS	DWELT	SWAYS	SWORE	AXIAL
OVERS	OWEST	SWEAR	SWORN	AXILE

AXING	EXTRA	EYING	NYMPH	XYLIC
AXIOM	EXUDE	EYRIE	PYGMY	XYLOL
AXION	EXULT	EYRIR	PYLON	XYLYL
AXLED	EXURB	GYOZA	PYRAL	XYSTI
AXLES	OXBOW	GYPSY	PYRES	XYSTS
AXMAN	OXEYE	HYDRA	PYXIS	XYZZY
AXMEN	OXIDE	HYDRO	SYLPH	AZIDE
AXONE	OXLIP	HYENA	SYNCH	AZINE
AXONS	OXTER	HYMEN	SYNCS	AZOIC
EXACT	BYLAW	HYPED	SYNOD	AZURE
EXALT	BYWAY	HYPER	SYRAH	AZURN
EXAMS	CYANS	HYRAX	SYRUP	AZURY
EXCEL	CYBER	LYING	SYSOP	CZARS
EXECS	CYCAD	LYMPH	TYING	OZONE
EXERT	CYCLE	LYNCH	TYPED	PZAZZ
EXILE	CYNIC	LYRIC	TYPES	
EXINE	CYSTS	MYLAR	TYPIC	
EXIST	CYTOL	MYNAH	TYPOS	
EXITS	DYADS	MYOPE	TYRAN	
EXODE	DYERS	MYOPY	TYRED	
EXONS	DYING	MYRRH	TYRES	
EXPAT	DYKES	MYTHS	TYROS	
EXPEL	DYKEY	MYTHY	VYING	
EXPOS	DYNES	NYALA	XYLAN	
EXTOL	EYERS	NYLON	XYLEM	

ABACA	ANALS	BEATS	CHAFE	CLAIM
ABACI	APACE	BEAUT	CHAFF	CLAMP
ABACK	APART	BLACK	CHAIN	CLAMS
ABAFT	ASANA	BLADE	CHAIR	CLANG
ABASE	ATAXY	BLAME	CHAIS	CLANK
ABASH	AVAIL	BLAND	CHALK	CLANS
ABASK	AVANT	BLANK	CHAMP	CLAPS
ABATE	AVAST	BLARE	CHAMS	CLARO
ABAYA	AWAIT	BLAST	CHANT	CLARY
ADAGE	AWAKE	BLAZE	CHAOS	CLASH
ADAPT	AWARD	BOARD	CHAPE	CLASP
AGAIN	AWARE	BOAST	CHAPS	CLASS
AGAMA	AWARN	BRACE	CHARD	CLAST
AGAPE	AWASH	BRAID	CHARE	CLAVE
AGARS	BEACH	BRAIN	CHARM	CLAWS
AGATE	BEADS	BRAKE	CHARS	CLAYS
AGAVE	BEADY	BRAND	CHART	COACH
ALACK	BEAKY	BRASH	CHARY	COALS
ALAMO	BEAMS	BRASS	CHASE	COALY
ALARM	BEAMY	BRAVE	CHASM	COAPT
ALARY	BEANO	BRAVO	CHAST	COAST
ALATE	BEANS	BRAWL	CHATS	COATE
AMAIN	BEARD	BRAWN	CHAYS	COATI
AMASS	BEARS	CEASE	CLACK	COATS
AMAZE	BEAST	CHADS	CLADE	CRABS

CRACK	DEANS	DWALE	FLAPS	GRANT
CRAFT	DEARN	DWARF	FLARE	GRAPE
CRAGS	DEARS	DYADS	FLASH	GRAPH
CRAKE	DEARY	ELAND	FLASK	GRASP
CRAME	DEATH	ELANS	FLAWS	GRASS
CRAMP	DIALS	ELATE	FOAMY	GRATE
CRAMS	DIANA	EMAIL	FRAIL	GRAVE
CRANE	DIARY	ENACT	FRAME	GRAVY
CRANK	DRABS	ENATE	FRANK	GRAZE
CRANS	DRAFF	EPACT	FRAUD	GUANO
CRAPS	DRAFT	ERASE	GIANT	GUARD
CRASH	DRAGS	EVADE	GLADE	GUAVA
CRASS	DRAIL	EXACT	GLAND	HEADS
CRATE	DRAIN	EXALT	GLARE	HEADY
CRAVE	DRAKE	EXAMS	GLASS	HEAPS
CRAWL	DRAMA	FEARS	GLAZE	HEARD
CRAYS	DRAMS	FEAST	GNASH	HEARS
CRAZE	DRANK	FEATS	GOALS	HEART
CRAZY	DRAPE	FLAGS	GRABS	HEATH
CYANS	DRAWL	FLAIL	GRACE	HEAVE
CZARS	DRAWN	FLAIR	GRADE	HEAVY
DEADS	DRAWS	FLAKE	GRAFT	HOARD
DEALE	DRAYS	FLAKY	GRAIL	HOARY
DEALS	DUALS	FLAME	GRAIN	IMAGE
DEALT	DWAAL	FLANK	GRAND	INANE

INAPT	LOANS	ORALS	PIANO	PRASE
IRATE	LOATH	ORANG	PLACE	PRATE
JEANS	MEADS	ORATE	PLAGE	PRAWN
KHAKI	MEALS	OVALS	PLAID	PSALM
KHANS	MEALY	OVARY	PLAIN	PZAZZ
KIANG	MEANS	OVATE	PLAIT	QUACK
KNACK	MEANT	PEACE	PLANE	QUAFF
KNAPS	MEANY	PEACH	PLANK	QUAIL
LEACH	MEATS	PEAKS	PLANS	QUAKE
LEADS	MEATY	PEAKY	PLANT	QUAKY
LEAFY	MIASM	PEALS	PLASH	QUALM
LEAKY	MIAUL	PEANS	PLASM	QUASH
LEANS	MOANS	PEARE	PLATE	QUASI
LEAPT	MOANY	PEARL	PLATS	REACH
LEARN	MOATS	PEARS	PLATT	REACT
LEASE	NEARE	PEART	PLAYA	READS
LEASH	NEARS	PEARY	PLAYS	READY
LEAST	NEATH	PEASE	PLAZA	REALM
LEAVE	NEATO	PEATS	POACH	REALS
LIANG	NEATS	PEATY	PRADS	REAME
LIARS	NYALA	PEAVY	PRAME	REAMS
LLAMA	OKAPI	PHAGE	PRAMS	REARM
LLANO	OKAYS	PHARM	PRANA	REARS
LOADS	OPALS	PHARO	PRANG	REATA
LOAMY	ORACY	PHASE	PRANK	RIALS

RIATA	SCAUP	SHARP	SMAIL	SPALL
ROACH	SEALS	SHART	SMALL	SPAMS
ROADS	SEAMS	SHAVE	SMARM	SPANG
ROARS	SEAMY	SHAWL	SMART	SPANK
ROAST	SEATS	SHAWM	SMASH	SPANS
SCABS	SHACK	SHAYS	SMAZE	SPARE
SCADS	SHADE	SKALD	SNACK	SPARK
SCALD	SHADS	SKANK	SNAFU	SPARS
SCALE	SHADY	SKARN	SNAGS	SPASM
SCALP	SHAFT	SKATE	SNAIL	SPATE
SCALY	SHAGS	SKATS	SNAKE	SPATS
SCAMP	SHAHS	SLABS	SNAKY	SPAWN
SCAMS	SHAKA	SLACK	SNAPS	SPAWS
SCANS	SHAKE	SLAGS	SNARE	SPAZZ
SCANT	SHAKO	SLAIN	SNARK	STABS
SCAPE	SHAKY	SLAKE	SNARL	STACK
SCAPI	SHALE	SLANG	SOAKS	STADE
SCARD	SHALL	SLANT	SOAPS	STAFF
SCARE	SHAME	SLAPS	SOAPY	STAGE
SCARF	SHAMS	SLASH	SOARS	STAGS
SCARP	SHANK	SLATE	SPACE	STAGY
SCARS	SHAPE	SLATS	SPACY	STAID
SCARY	SHARD	SLATY	SPADE	STAIN
SCATH	SHARE	SLAVE	SPAHI	STAIR
SCATT	SHARK	SMACK	SPAIN	STAKE

STALE	SWANK	THAWS	TRAYS	YEAST
STALK	SWANS	THAWY	TSARS	ZEALE
STALL	SWAPE	TIARA	TWAIN	ZEALS
STAMP	SWAPS	TOADS	TWANG	ABBAT
STAND	SWARD	TOADY	TWANK	ABBEY
STANE	SWARM	TOAST	UGALI	ABBOT
STANK	SWART	TRACE	UKASE	ALBUM
STARE	SWASH	TRACH	UMAMI	AMBER
STARK	SWATH	TRACK	UNAPT	AMBIT
STARS	SWATS	TRACT	USAGE	AMBLE
START	SWAYS	TRADE	VIAND	AMBON
STASH	TEACH	TRAIL	WEARS	AMBOS
STATE	TEADE	TRAIN	WEARY	AMBRY
STATS	TEAED	TRAIT	WEAVE	ARBOR
STAVE	TEAKS	TRAMP	WHACK	BABEL
STAYS	TEALS	TRAMS	WHALE	BIBLE
SUAVE	TEAMS	TRANQ	WHANG	BOBBY
SWABS	TEARE	TRANS	WHARF	BUBBA
SWAGE	TEARS	TRANT	WRACK	CABAL
SWAGS	TEARY	TRAPS	WRAPS	CABBY
SWAIN	TEASE	TRAPT	WRATH	CABER
SWALE	TEATS	TRASH	XOANA	CABIN
SWAMI	THANE	TRASS	YEARE	CABLE
SWAMP	THANK	TRAVE	YEARN	COBBS
SWANG	THATS	TRAWL	YEARS	COBBY

COBIA	FABLE	NABES	RIBBY	TUBAS
COBRA	FIBER	NABLA	ROBED	TUBBY
CUBBY	FIBRE	NABOB	ROBES	TUBED
CUBEB	FUBAR	NEBBY	ROBIN	TUBER
CUBED	GABBY	NOBBY	ROBOT	TUBES
CUBER	GABLE	NOBLE	RUBES	UMBER
CUBES	GOBBY	NOBLY	RUBLE	UMBRA
CUBIC	HABIT	NUBBY	SABER	UNBAN
CUBIT	HOBBY	OMBRE	SABLE	UNBOX
CYBER	HUBBY	OMBUD	SABOT	URBAN
DEBAR	IMBED	ORBED	SABRA	VIBES
DEBIT	IMBUE	ORBIT	SABRE	XEBEC
DEBTS	JABOT	OXBOW	SEBUM	YOBBO
DEBUG	JIBBS	PUBES	SIBYL	ZEBRA
DEBUT	JIBED	PUBIC	SOBBY	ACCEL
DOBBY	JIBES	PUBIS	SOBER	ACCUS
DOBRA	KEBAB	RABBI	TABBY	ALCID
DOBRO	LABEL	RABIC	TABES	ALCOS
EBBED	LABIA	RABID	TABLA	ANCHO
ELBOW	LABOR	REBAR	TABLE	ANCON
EMBAY	LIBEL	REBBE	TABOO	ARCED
EMBED	LIBRA	REBEC	TABOR	ARCHY
EMBER	LOBBY	REBEL	TABUN	ASCOT
EMBOG	LUBED	REBUS	TIBIA	ASCUS
EMBUS	MOBES	REBUT	TUBAL	BACON

BOCHE	DECOY	FOCAL	LUCID	NACRE
BUCKS	DECRY	FOCUS	LUCKY	NECKE
CACAO	DICER	HACKS	LUCRE	NECKS
CACAS	DICES	HACKY	MACAW	NECRO
CACHE	DICEY	HECKA	MACES	NICAD
CACTI	DICKS	INCEL	MACHO	NICER
CECAL	DICKY	INCUR	MACLE	NICHE
CECUM	DICOT	INCUS	MACON	NICKS
COCAS	DICTA	ITCHY	MACRO	OCCUR
COCCI	DICTY	JACAL	MECCA	ONCER
COCKS	DOCKS	JACKS	MECHA	ONCET
COCKY	DUCAT	JACKY	MICAS	OUCHE
COCOA	DUCES	JACOB	MICKS	PACED
COCOS	DUCHY	JOCKS	MICRO	PACER
CYCAD	DUCKS	JOCKY	MOCHA	PACES
CYCLE	DUCKY	KECKS	MOCHI	PACEY
DACHA	DUCTS	KICKS	MOCKS	PACKS
DACKS	ECCHI	KICKY	MUCAL	PACTS
DECAD	EMCEE	LACED	MUCHO	PECAN
DECAF	EXCEL	LACKS	MUCID	PECKE
DECAL	FACED	LICIT	MUCIN	PECKS
DECAY	FACES	LOCAL	MUCKY	PICCY
DECKS	FACET	LOCKS	MUCRO	PICKS
DECON	FACTS	LOCUM	MUCUS	PICKY
DECOR	FECES	LOCUS	NACHO	PICOT

PICTS	RUCHE	ULCER	ANDRO	CODED
PICUL	SACKS	UNCLE	ARDOR	CODER
POCKS	SACRA	UNCOS	ASDIC	CODES
PUCES	SECCO	UNCUT	AUDAX	CODEX
PUCKS	SECTS	VICAR	AUDIO	CODON
RACED	SICKO	VICES	AUDIT	CUDDY
RACER	SOCKS	VOCAL	BADGE	DADAS
RACES	SOCLE	WACKE	BADLY	DADDY
RACKS	SUCKA	WACKO	BEDEW	DADOS
RACON	SUCKS	WACKY	BEDIM	DIDDY
RECAP	SUCKY	WICCA	BIDDY	DIDIE
RECCE	SUCRE	YACHT	BIDET	DIDOS
RECIT	TACHE	YUCCA	BODGE	DODGE
RECON	TACHS	YUCKS	BUDDY	DODGY
RECTA	TACIT	YUCKY	BUDGE	DUDES
RECTO	TACKS	ADDAX	CADDY	EIDER
RECUR	TACKY	ADDED	CADET	EIDOS
RICER	TACOS	ADDER	CADGE	ELDER
RICES	TACTS	ADDLE	CADRE	ENDED
RICHE	TECHS	AIDED	CEDAR	ENDOW
RICIN	TECHY	AIDER	CEDED	ENDUE
RICKS	TECTA	AIDES	CEDER	FADDY
ROCHE	TICKS	ALDER	CIDER	FADED
ROCKS	TICKY	ALDOL	CODAS	FADES
ROCKY	TUCKS	ANDED	CODEC	FUDGE

GIDDY	LODGE	NODED	RADIX	SIDES
GODLY	LUDIC	NODES	RADON	SIDLE
HADES	MADAM	NODUS	REDAN	SODAS
HEDGE	MADLY	NUDER	REDDS	SODDY
HEDON	MEDAL	NUDES	REDDY	SUDOR
HIDER	MEDIA	NUDGE	REDID	SUDSY
HIDES	MEDIC	NUDIE	REDOS	TEDDY
HYDRA	MIDDY	ODDER	REDOX	TIDAL
HYDRO	MIDGE	ODDLY	REDUX	TIDED
INDEX	MIDIS	OLDEN	RIDER	TIDES
INDIA	MIDST	OLDER	RIDES	TODAY
INDIE	MODAL	OLDIE	RIDGE	TODDY
JADED	MODEL	ORDER	RIDGY	UNDER
JADES	MODEM	PADDY	RIDIC	UNDUE
JUDAH	MODES	PADRE	RODEO	VIDEO
JUDGE	MODUS	PEDAL	RODES	VODKA
JUDGY	MUDAR	PEDIS	RUDDY	WADDY
KEDGE	MUDDY	PODGE	RUDER	WADER
KIDDO	MUDGE	PODGY	SADES	WEDGE
KIDLY	MUDRA	PODIA	SADHU	WEDGY
KUDOS	NADIR	PUDGE	SADLY	WIDEN
LADDU	NEDDY	PUDGY	SEDAN	WIDER
LADEN	NIDUS	RADAR	SEDER	WIDOW
LADLE	NODAL	RADII	SEDGE	WIDTH
LEDGE	NODDY	RADIO	SEDUM	WODGE

YODEL	ARECA	CHEEK	CREDO	DREAM
ABEAM	ARENA	CHEEP	CREDS	DREAR
ABEAR	AREPA	CHEER	CREED	DRECK
ABELE	ARETE	CHEEZ	CREEK	DREGS
ABEND	AVENS	CHEFS	CREEL	DRESS
ABETS	AVERS	CHELA	CREEP	DREYS
ACERB	AVERT	CHEMO	CREMS	DUELS
ADEPT	AXELS	CHERT	CREPE	DUETS
AGEND	BEECH	CHESS	CREPT	DUETT
AGENT	BEEFY	CHEST	CREPY	DWEEB
AGERS	BLEAK	CHEWS	CRESC	DWELL
AHEAD	BLEAR	CHEWY	CRESS	DWELT
AKENS	BLEAT	CLEAN	CREST	DYERS
ALEPH	BLECH	CLEAR	CREWS	EDEMA
ALERT	BLEED	CLEAT	DEEDE	EGEST
AMEBA	BLEEP	CLEEK	DEEDS	EJECT
AMEND	BLEND	CLEFT	DEEMS	ELECT
AMENS	BLESS	CLEPE	DEEPS	ELEGY
AMENT	BLEST	CLERK	DEERE	ELEMI
ANELE	BREAD	CLEVE	DEERS	EMEER
ANENT	BREAK	CLEWS	DEETS	EMEND
APERS	BREED	COEDS	DIENE	EMERG
APERY	CHEAP	CREAK	DIETS	EMERY
AREAL	CHEAT	CREAM	DOERS	ENEMA
AREAS	CHECK	CREAT	DREAD	ENEMY

ERECT	GEESE	KEEPS	OCEAN	PEERS
EVENS	GLEAM	KEEVE	ODEUM	PEEVE
EVENT	GLEAN	KNEAD	OLEUM	PIECE
EVERE	GREAT	KNEED	OMEGA	PIERS
EVERT	GREED	KNEEL	OMENS	PIETS
EVERY	GREEK	KNEES	ONELY	PIETY
EXECS	GREEN	KNELL	ONERS	PLEAD
EXERT	GREET	KNELT	ONERY	PLEAS
EYERS	GUESS	KVELL	ONEST	PLEAT
FEEDS	GUEST	LEECH	OPENS	PLEBE
FEELS	HEELS	LEERY	OPERA	PLEBS
FIELD	HYENA	LIEGE	OPERS	POEME
FIEND	IDEAL	LIENS	OREAD	POEMS
FIERY	IDEAS	MEETS	OVENS	POESY
FLECK	INEPT	MIENS	OVERS	POETE
FLEEK	INERT	NEEDS	OVERT	POETS
FLEER	ITEMS	NEEDY	OWEST	PREDS
FLEET	JEEPS	NEEMB	OXEYE	PREEN
FLESH	JEERS	NEEMS	PAEAN	PREGO
FREAK	JOEYS	NIECE	PAEDO	PRESS
FREED	KEEKS	NIEVE	PAEON	PREST
FREER	KEELS	OBEAH	PEELS	PREXY
FRESH	KEENE	OBELI	PEENS	PSEUD
FUELS	KEENS	OBESE	PEEPE	QUEAN
GEEKY	KEEPE	OBEYS	PEEPS	QUEEF

QUEEN	SEEMS	SLEET	STEAM	SWEPT
QUEER	SEEPS	SLEPT	STEAN	TEEMS
QUELL	SEERS	SLEYS	STEED	TEENS
QUERY	SHEAF	SMEAR	STEEK	TEENY
QUEST	SHEAR	SMELL	STEEL	TEETH
QUEUE	SHEDS	SMELT	STEEP	THEBE
REEDE	SHEEN	SMEWS	STEER	THECA
REEDS	SHEEP	SNEAK	STEIN	THEED
REEDY	SHEER	SNECK	STELA	THEES
REEFS	SHEET	SNEER	STELE	THEFT
REEFY	SHEIK	SNELL	STEMS	THEGN
REEKS	SHELF	SPEAK	STENO	THEIR
REEKY	SHELL	SPEAR	STENT	THEME
REELS	SHERO	SPECK	STEPS	THERE
REENS	SHETH	SPECS	STERN	THERM
REEVE	SIEGE	SPEED	STEWS	THESE
RHEUM	SIENS	SPEEL	SUEDE	THESP
SCENA	SIENT	SPELL	SUERS	THETA
SCEND	SIEVE	SPELT	SUETY	THEWS
SCENE	SKEAN	SPEND	SWEAR	THEWY
SCENT	SKEET	SPENT	SWEAT	TIERS
SEEDE	SKEIN	SPERM	SWEDE	TREAD
SEEDS	SLEDS	STEAD	SWEEP	TREAT
SEEDY	SLEEK	STEAK	SWEET	TREED
SEEKS	SLEEP	STEAL	SWELL	TREEN

TREES	WHELP	GAFFE	PUFFY	TUFTS
TREKS	WHERE	GIFTS	RAFTS	TUFTY
TREND	WIELD	GOFER	REFER	UNFIT
TRESS	WREAK	HEFTY	REFIT	UNFIX
TRETS	WRECK	HUFFY	REFIX	UNFUN
TREWS	WREST	INFER	REFUT	WAFER
TREYS	YIELD	INFIX	RIFER	WIFEY
TWEAK	AFFIX	JIFFS	RIFFS	AEGER
TWEED	AWFUL	JIFFY	RIFLE	AEGIS
TWEEN	BEFIT	KAFIR	RIFTS	AGGIE
TWEET	BEFOG	KEFIR	RUFFE	AGGRO
TWERK	BOFFO	LEFTY	RUFFS	ALGAE
TWERP	BUFFO	LIFER	SAFER	ALGAL
UPEND	CAFES	LIFTS	SAFES	ALGID
USERS	CAFFS	LOFTY	SOFAR	ALGIN
VIEWS	CUFFS	MAFIA	SOFAS	ALGOR
WEEDS	DAFFS	MAFIC	SOFTA	ANGEL
WEEDY	DAFFY	MIFFS	SOFTS	ANGER
WEENY	DEFER	MUFFS	SOFTY	ANGLE
WEEPY	DEFIB	MUFTI	SUFIS	ANGRY
WHEAL	DEFOG	NIFFY	TAFFY	ANGST
WHEAT	DIFFS	NIFTY	TIFFS	ARGIL
WHEEL	ELFIN	OFFAL	TOFUS	ARGON
WHELK	FIFTH	OFFED	TUFAS	ARGOT
WHELM	FIFTY	OFFER	TUFFS	ARGUE

AUGER	DAGGA	JAGER	NIGGA	ROGER
AUGHT	DEGUT	JAGGS	NIGHT	ROGUE
AUGUR	DIGIT	JAGGY	ORGAN	ROGUY
AVGAS	DOGES	JIGGY	ORGIC	RUGBY
BAGEL	DOGGE	LAGER	OUGHT	SAGAR
BAGGY	DOGGY	LEGAL	PAGAN	SAGAS
BEGAN	DOGIE	LEGIT	PAGED	SAGES
BEGET	DOGMA	LIGHT	PAGER	SAGGY
BEGIN	EAGER	LOGAN	PAGES	SAGUM
BEGOT	EAGLE	LOGIC	PAGRI	SEGUE
BEGUN	EAGRE	LOGIN	PEGGY	SIGHS
BIGHT	EDGED	LOGON	PIGGY	SIGHT
BIGOT	EDGER	LOGOS	PIGMY	SIGIL
BOGAN	EDGES	MAGES	POGEY	SIGMA
BOGEY	EGGAR	MAGIC	POGOS	SIGNA
BOGGY	EGGED	MAGMA	PYGMY	SIGNS
BOGLE	EIGHT	MAGUS	RAGED	SOGGY
BOGUS	ERGON	MIGHT	RAGER	SUGAR
BUGGY	ERGOT	MOGGY	RAGES	TAGGY
BUGLE	FIGHT	MOGUL	RAGGY	TIGER
CAGED	FOGEY	MUGGY	REGAL	TIGHT
CAGES	FOGGY	NAGAS	REGEN	TIGON
CAGEY	FUGGY	NAGGY	RIGHT	TIGRE
CIGAR	FUGUE	NEGRO	RIGID	TOGAE
CIGGY	INGOT	NEGUS	RIGOR	TOGAS

URGED	ASHEN	OTHER	ALIBI	ASIDE
URGES	ASHER	PSHAW	ALIEN	ATILT
VAGUE	ASHES	REHAB	ALIGN	AVIAN
VEGAN	CAHOW	SAHIB	ALIKE	AVION
VIGIL	COHAB	SCHMO	ALIVE	AVISO
VIGOR	DAHLS	SCHWA	AMICE	AWING
VOGUE	ECHOS	TEHEE	AMICI	AXIAL
WAGED	EPHAH	USHER	AMIDE	AXILE
WAGER	EPHOD	WAHOO	AMIGA	AXING
WAGES	EPHOR	YAHOO	AMIGO	AXIOM
WAGON	ETHER	ABIDE	AMINE	AXION
WIGHT	ETHIC	ACIDS	AMINO	AZIDE
YEGGS	ETHOS	ACIDY	AMISS	AZINE
YOGAS	ETHYL	ACING	AMITY	BAIRN
YOGIC	ICHOR	ACINI	ANILE	BEIGE
YOGIN	JIHAD	ADIEU	ANIMA	BEING
YOGIS	JOHNS	ADIOS	ANIME	BLIMP
ABHOR	LAHAR	AFIRE	ANION	BLIND
ACHED	MAHAL	AGILE	ANISE	BLING
ACHES	MAHOE	AGING	APIAN	BLINK
ACHOO	MOHEL	AGIST	APING	BLISS
APHID	NIHIL	AGITA	APISH	BLITZ
APHIS	OCHER	AHING	ARIAS	BOILS
ARHAT	OCHRE	AKITA	ARILS	BOING
ASHED	OGHAM	ALIAS	ARISE	BRIBE

BRICK	CHINA	COINS	DRIER	EXIST
BRIDE	CHINE	CRIBS	DRIES	EXITS
BRIEF	CHINK	CRICK	DRIFT	EYING
BRIER	CHINO	CRIED	DRILL	FAILS
BRILL	CHINS	CRIER	DRINK	FAINT
BRINE	CHIPS	CRIES	DRIPS	FAIRY
BRING	CHIRO	CRIME	DRIVE	FAITH
BRINK	CHIRP	CRIMP	DYING	FEIGN
BRINY	CHIRR	CRIMS	EDICT	FEINT
BRISK	CHITS	CRIPS	EDIFY	FEIST
BUILD	CHIVE	CRISE	EDITS	FLICK
BUILT	CHIVY	CRISP	EJIDO	FLIER
CAIRN	CLICK	DAILY	EKING	FLIES
CEIBA	CLIFF	DAIRY	ELIDE	FLING
CHIBI	CLIFT	DAISY	ELITE	FLINT
CHICA	CLIMB	DEICE	EMIRS	FLIRT
CHICK	CLIME	DEIFY	EMITS	FOIST
CHICS	CLINE	DEIGN	EPICK	FRIAR
CHIDE	CLING	DEISM	EPICS	FRICK
CHIEF	CLINK	DEIST	ERICA	FRIED
CHILD	CLIPS	DEITY	EVICT	FRILL
CHILE	COIFS	DJINN	EVILL	FRISK
CHILI	COIGN	DOILY	EVILS	FRITZ
CHILL	COILS	DOING	EXILE	FRIZZ
CHIME	COINE	DRIED	EXINE	GAILY

GAINS	HEIST	MAINS	OPINE	PRICK
GLIDE	HOICK	MAIRE	OPIUM	PRICY
GLINT	HOIST	MAIST	ORIBI	PRIDE
GLITZ	ICILY	MAIZE	ORIEL	PRIED
GOING	ICING	MOILE	OSIER	PRIER
GRIEF	IDIOM	MOILS	OVINE	PRIGS
GRIFT	IDIOT	MOIRE	OWING	PRILL
GRIKE	JAILS	MOIST	OXIDE	PRIME
GRILL	JOINS	NAIAD	PAILS	PRIMO
GRIME	JOINT	NAILS	PAINS	PRIMP
GRIMY	JOIST	NAILY	PAINT	PRINK
GRIND	JUICE	NAIRA	PAIRE	PRINT
GRINS	JUICY	NAIVE	PAIRS	PRION
GRIOT	KAILS	NEIGH	PAISA	PRIOR
GRIPE	KNIFE	NOICE	PHIAL	PRISE
GRITH	KNITS	NOISE	PHISH	PRISM
GRITS	KNIVE	NOISY	PLICA	PRIVY
GUIDE	LAIRD	OBITS	PLIER	PRIZE
GUILD	LAITY	ODIST	PLIES	QUICK
GUILE	LOINS	ODIUM	PLINK	QUIET
GUILT	LYING	OGIVE	POILU	QUILL
GUISE	MAIDE	OHING	POINT	QUILT
HAIKU	MAIDS	OLIVE	POISE	QUIPS
HAIRY	MAILE	OMITS	PRIAL	QUIRK
HEIRS	MAILS	ONION	PRICE	QUITE

QUITS	SHIER	SKIPS	SNIFT	STICK
RAIDS	SHIES	SKIRR	SNIPE	STIES
RAILE	SHIFT	SKIRT	SNIPS	STIFF
RAILS	SHILL	SKITE	SOILE	STIKE
RAINS	SHINE	SKITS	SOILS	STILB
RAINY	SHINS	SKIVE	SPICA	STILE
RAISE	SHINY	SLICE	SPICE	STILL
RAITA	SHIPS	SLICK	SPICY	STILT
REIFY	SHIRE	SLIDE	SPIED	STIME
REIGN	SHIRK	SLIME	SPIEL	STIMY
REIKI	SHIRT	SLIMS	SPIES	STING
REINS	SHITE	SLIMY	SPIFF	STINK
RHINO	SHITS	SLING	SPIKE	STINT
ROIDS	SHIVA	SLINK	SPIKY	STIPE
ROILY	SHIVE	SLIPS	SPILE	STIRK
RUINS	SHIVS	SLITE	SPILL	STIRS
SAILE	SKIDS	SLITS	SPILT	STIVE
SAILS	SKIER	SLIVE	SPINE	SUING
SAINT	SKIES	SMILE	SPINS	SUITE
SCION	SKIFF	SMIRK	SPINY	SUITS
SEINE	SKILL	SMITE	SPIRE	SWIFT
SEINS	SKILS	SMITH	SPITE	SWIGS
SEISM	SKIMP	SNICK	SPITS	SWILL
SEITY	SKINS	SNIDE	SPITZ	SWIMS
SEIZE	SKINT	SNIFF	SPIVS	SWINE

SWING	TRICK	UNIFY	WHIRR	ANKLE
SWINK	TRIED	UNION	WHISH	ASKED
SWIPE	TRIER	UNITE	WHISK	ASKER
SWIRL	TRIES	UNITS	WHITE	ASKES
SWISH	TRIGS	UNITY	WHITY	ASKEW
SWISS	TRIKE	URINE	WHIZZ	BAKED
SWIZZ	TRILL	USING	WRICK	BAKER
TAIGA	TRIMS	UTILE	WRING	BIKER
TAILS	TRINE	VEINS	WRIST	BOKEH
TAINT	TRIOS	VEINY	WRITE	CAKED
THICK	TRIPE	VOICE	ZAIRE	CAKES
THIEF	TRIPS	VOILA	BIJOU	CAKEY
THIGH	TRITE	VYING	CAJUN	COKED
THILL	TWICE	WAIST	ENJOY	COKER
THING	TWICT	WAITS	HAJJI	COKES
THINK	TWIGS	WAIVE	HIJAB	DEKES
THINS	TWILL	WEIGH	HIJRA	DEKKO
THIOL	TWINE	WEIRD	MAJOR	DIKER
THIRD	TWINS	WHICH	MOJOS	DIKES
TOILE	TWINY	WHIFF	RAJAH	DUKES
TOILS	TWIRL	WHILE	RAJAS	DYKES
TRIAD	TWIST	WHIMS	REJIG	DYKEY
TRIAL	TWITE	WHINE	ALKIE	ELKES
TRIBE	TWITS	WHINY	ALKYD	ESKER
TRICE	TYING	WHIRL	ALKYL	FAKED

FAKER	NAKER	SAKES	AGLET	BILGE
FAKIR	NAKFA	SOKEN	AGLOW	BILLS
HIKER	NUKER	SOKES	AILED	BILLY
HOKEY	NUKES	SOKOL	ALLAY	BULGE
HOKKU	OAKED	TAKED	ALLEY	BULKY
HOKUM	OAKEN	TAKEN	ALLOT	BULLS
IRKED	OAKUM	TAKER	ALLOW	BULLY
JAKES	PEKOE	TAKES	ALLOY	BYLAW
JOKED	PIKED	TAKIN	ALLYL	CALFS
JOKER	PIKER	TIKKA	ATLAS	CALIF
JOKES	PIKES	TOKED	AXLED	CALIX
JOKEY	POKED	TOKEN	AXLES	CALKS
JUKED	POKER	TOKES	BALDY	CALLA
JUKES	POKES	WAKEN	BALKY	CALLI
KAKAS	POKEY	YAKKY	BALLS	CALLS
KIKES	POKIE	YAKOW	BALLY	CALMS
LIKED	PUKER	YOKED	BALMY	CALMY
LIKEN	PUKES	YOKEL	BELAY	CALYX
LIKES	PUKKA	YOKES	BELCH	CELEB
MAKER	RAKED	YUKKY	BELIE	CELLA
MAKES	RAKER	ZAKAT	BELLE	CELLI
MIKED	RAKES	AALII	BELLS	CELLO
MIKES	REKEY	ABLED	BELLY	CELLS
MOKES	ROKES	ABLER	BELOW	CELTS
NAKED	SAKER	ABLES	BILBY	CILIA

COLAS	DOLOR	GELID	IGLOO	MALES
COLDS	DOLTS	GILET	INLAY	MALLS
COLES	DULLY	GOLEM	INLET	MALMS
COLIC	DULSE	GOLLY	ISLAM	MALTA
COLON	EELED	GULCH	ISLET	MALTS
COLOR	EELER	GULLY	JALAP	MALTY
COLTS	FALLS	HALAL	JALEO	MELEE
CULEX	FALSE	HALTS	JELLY	MELON
CULLS	FELLA	HALVE	JILTS	MELTY
CULLY	FELON	HELIX	JOLLY	MILCH
CULTS	FILCH	HELLA	JOLTS	MILDS
CULTY	FILED	HELLO	JOLTY	MILER
DALES	FILES	HELPS	JULEP	MILES
DALLY	FILET	HELVE	KALES	MILKO
DELAY	FILLS	HILLS	KELLS	MILKS
DELFT	FILLY	HILLY	KELLY	MILKY
DELLS	FILMS	HOLDS	KILIM	MILLS
DELTA	FILMY	HOLER	KILLS	MILOS
DELVE	FILTH	HOLES	KILNS	MOLAL
DILDO	FOLDS	HOLEY	KILOS	MOLAR
DILLS	FOLIO	HOLLO	KILTS	MOLDS
DILLY	FOLKS	HOLLY	LILAC	MOLDY
DOLLS	FOLLY	HULKY	LOLLY	MOLES
DOLLY	FULLY	IBLIS	MALAI	MOLLY
DOLMA	GALAH	IDLER	MALAR	MOLTS

MULCH	PALLY	PULES	SALAT	SOLAR
MULCT	PALMS	PULLS	SALEP	SOLDO
MULES	PALMY	PULLY	SALES	SOLER
MULEY	PALSY	PULPS	SALLY	SOLES
MULGA	PELMA	PULPY	SALMI	SOLID
MULLA	PHLOX	PULSE	SALON	SOLON
MULLS	PILAF	PYLON	SALSA	SOLOS
MULTI	PILED	QILIN	SALTS	SOLUS
MYLAR	PILER	RALLY	SALTY	SOLVE
NELLY	PILES	RELAX	SALVE	SPLAT
NULLS	PILIS	RELAY	SALVO	SPLAY
NYLON	PILLS	RELIC	SELFS	SPLIT
OGLED	PILLY	RELLY	SELLE	SPLOT
OGLER	PILOT	RILED	SELLS	SULKS
OGLES	PILUS	RILEY	SELLY	SULKY
OILED	POLAR	RILLE	SELVA	SULLY
OILER	POLES	RILLS	SILES	SULUS
OLLIE	POLIO	ROLES	SILEX	SYLPH
OWLER	POLIS	ROLLS	SILKS	TALCS
OWLET	POLKA	ROLLY	SILKY	TALCY
OXLIP	POLLS	RULED	SILLS	TALED
PALEA	POLLY	RULER	SILLY	TALES
PALED	POLOS	RULES	SILOS	TALKE
PALES	POLYP	SALAD	SILVA	TALKS
PALLS	PULER	SALAL	SOLAN	TALKY

TALLY	UNLIT	YELLS	CAMES	DAMES
TALMA	VALET	YELPS	CAMOS	DAMNS
TALON	VALID	YOLKS	CAMPI	DEMIT
TALUS	VALOR	YOLKY	CAMPO	DEMOB
TELCO	VALUE	ZILCH	CAMPS	DEMOI
TELEX	VALVE	ACMES	CAMPY	DEMON
TELIC	VELUM	ADMAN	COMAE	DEMOS
TELLS	VILLA	ADMIN	COMAS	DEMUR
TELLY	VOLAR	ADMIT	COMBE	DIMER
TELOS	VULGO	ADMIX	COMBO	DIMES
TILDE	VULVA	AIMED	COMBS	DIMLY
TILED	WALES	AIMER	COMER	DIMPS
TILER	WALKS	ARMED	COMES	DOMED
TILES	WALLS	ARMIE	COMET	DOMES
TILLS	WALTZ	ARMOR	COMFY	DUMBO
TILLY	WELLY	ATMAN	COMIC	DUMMY
TILTH	WELSH	ATMOS	COMIX	DUMPS
TILTS	WILDS	AXMAN	COMMA	DUMPY
TOLAR	WILES	AXMEN	COMMO	ELMEN
TOLED	WILLY	BIMBO	COMMS	EMMER
TOLES	XYLAN	BUMPS	COMMY	EMMET
TOLLS	XYLEM	BUMPY	COMPO	ERMIN
TULIP	XYLIC	CAMAS	COMPS	FAMED
TULLE	XYLOL	CAMEL	CUMIN	FEMME
UNLAY	XYLYL	CAMEO	DAMAR	FUMES

GAMER	JUMPY	MIMIC	PUMAS	SAMPS
GAMES	KAMAL	MOMMA	PUMPS	SEMEN
GAMIN	KAMES	MOMMY	RAMED	SEMIS
GAMMY	KEMPT	MOMSY	RAMEN	SIMAS
GAMUT	LAMIA	MUMMY	RAMIE	SIMBA
GIMPY	LEMAN	MUMPS	RAMPS	SIMON
GUMBO	LEMON	MUMSY	RAMUS	SIMPS
GUMMY	LIMBO	NAMED	REMEX	SIMUL
HAMMY	LIMBS	NAMER	REMIT	SOMAN
HOMES	LIMEY	NAMES	REMIX	SOMAS
HOMEY	LIMIT	NIMBY	RIMED	SUMAC
HOMIE	LUMIC	NOMAD	RIMER	SUMMA
HUMAN	LUMPY	NOMAN	RIMES	SUMPS
HUMID	LYMPH	NOMEN	ROMAN	TAMAS
HUMOR	MAMAS	NOMES	ROMEO	TAMED
HUMUS	MAMBA	NUMEN	ROMPS	TAMER
HYMEN	MAMBO	NYMPH	RUMBA	TAMES
IMMIX	MAMMA	OHMIC	RUMEN	TAMIS
JAMBS	MAMMY	OOMPH	RUMMY	TAMMY
JAMMY	MEMES	ORMER	RUMOR	TAMPS
JEMMY	MEMOS	OSMOL	RUMPS	TEMPI
JIMMY	MIMED	PAMPA	SAMBA	TEMPO
JUMBO	MIMEO	PIMPS	SAMBO	TEMPS
JUMBY	MIMER	POMMY	SAMEY	TEMPT
JUMPS	MIMES	POMPS	SAMMY	TIMED

TIMER	ANNAS	BONGO	CONES	DINGY
TIMES	ANNEX	BONNY	CONEY	DINKS
TIMID	ANNOY	BONUS	CONGA	DINKY
TOMBS	ANNUL	BUNCH	CONIC	DINOS
TOMES	APNEA	BUNCO	CONKS	DINTS
TUMID	AUNTS	BUNNY	CONKY	DONEE
TUMMY	AUNTY	CANAL	CONST	DONGS
TUMOR	AWNED	CANDY	CONTE	DONNA
TUMPS	AWNER	CANED	CUNTS	DONOR
UNMAN	BANAL	CANES	CYNIC	DONUT
UNMET	BANDO	CANID	DANCE	DUNAM
VOMIT	BANDY	CANNA	DANDY	DUNCE
WIMPY	BANGS	CANNY	DANIO	DUNES
WOMAN	BANNS	CANOE	DANKS	DUNGS
WOMEN	BENCH	CANON	DENAR	DUNKS
YAMEN	BENDY	CANTO	DENEB	DUNNY
YUMMO	BINDI	CANTS	DENES	DYNES
YUMMY	BINDS	CANTY	DENIM	ENNUI
ZAMIA	BINGE	CENSE	DENSE	ERNES
ZOMBI	BINGO	CENTO	DENTS	FANCY
ACNED	BONCE	CENTS	DINAR	FANGS
ACNES	BONDS	CINCH	DINER	FANNE
AMNIA	BONER	CONCH	DINGE	FANNY
AMNIO	BONES	CONDO	DINGO	FENCE
ANNAL	BONEY	CONED	DINGS	FINAL

FINDS	HANDY	JUNKY	LINKS	MANUS
FINED	HANGS	JUNTA	LONER	MENDS
FINER	HENCE	JUNTO	LONGS	MENSA
FINES	HENCH	KANAS	LUNAR	MENSE
FINIS	HENNA	KANJI	LUNCH	MENUS
FUNDI	HINGE	KENAF	LUNGE	MINCE
FUNDS	HINKY	KENDO	LUNGI	MINCY
FUNGI	HINTS	KENTE	LUNGS	MINDE
FUNKY	HONED	KINDE	LYNCH	MINDS
FUNNY	HONEY	KINDS	MANAT	MINED
GANJA	HONOR	KINDY	MANED	MINER
GENES	HUNCH	KINGS	MANES	MINES
GENIC	HUNKS	KININ	MANGA	MINGY
GENIE	HUNKY	KINKS	MANGE	MINIM
GENRE	INNER	KINKY	MANGO	MINKS
GENTS	JANES	LANAI	MANGY	MINNY
GENUS	JANUS	LANCE	MANIA	MINOR
GONAD	JENNY	LANDS	MANIC	MINTS
GONER	JINGO	LANKY	MANIS	MINTY
GONNA	JINKS	LENDS	MANLY	MINUS
GONZO	JINNI	LINED	MANNA	MINXY
GUNGE	JONAH	LINEN	MANNY	MONAD
GUNGY	JONES	LINER	MANOR	MONDO
GUNKY	JUNCO	LINES	MANSE	MONES
HANDS	JUNKS	LINGO	MANTA	MONEY

MONGO	PANEL	PINKO	RANEE	RUNES
MONGS	PANES	PINKS	RANGA	RUNGS
MONKS	PANGA	PINKY	RANGE	RUNIC
MONTE	PANGS	PINNA	RANGI	RUNNY
MONTH	PANIC	PINNY	RANGY	RUNTS
MUNCH	PANNE	PINOT	RANIS	RUNTY
MUNGO	PANSY	PINTO	RANKE	SANDO
MYNAH	PANTO	PINTS	RANKS	SANDS
NANAS	PANTS	PINUP	RANTS	SANDY
NANCY	PANTY	PONCE	RENAL	SANTO
NANNY	PENAL	PONDS	RENEW	SENDS
NINES	PENCE	PONDY	RENIG	SENES
NINJA	PENES	PONGS	RENIN	SENNA
NINNY	PENIS	PONGY	RENTS	SENOR
NINON	PENNA	PUNCH	RINDS	SENSE
NINTH	PENNE	PUNIC	RINDY	SENTE
NONAD	PENNI	PUNKS	RINED	SENTI
NONCE	PENNY	PUNKY	RINES	SENTS
NONES	PENTS	PUNNY	RINGS	SINCE
NONET	PINAY	PUNTS	RINKS	SINES
OUNCE	PINCH	PUNTY	RINSE	SINEW
OWNED	PINES	QANAT	RONDE	SINGE
OWNER	PINEY	RANCH	RONDO	SINGS
PANDA	PINGO	RANDS	RONIN	SINKS
PANED	PINGS	RANDY	RUNED	SINUS

SONAR	TENDU	TONIC	WINZE	ABOIL
SONDE	TENET	TONNE	WONGA	ABORD
SONES	TENGE	TONUS	WONKY	ABORE
SONGS	TENNO	TUNAS	XENIA	ABORN
SONIC	TENON	TUNED	XENIC	ABORT
SONNY	TENOR	TUNER	XENON	ABOUT
SUNNA	TENSE	TUNES	XENYL	ABOVE
SUNNI	TENTH	TUNIC	YANKS	ACORN
SUNNY	TENTS	TUNNY	YENTA	ADOBE
SUNUP	TENUE	VENAL	YONIC	ADOBO
SYNCH	TINCT	VENGE	YONIS	ADOPT
SYNCS	TINED	VENOM	YONKS	ADORE
SYNOD	TINES	VENUE	ZINCO	ADORN
TANGA	TINGE	VENUS	ZINCS	AEONS
TANGI	TINGS	VINES	ZINCY	AFOOT
TANGO	TINKS	VINYL	ZINGS	AFORE
TANGS	TINNY	WANED	ZINGY	AFOUL
TANGY	TINTS	WANNA	ZINKY	AGONE
TANKA	TONAL	WANTS	ZONAL	AGONS
TANKS	TONDO	WENCH	ZONED	AGONY
TANKY	TONED	WINCE	ZONER	AGORA
TANSY	TONER	WINCH	ZONES	AHOLD
TANTO	TONES	WINDS	ZONKS	AIOLI
TENCH	TONGA	WINDY	ZONKY	ALOED
TENDS	TONGS	WINGS	ABODE	ALOES

ALOFT	AWOKE	BOOTY	CLOCK	CROCK
ALOHA	AWORK	BOOZE	CLODS	CROFT
ALONE	AXONE	BOOZY	CLOGS	CRONE
ALONG	AXONS	BROAD	CLOMP	CRONY
ALOOF	AZOIC	BROIL	CLONE	CROOK
ALOUD	BIOME	BROKE	CLONK	CROON
AMOKS	BIOTA	BROOD	CLOSE	CROPS
AMOLE	BLOAT	BROOK	CLOTH	CRORE
AMONG	BLOCK	BROOM	CLOTS	CROSS
AMOUR	BLOGS	BROTH	CLOUD	CROUP
ANODE	BLOKE	BROWN	CLOUT	CROWD
ANOLE	BLOND	CHOCK	CLOVE	CROWN
ANOMY	BLOOD	CHOCS	CLOWN	CROWS
APOLS	BLOOM	CHODE	COOED	CROZE
AROHA	BLOWN	CHOIR	COOER	DHOBI
AROID	BLOWS	CHOKE	COOKS	DHOLE
AROMA	BLOWY	CHOKY	COOKY	DHOTI
AROSE	BOOBS	CHOLO	COOLE	DIODE
ATOLL	BOOBY	CHOMP	COOLY	DOOLY
ATOMS	BOOKS	CHOPS	COONS	DOOMS
ATOMY	BOOMY	CHORD	COOPS	DOOMY
ATONE	BOONG	CHORE	COOPT	DOORS
ATOPY	BOOST	CHOSE	COOTS	DOOZY
AVOID	BOOTH	CHOWS	COOTY	DROID
AVOWS	BOOTS	CLOAK	CROAK	DROIT

DROLL	FLOAT	GLOOM	HOOEY	MOOCH
DRONE	FLOCK	GLOOP	HOOKY	MOODS
DROOL	FLOOD	GLORY	HOOVE	MOODY
DROOP	FLOOR	GLOSS	ICONS	MOOER
DROPS	FLORA	GLOVE	IRONS	MOOLA
DROSS	FLOSS	GNOME	IRONY	MOONS
DROVE	FLOUR	GOOCH	IVORY	MOONY
DROWN	FLOUT	GOODS	KHOUM	MOORS
DUOMO	FLOWS	GOODY	KIOSK	MOORY
EBONS	FLOWY	GOOEY	KNOCK	MOOSE
EBONY	FOODS	GOOFY	KNOLL	MOOTS
ELOPE	FOOLS	GOOSE	KNOTS	MUONS
EMOJI	FROCK	GROAN	KNOUT	MYOPE
EMOTE	FROND	GROIN	KNOWE	MYOPY
ENOKI	FRONT	GROOM	KNOWN	NEONS
ENORM	FROST	GROPE	KNOWS	NOOBS
EPOCH	FROTH	GROSS	KOOKY	NOOBY
EPODE	FROWN	GROUP	LOOBY	NOOKS
EPOXY	FROZE	GROUT	LOOFA	NOOKY
ERODE	GEODE	GROVE	LOOKS	NOONE
EROSE	GHOST	GROWL	LOOMS	NOONS
EVOKE	GHOUL	GROWN	LOONY	NOOSE
EXODE	GLOAT	GROWS	LOOPY	OBOES
EXONS	GLOBE	GYOZA	LOOSE	ODORS
FJORD	GLOMP	HOOCH	MEOWS	ODOUR

OLOGY	POORE	QUOTE	SCORN	SHOWY
OVOID	POOTS	REORG	SCOTS	SKOAL
OVOLO	PROBE	RHOMB	SCOUR	SKOSH
OZONE	PROBS	RIOTS	SCOUT	SLOBS
PEONS	PROEM	ROODS	SCOWL	SLOES
PEONY	PROFS	ROOFS	SCOWS	SLOGS
PHONE	PROLE	ROOFY	SHOAL	SLOKA
PHONO	PROMO	ROOKE	SHOAT	SLOOP
PHONS	PROMS	ROOKS	SHOCK	SLOPE
PHONY	PRONE	ROOKY	SHOER	SLOPS
PHOTO	PRONG	ROOME	SHOES	SLOSH
PIONS	PRONS	ROOMS	SHOJI	SLOTH
PIOUS	PROOF	ROOMY	SHONE	SLOTS
PLONK	PROPS	ROOST	SHOOK	SLOWS
PLOTS	PROSE	ROOTS	SHOON	SMOCK
PLOWS	PROSS	ROOTY	SHOOP	SMOKE
PLOYS	PROSY	SCOBS	SHOOT	SMOKO
POOCH	PROTO	SCOFF	SHOPS	SMOKY
POODS	PROUD	SCOLD	SHORE	SMOLT
POOFS	PROVE	SCONE	SHORT	SNOBS
POOFY	PROWL	SCOOP	SHOTS	SNOOD
POOKA	PROWS	SCOOT	SHOUT	SNOOK
POOLS	PROXY	SCOPA	SHOVE	SNOOP
POONS	QUOIN	SCOPE	SHOWN	SNOOT
POOPS	QUOTA	SCORE	SHOWS	SNORE

SNORT	STOIC	SWOOP	TROTS	ZOOTY
SNOTS	STOKE	SWOPS	TROUT	ALPHA
SNOUT	STOLE	SWORD	TROVE	AMPED
SNOWS	STOMA	SWORE	TROWS	AMPLE
SNOWY	STOMP	SWORN	VIOLA	AMPLY
SOOKS	STONE	SWOTS	VLOGS	AMPUL
SOOKY	STONG	THOLE	WHOLE	APPAL
SOOTH	STONK	THONG	WHOMP	APPAR
SOOTY	STONY	THORN	WHOOP	APPEL
SPOIL	STOOD	THORO	WHORE	APPLE
SPOKE	STOOK	THORP	WHORL	APPLY
SPOOF	STOOL	THOUS	WHOSE	ASPEN
SPOOK	STOOP	TOOKE	WOODS	ASPER
SPOOL	STOPE	TOOLS	WOODY	ASPIC
SPOON	STOPS	TOONS	WOOED	ASPIE
SPOOR	STORE	TOOTH	WOOER	CAPED
SPORE	STORK	TOOTS	WOOLY	CAPER
SPORK	STORM	TRODE	WOOZY	CAPES
SPORT	STORY	TRODS	WRONG	CAPON
SPOTS	STOTE	TROLL	WROTE	CAPUT
SPOUT	STOUP	TROMP	WROTH	COPAL
STOAT	STOUT	TRONA	ZLOTY	COPAY
STOCK	STOVE	TROOP	ZOOID	COPED
STOEP	SWOLE	TROPE	ZOOMS	COPES
STOGY	SWOON	TROTH	ZOOMY	COPRA

COPSE	GAPER	LIPID	POPSY	SAPOR
COPSY	GYPSY	MAPLE	PUPAE	SAPPY
CUPEL	HAPPY	MOPED	PUPAL	SEPAL
CUPID	HIPPO	MOPER	PUPAS	SEPIA
CUPPA	HIPPY	MOPES	PUPIL	SEPOY
CUPPY	HOPED	MOPEY	PUPPY	SEPTA
DEPOT	HOPES	MOPPY	RAPED	SEPTS
DEPTH	HYPED	NAPPE	RAPER	SIPES
DEPTS	HYPER	NAPPY	RAPES	SIPPY
DIPPY	IMPEL	NIPPY	RAPHE	SOPHS
DIPSO	IMPEX	NOPAL	RAPID	SOPHY
DOPED	IMPLY	PAPAL	RAPPA	SOPOR
DOPER	INPUT	PAPAS	REPAY	SOPPY
DOPES	JAPAN	PAPER	REPEL	SUPER
DOPEY	JAPED	PAPPY	REPLY	TAPED
DUPED	JAPER	PEPLA	REPOS	TAPER
DUPER	JAPES	PEPPY	REPOT	TAPES
DUPES	KAPOK	PIPER	REPRO	TAPET
DUPPY	KAPPA	PIPES	RIPEN	TAPIR
EMPTY	KAPUT	PIPET	RIPER	TAPIS
ESPER	KAPUT	PIPIT	RIPES	TEPAL
EXPAT	KIPED	PIPPY	ROPER	TEPEE
EXPEL	KIPES	POPES	ROPES	TEPID
EXPOS	LAPSE	POPPA	RUPEE	TIPPY
GAPED	LEPER	POPPY	SAPID	TIPSY

TOPAZ	ZIPPY	AURAL	BURRY	CHRON
TOPER	NIQAB	AURAS	BURST	CIRCA
TOPIC	PIQUE	AURIC	CARAT	CIRCS
TOPOS	ROQUE	BARBS	CARDI	CORAL
TOPPY	TOQUE	BARED	CARDS	CORDS
TUPIK	TUQUE	BARGE	CARED	CORDY
TYPED	AARTI	BARMY	CARER	CORER
TYPES	ACRED	BARON	CARES	CORES
TYPIC	ACRES	BERET	CARET	COREY
TYPOS	ACRID	BERRY	CARGO	CORGI
UNPEG	AERIE	BERTH	CARLE	CORKS
UPPED	AFROS	BERYL	CARNY	CORKY
UPPER	AGREE	BIRCH	CAROB	CORNS
VAPID	AIRED	BIRDS	CAROL	CORNU
VAPOR	AIRES	BIRSE	CAROM	CORNY
VIPER	AMRIT	BIRTH	CARPI	COROL
WIPED	AORTA	BORAX	CARPS	CORPS
WIPER	APRON	BORED	CARRS	CORSE
WIPES	ARRAS	BORNE	CARRY	CORVE
YAPPS	ARRAY	BURKA	CARTE	CURBS
YAPPY	ARRIS	BURKE	CARTS	CURDS
YIPPY	ARROW	BURLY	CARUS	CURDY
YUPPY	ARROZ	BURNS	CARVE	CURED
ZAPPY	ATRIA	BURNT	CERIC	CURER
ZIPPO	AURAE	BURRO	CERTS	CURES

CURET	DIRKE	FARCE	GIRLS	HURTS
CURIA	DIRKS	FARED	GIRLY	HYRAX
CURIE	DIRTY	FARES	GIRTH	JERKS
CURIO	DORKS	FARSI	GORGE	JERKY
CURLS	DORKY	FERAL	GORSE	JERRY
CURLY	DORMS	FERRY	HARAM	JIRGA
CURRY	DORSA	FIRED	HARDS	JORUM
CURSE	DURAL	FIREE	HARDY	JURAL
CURST	DURRA	FIRMS	HAREM	JURAT
CURVE	DURUM	FIRST	HARMS	JUROR
CURVY	EARED	FIRTH	HARPY	KARAT
DARBY	EARLE	FORAY	HARRY	KARMA
DARED	EARLS	FORCE	HARSH	KARRI
DARER	EARLY	FORGE	HERBS	KARST
DARES	EARNS	FORGO	HERON	KARTS
DARKE	EARNT	FORMS	HERTZ	KERFS
DARKS	EARTH	FORTE	HIRED	KERRY
DARKY	EERIE	FORTH	HORDE	LARDY
DARTS	EGRET	FORTY	HORNS	LARGE
DERBY	ENROL	FORUM	HORNY	LARKY
DERMA	ERRED	FUROR	HORSE	LARVA
DERMS	ERROR	FURRY	HORSY	LORDY
DERNS	EUROS	FURZE	HURLY	LORRY
DERPY	EYRIE	GARBO	HURRY	LURCH
DIRGE	EYRIR	GERMS	HURST	LURED

LURER	MERLE	NERDO	PARLE	PORNO
LURES	MERRY	NERDS	PAROL	PORNS
LURID	MIRED	NERDY	PARRY	PORNY
LYRIC	MIREX	NERTS	PARSE	PORTA
MARCH	MIRID	NERVE	PARTS	PORTS
MARCS	MIRTH	NERVY	PARTY	PURED
MARDY	MORAL	NORIA	PERCH	PUREE
MARES	MORAY	NORMA	PERDU	PURER
MARGE	MOREL	NORMS	PERIL	PURGE
MARGO	MORES	NORTH	PERKS	PURIS
MARIA	MORNS	NURSE	PERKY	PURRS
MARKE	MORON	OARED	PERPS	PURRY
MARKS	MORPH	OCREA	PERQS	PURSE
MARLE	MORTS	OGRES	PERRY	PURSY
MARLY	MURAL	OKRAS	PERSE	PYRAL
MARRY	MUREX	ORRIS	PERVE	PYRES
MARSH	MURID	PARCH	PERVS	RARER
MARTS	MURKY	PARED	PERVY	RERUN
MERCH	MURRE	PAREN	PORCH	RURAL
MERCS	MURUS	PARER	PORED	SARAH
MERCY	MYRRH	PAREU	PORER	SAREE
MERDE	NARCO	PARGE	PORES	SARGE
MERES	NARES	PARKA	PORGY	SARIN
MERGE	NARKS	PARKS	PORIN	SARIS
MERIT	NARKY	PARKY	PORKY	SARKS

SARKY	SERVO	STRAW	TARTY	TORSK
SAROD	SHRED	STRAY	TERAI	TORSO
SCRAG	SHREW	STREW	TERCE	TORTE
SCRAM	SHRUB	STRIA	TERGA	TORTS
SCRAN	SHRUG	STRIP	TERMS	TORUS
SCRAP	SIREE	STROP	TERRA	TURBO
SCREE	SIREN	STRUM	TERRY	TURFS
SCREW	SIRES	STRUT	TERSE	TURFY
SCRIM	SORBS	SURAH	THREE	TURNS
SCRIP	SORES	SURAS	THREW	TURPS
SCROD	SOROR	SURDS	THRID	TYRAN
SCROW	SORRY	SURGE	THROB	TYRED
SCRUB	SORTA	SURLY	THROE	TYRES
SCRUM	SORTE	SYRAH	THROW	TYROS
SERAC	SORTS	SYRUP	THRUM	VERBS
SERAI	SORUS	TARDY	TIRED	VERGE
SERES	SPRAG	TARED	TIRES	VERSE
SERFS	SPRAT	TARES	TIROS	VERSO
SERGE	SPRAY	TARNS	TORAN	VERVE
SERIE	SPREE	TAROT	TORCH	VIRAL
SERIF	SPRIG	TARPS	TORES	VIRGA
SERIN	SPRIT	TARRE	TORIC	VIRUS
SEROW	SPROG	TARRY	TORII	WARES
SERUM	SPRUE	TARSI	TORSE	WARNS
SERVE	STRAP	TARTS	TORSI	WARTY

WIRED	ARSON	CASTS	DUSTY	HOSTS
WIRRA	ASSAI	CESTA	EASED	HUSKY
WORDS	ASSAY	CISCO	EASEL	HUSSY
WORDY	ASSES	CISSY	EASER	INSET
WORKS	ASSET	COSIE	EASES	ISSUE
WORLD	BASAL	COSMO	EASTS	JESTS
WORMY	BASED	COSTA	ENSKY	JESUS
WORRY	BASES	COSTS	ENSUE	JUSTS
WORSE	BASIC	CUSHY	EOSIN	KASHA
WORST	BASIL	CUSPS	ESSAY	KISSY
WORTH	BASIN	CYSTS	ESSES	LASER
WURST	BASIS	DESEX	FISHY	LASSO
XERIC	BASTE	DESIS	FOSSE	LASTS
XEROX	BESET	DESKS	FUSED	LISTS
XERUS	BISON	DISAD	FUSSY	LOSEL
YARDS	BOSOM	DISCO	FUSTY	LOSER
YARER	BOSSY	DISCS	GASPS	LOSES
YARNS	BUSBY	DISHY	GASSY	LUSTY
YORKS	BUSHY	DISIR	GESTE	MASER
ZEROS	BUSTY	DISKS	GUSHY	MASHY
AISLE	CASAS	DOSAS	GUSTO	MASKS
APSIS	CASED	DOSES	GUSTY	MASON
ARSED	CASES	DUSKS	HASTE	MASSA
ARSES	CASKS	DUSKY	HASTY	MASSY
ARSIS	CASTE	DUSTS	HISSY	MASTS

MESAS	MUSTS	PESOS	RISEN	TASES
MESHY	MUSTY	PESTO	RISER	TASKS
MESIC	NASAL	PESTS	RISES	TASTE
MESNE	NASTY	PESTY	RISHI	TASTY
MESON	NESTS	PISCO	RISKS	TESLA
MESSY	NISEI	PISSY	RISKY	TESTA
MISER	NISSE	PISTE	ROSEN	TESTS
MISES	NOSED	POSED	ROSES	TESTY
MISSY	NOSER	POSER	ROSIN	TOSSY
MISTS	NOSES	POSES	RUSES	TUSKS
MISTY	NOSEY	POSIT	RUSHY	TUSKY
MOSEY	OASES	POSSE	RUSKS	UNSAY
MOSSY	OASIS	POSTS	RUSTS	UNSET
MOSTS	OASTS	PUSHY	RUSTY	UNSEX
MUSED	ONSET	PUSSY	SASSE	UPSET
MUSER	OPSIN	RASES	SASSY	VASTY
MUSES	OUSTS	RASHY	SISAL	VISIT
MUSET	PASEO	RASPS	SISES	VISOR
MUSHY	PASHA	RASPY	SISSY	VISTA
MUSIC	PASSE	RASTA	SISTA	WASHY
MUSIT	PASTA	RESES	SUSHI	WASPY
MUSKS	PASTE	RESET	SUSUS	WASTE
MUSKY	PASTS	RESIN	SYSOP	WISER
MUSOS	PASTY	RESIT	TASED	WISPY
MUSSY	PESKY	RESTS	TASER	XYSTI

XYSTS	ATTAR	CITAL	DOTER	FETUS
YESES	ATTIC	CITED	DOTES	FUTON
ZESTS	AUTOS	CITER	DOTTY	GETUP
ZESTY	BATCH	CITES	DUTCH	GOTTA
ACTED	BATHE	CITIE	DUTIE	GUTSY
ACTER	BATHS	COTES	EATED	GUTTY
ACTIN	BATIK	COTTA	EATEN	HATCH
ACTOR	BATON	CUTER	EATER	HATED
AFTER	BATTY	CUTES	ENTER	HATER
AITCH	BETTY	CUTIE	ENTIA	HATES
ALTAR	BITCH	CUTIN	ENTRE	HETRO
ALTER	BITES	CUTIS	ENTRY	HITCH
ALTOS	BITSY	CUTUP	ESTER	HOTEL
ANTED	BITTY	CYTOL	ESTOC	HOTLY
ANTES	BOTCH	DATED	ESTOP	HUTCH
ANTIC	BOTHY	DATER	EXTOL	INTEL
ANTRA	BOTOX	DATES	EXTRA	INTER
ANTRE	BOTTY	DATUM	FATAL	INTRA
ANTSY	BUTCH	DETER	FATED	INTRO
APTER	BUTTE	DETOX	FATES	JETTY
APTLY	BUTTY	DITCH	FATLY	JUTTY
ARTEL	CATCH	DITSY	FATTY	KETCH
ARTSY	CATER	DITTO	FETAL	KITED
ASTER	CATES	DITTY	FETCH	KITES
ASTIR	CATTY	DITZY	FETID	LATCH

LATER	MITER	NETTY	OTTER	POTCH
LATEX	MITES	NITES	OUTDO	POTOO
LATIN	MITRE	NITID	OUTED	POTTO
LATTE	MITTS	NITRO	OUTER	POTTY
LETCH	MOTED	NOTAM	OUTGO	PUTTO
LETUP	MOTEL	NOTCH	OUTRE	PUTTS
LITHE	MOTES	NOTED	OXTER	PUTTY
LOTUS	MOTET	NOTER	PATCH	RATCH
MATCH	MOTHS	NOTES	PATED	RATED
MATED	MOTHY	NOTIF	PATEN	RATEL
MATER	MOTIF	NOTUM	PATER	RATER
MATES	MOTOR	NUTSY	PATES	RATES
MATEY	MOTTE	NUTTY	PATHS	RATHE
MATHS	MOTTO	OATER	PATIN	RATIO
MATTE	MUTED	OATHS	PATIO	RATTY
MATTY	MUTER	OCTAD	PATSY	RETCH
MATZO	MUTES	OCTAL	PATTY	RETRO
METAL	MUTIS	OCTET	PETAL	RETRY
METER	MYTHS	OFTEN	PETER	RITES
METES	MYTHY	OFTER	PETIT	RITZY
METIC	NATAL	ONTIC	PETTY	ROTAS
METRE	NATCH	OOTID	PITCH	ROTES
METRO	NATES	OPTED	PITHY	ROTIS
METTS	NATTY	OPTER	PITON	ROTOR
MITCH	NETTS	OPTIC	PITTA	RUTIN

RUTTY	TITLE	YETTS	BLUFF	CHURL
SATAN	TITTY	ZITTY	BLUNT	CHURN
SATAY	TOTAL	ABUSE	BLURB	CHURR
SATED	TOTED	ABUTS	BLURT	CHUTE
SATES	TOTEM	ABUTT	BLUSH	CLUBS
SATIN	TOTER	ABUZZ	BOUGH	CLUCK
SATYR	TOTES	ACUTE	BOUND	CLUES
SETAE	TUTEE	ADULT	BOURG	CLUEY
SETTS	TUTOR	ADUST	BOURN	CLUMP
SETUP	TUTTI	AGUED	BOUTS	CLUNG
SHTIK	ULTRA	AGUES	BRUIT	CLUNK
SHTUP	UNTIE	AJUGA	BRUME	COUCH
SITAR	UNTIL	ALUMN	BRUNT	COUGH
SITES	UTTER	ALUMS	BRUSH	COULD
SITUS	VATIC	AMUCK	BRUTE	COUNT
SUTRA	VETCH	AMUSE	CAULK	COUPE
TATER	VITAL	ANURY	CAUSE	COUPS
TATHS	VOTED	AQUAE	CHUBS	COURS
TATTS	VOTER	AQUAS	CHUCK	COURT
TATTY	WATCH	AZURE	CHUFA	COUTH
TETRA	WATER	AZURN	CHUFF	CRUCK
TITAN	WITCH	AZURY	CHUGS	CRUDE
TITCH	WITHY	BAULK	CHUMP	CRUDS
TITER	WITTY	BHUMI	CHUMS	CRUDY
TITHE	YETIS	BLUES	CHUNK	CRUEL

CRUES	ELUDE	FOUND	INUIT	MOUTH
CRUET	ELUTE	FOUNT	INURE	NEUME
CRUMB	EMULE	FRUIT	INURN	NEUMS
CRUMP	EQUAL	FRUMP	JAUNT	NEURO
CRUNK	EQUID	GAUDY	JOUAL	NOUNS
CRUOR	EQUIP	GAUGE	JOULE	NOUNY
CRURA	ERUCT	GAUNT	JOURS	OCULI
CRUSE	ERUPT	GAUZE	JOUST	OVULE
CRUSH	ETUDE	GAUZY	KAURI	PAUCE
CRUST	EXUDE	GLUED	KNURL	PAUSE
DAUBE	EXULT	GLUEY	LAUGH	PLUCK
DAUBS	EXURB	GOUGE	LOUGH	PLUGS
DAUNT	FAUGH	GOUND	LOUIS	PLUMB
DEUCE	FAULT	GOURD	LOUSE	PLUME
DOUBT	FAUNA	GRUEL	LOUSY	PLUMP
DOUGH	FLUFF	GRUFF	MAULS	PLUMS
DOULA	FLUID	GRUMP	MAUND	PLUMY
DOUSE	FLUKE	GRUNT	MAUVE	PLUNK
DRUGS	FLUKY	HAULM	MOULD	PLUSH
DRUID	FLUME	HAULT	MOULT	PLUTE
DRUMS	FLUMP	HAUNT	MOUND	POUCH
DRUNK	FLUNG	HAUTE	MOUNT	POUFS
DRUPE	FLUNK	HOUND	MOURN	POULT
EDUCE	FLUSH	HOURS	MOUSE	POUND
EDUCT	FLUTE	HOUSE	MOUSY	POUTS

POUTY	SCUTE	SOUGH	STUFF	TRUES
PRUDE	SCUZZ	SOULE	STUMP	TRULL
PRUNE	SHUCK	SOULS	STUMS	TRULY
REUSE	SHULS	SOUND	STUNG	TRUMP
RHUMB	SHUNT	SOUPS	STUNT	TRUNK
ROUGE	SHUSH	SOUPY	STUPA	TRUSS
ROUGH	SHUTS	SOURS	STUPE	TRUST
ROUND	SKULK	SOUSE	SWUNG	TRUTH
ROUSE	SKULL	SOUTH	TAUNT	UNUSE
ROUST	SKUNK	SPUME	TAUPE	USUAL
ROUTE	SLUFF	SPUMY	THUDS	USURP
ROUTS	SLUGS	SPUNK	THUGS	USURY
SAUCE	SLUMP	SPURN	THUJA	UVULA
SAUCY	SLUMS	SPURS	THUMB	VAULT
SAULT	SLUNK	SPURT	THUMP	VAUNT
SAUNA	SLURP	SQUAB	THUNK	VOUCH
SAURY	SLURS	SQUAD	TOUCH	WAULK
SAUTE	SLUSH	SQUAT	TOUGH	WHUMP
SCUBA	SLUTS	SQUAW	TOURS	WOULD
SCUDO	SMURF	SQUIB	TOUSY	WOUND
SCUFF	SMUTS	SQUID	TOUTS	WRUNG
SCULL	SNUBS	STUBS	TRUCE	YOUNG
SCUMS	SNUCK	STUCK	TRUCK	YOURS
SCURF	SNUFF	STUDS	TRUED	YOUSE
SCUTA	SNUGS	STUDY	TRUER	YOUTH

ANVIL	DIVES	JIVES	NAVVY	RIVES
BEVEL	DIVIS	JIVEY	NEVER	RIVET
BEVVY	DIVOT	JUVIE	NEVES	ROVER
CAVER	DIVVY	LEVEE	NEVUS	SAVED
CAVES	DOVES	LEVEL	NIVAL	SAVER
CAVIL	DUVET	LEVER	NOVAE	SAVES
CIVET	EAVES	LIVED	NOVAS	SAVIN
CIVIC	ELVER	LIVEN	NOVEL	SAVOR
CIVIL	ELVES	LIVER	NOVUM	SAVOY
CIVVY	ENVOI	LIVES	OAVES	SAVVY
COVEN	ENVOY	LIVID	PAVED	SEVEN
COVER	FAVOR	LOVED	PAVER	SEVER
COVES	FEVER	LOVER	PIVOT	VIVID
COVET	GAVEL	LOVES	RAVEL	WAVED
COVEY	GIVEN	MAVEN	RAVEN	WAVER
COVIN	GIVER	MAVIN	RAVER	WAVES
DAVID	GIVES	MAVIS	RAVES	WAVEY
DAVIT	HAVEN	MOVED	RAVIN	WOVEN
DEVAS	HAVES	MOVER	REVEL	ALWAY
DEVEL	HAVOC	MOVES	REVER	BAWDY
DEVIL	HIVES	MOVIE	REVUE	BOWED
DEVON	HOVEL	NAVAL	RIVAL	BOWEL
DIVAN	HOVER	NAVEL	RIVEL	BOWER
DIVAS	JIVED	NAVES	RIVEN	BYWAY
DIVER	JIVER	NAVIE	RIVER	COWED

COWER	LOWLY	ROWEL	YOWLS	NEXUM
COWLS	MAWED	ROWEN	AUXIN	NEXUS
CRWTH	MEWLS	ROWER	BOXED	NIXED
DAWNS	MOWER	SAWER	BOXER	NIXES
DEWAN	NAWAB	SEWER	BOXES	NIXIE
DEWAR	NEWEL	SOWED	BUXOM	PIXEL
DOWDS	NEWER	SOWER	COXAE	PIXIE
DOWDY	NEWES	TAWNY	COXAL	POXES
DOWEL	NEWIE	TAWSE	COXED	PYXIS
DOWER	NEWLY	TOWED	COXES	SEXER
DOWNS	NEWSY	TOWEE	DIXIE	SEXES
DOWNY	NEWTS	TOWEL	DOXIE	SIXER
DOWRY	NGWEE	TOWER	DUXES	SIXES
DOWSE	NOWAY	TOWNE	FIXED	SIXTH
FEWER	NOWED	TOWNS	FIXER	SIXTY
GAWKY	PAWED	TOWNY	FIXES	TAXED
HOWDY	PAWER	TOWRE	HEXAD	TAXER
JAWED	PAWKY	UNWED	LEXIS	TAXES
JEWED	PAWNS	VOWED	MAXIM	TAXIS
JEWEL	PEWEE	VOWEL	MAXIS	TAXON
JEWRY	POWER	WOWED	MIXED	TAXOR
JOWLS	RAWER	YAWED	MIXER	TEXAS
JOWLY	ROWAN	YAWNS	MIXES	TEXTS
LAWKS	ROWDY	YAWNY	MIXUP	TOXIC
LOWER	ROWED	YAWPS	MOXIE	TOXIN

VEXED	FLYBY	RHYME	BUZZY	NAZIS
VIXEN	FLYER	RIYAL	COZEN	OOZED
WAXEN	FOYER	ROYAL	COZIE	OOZES
ZAXES	GLYPH	SAYER	DAZED	OUZEL
ABYSM	IDYLL	SHYER	DAZES	PIZZA
ABYSS	JOYED	SHYLY	DIZZY	PIZZE
ACYLS	KAYAK	SKYEY	DOZEN	RAZED
ASYLA	KEYED	SLYLY	DOZER	RAZER
ASYNC	KEYER	SLYPE	DOZES	RAZOR
BAYOU	LAYER	SPYAL	ENZYM	SIZER
BOYAR	LOYAL	STYLE	FAZED	SIZES
BUYER	MAYBE	STYMY	FIZZY	TAZZA
CHYLE	MAYOR	TAYRA	FUZZY	TAZZE
CHYME	MAYOS	THYME	GAZED	TIZZY
COYER	NOYAU	THYMI	GAZES	UNZIP
COYLY	PAYED	THYMY	GIZMO	XYZZY
COYPU	PAYEE	TIYIN	HAZED	
CRYER	PAYER	TOYED	HAZEL	
CRYPT	PAYOR	TOYER	JAZZY	
DAYER	PHYLA	TOYON	KAZOO	
DOYEN	PLYER	TRYED	MAZER	
DRYAD	PRYER	TRYER	MAZES	
DRYER	PSYCH	TRYST	MEZZO	
DRYLY	RAYED	WRYLY	MUZZY	
ETYMA	RAYON	ZAYIN	NAZES	

ABBAT

ABEAM	ASSAY	BROAD	COMAS	DIVAN
ABEAR	ATLAS	BYLAW	COPAL	DIVAS
ADDAX	ATMAN	BYWAY	COPAY	DOSAS
ADMAN	ATTAR	CABAL	CORAL	DREAD
AHEAD	AUDAX	CACAO	COXAE	DREAM
ALGAE	AURAE	CACAS	COXAL	DREAR
ALGAL	AURAL	CAMAS	CREAK	DRYAD
ALIAS	AURAS	CANAL	CREAM	DUCAT
ALLAY	AVGAS	CARAT	CREAT	DUNAM
ALTAR	AVIAN	CASAS	CROAK	DURAL
ALWAY	AXIAL	CECAL	CYCAD	DWAAL
ANNAL	AXMAN	CEDAR	DADAS	EGGAR
ANNAS	BANAL	CHEAP	DAMAR	EMBAY
APIAN	BASAL	CHEAT	DEBAR	EPHAH
APPAL	BEGAN	CIGAR	DECAD	EQUAL
APPAR	BELAY	CITAL	DECAF	ESSAY
AQUAE	BLEAK	CLEAN	DECAL	EXPAT
AQUAS	BLEAR	CLEAR	DECAY	FATAL
AREAL	BLEAT	CLEAT	DELAY	FERAL
AREAS	BLOAT	CLOAK	DENAR	FETAL
ARHAT	BOGAN	COCAS	DEVAS	FINAL
ARIAS	BORAX	CODAS	DEWAN	FLOAT
ARRAS	BOYAR	COHAB	DEWAR	FOCAL
ARRAY	BREAD	COLAS	DINAR	FORAY
ASSAI	BREAK	COMAE	DISAD	FREAK

FRIAR	JUDAH	MAMAS	NIQAB	PECAN
FUBAR	JURAL	MANAT	NIVAL	PEDAL
GALAH	JURAT	MEDAL	NODAL	PENAL
GLEAM	KAKAS	MESAS	NOMAD	PETAL
GLEAN	KAMAL	METAL	NOMAN	PHIAL
GLOAT	KANAS	MICAS	NONAD	PILAF
GONAD	KARAT	MODAL	NOPAL	PINAY
GREAT	KAYAK	MOLAL	NOTAM	PLEAD
GROAN	KEBAB	MOLAR	NOVAE	PLEAS
HALAL	KENAF	MONAD	NOVAS	PLEAT
HARAM	KNEAD	MORAL	NOWAY	POLAR
HEXAD	LAHAR	MORAY	NOYAU	PRIAL
HIJAB	LANAI	MUCAL	OBEAH	PSHAW
HUMAN	LEGAL	MUDAR	OCEAN	PUMAS
HYRAX	LEMAN	MURAL	OCTAD	PUPAE
IDEAL	LILAC	MYLAR	OCTAL	PUPAL
IDEAS	LOCAL	MYNAH	OFFAL	PUPAS
INLAY	LOGAN	NAGAS	OGHAM	PYRAL
ISLAM	LOYAL	NAIAD	OKRAS	QANAT
JACAL	LUNAR	NANAS	OREAD	QUEAN
JALAP	MACAW	NASAL	ORGAN	RADAR
JAPAN	MADAM	NATAL	PAEAN	RAJAH
JIHAD	MAHAL	NAVAL	PAGAN	RAJAS
JONAH	MALAI	NAWAB	PAPAL	REBAR
JOUAL	MALAR	NICAD	PAPAS	RECAP

REDAN	SCRAP	SPEAK	SWEAR	TWEAK
REGAL	SEDAN	SPEAR	SWEAT	TYRAN
REHAB	SEPAL	SPLAT	SYRAH	UNBAN
RELAX	SERAC	SPLAY	TAMAS	UNLAY
RELAY	SERAI	SPRAG	TEPAL	UNMAN
RENAL	SETAE	SPRAT	TERAI	UNSAY
REPAY	SHEAF	SPRAY	TEXAS	URBAN
RIVAL	SHEAR	SPYAL	TIDAL	USUAL
RIYAL	SHOAL	SQUAB	TITAN	VEGAN
ROMAN	SHOAT	SQUAD	TODAY	VENAL
ROTAS	SIMAS	SQUAT	TOGAE	VICAR
ROWAN	SISAL	SQUAW	TOGAS	VIRAL
ROYAL	SITAR	STEAD	TOLAR	VITAL
RURAL	SKEAN	STEAK	TONAL	VOCAL
SAGAR	SKOAL	STEAL	TOPAZ	VOLAR
SAGAS	SMEAR	STEAM	TORAN	WHEAL
SALAD	SNEAK	STEAN	TOTAL	WHEAT
SALAL	SODAS	STOAT	TREAD	WOMAN
SALAT	SOFAR	STRAP	TREAT	WREAK
SARAH	SOFAS	STRAW	TRIAD	XYLAN
SATAN	SOLAN	STRAY	TRIAL	YOGAS
SATAY	SOLAR	SUGAR	TUBAL	ZAKAT
SCRAG	SOMAN	SUMAC	TUBAS	ZONAL
SCRAM	SOMAS	SURAH	TUFAS	ADOBE
SCRAN	SONAR	SURAS	TUNAS	ADOBO

ALIBI	DARBY	LOBBY	SCUBA	AMICE
AMEBA	DAUBE	LOOBY	SIMBA	AMICI
BARBS	DAUBS	MAMBA	SLABS	AMUCK
BILBY	DERBY	MAMBO	SLOBS	APACE
BIMBO	DHOBI	MAYBE	SNOBS	ARECA
BOBBY	DOBBY	NEBBY	SNUBS	BATCH
BOOBS	DOUBT	NIMBY	SOBBY	BEACH
BOOBY	DRABS	NOBBY	SORBS	BEECH
BRIBE	DUMBO	NOOBS	STABS	BELCH
BUBBA	FLYBY	NOOBY	STUBS	BENCH
BUSBY	GABBY	NUBBY	SWABS	BIRCH
CABBY	GARBO	ORIBI	TABBY	BITCH
CEIBA	GLOBE	PLEBE	THEBE	BLACK
CHIBI	GOBBY	PLEBS	TOMBS	BLECH
CHUBS	GRABS	PROBE	TRIBE	BLOCK
CLUBS	GUMBO	PROBS	TUBBY	BONCE
COBBS	HERBS	RABBI	TURBO	BOTCH
COBBY	HOBBY	REBBE	VERBS	BRACE
COMBE	HUBBY	RIBBY	YOBBO	BRICK
COMBO	JAMBS	RUGBY	ZOMBI	BUNCH
COMBS	JIBBS	RUMBA	ABACA	BUNCO
CRABS	JUMBO	SAMBA	ABACI	BUTCH
CRIBS	JUMBY	SAMBO	ABACK	CATCH
CUBBY	LIMBO	SCABS	AITCH	CHECK
CURBS	LIMBS	SCOBS	ALACK	CHICA

CHICK	DISCS	FILCH	LATCH	NIECE
CHICS	DITCH	FLECK	LEACH	NOICE
CHOCK	DRECK	FLICK	LEECH	NONCE
CHOCS	DUNCE	FLOCK	LETCH	NOTCH
CHUCK	DUTCH	FORCE	LUNCH	ORACY
CINCH	EDICT	FRICK	LURCH	OUNCE
CIRCA	EDUCE	FROCK	LYNCH	PARCH
CIRCS	EDUCT	GOOCH	MARCH	PATCH
CISCO	EJECT	GRACE	MARCS	PAUCE
CLACK	ELECT	GULCH	MATCH	PEACE
CLICK	ENACT	HATCH	MECCA	PEACH
CLOCK	EPACT	HENCE	MERCH	PENCE
CLUCK	EPICK	HENCH	MERCS	PERCH
COACH	EPICS	HITCH	MERCY	PICCY
COCCI	EPOCH	HOICK	MILCH	PIECE
CONCH	ERECT	HOOCH	MINCE	PINCH
COUCH	ERICA	HUNCH	MINCY	PISCO
CRACK	ERUCT	HUTCH	MITCH	PITCH
CRICK	EVICT	JUICE	MOOCH	PLACE
CROCK	EXACT	JUICY	MULCH	PLICA
CRUCK	EXECS	JUNCO	MULCT	PLUCK
DANCE	FANCY	KETCH	MUNCH	POACH
DEICE	FARCE	KNACK	NANCY	PONCE
DEUCE	FENCE	KNOCK	NARCO	POOCH
DISCO	FETCH	LANCE	NATCH	PORCH

POTCH	SLICK	TERCE	WINCE	BENDY
POUCH	SMACK	THECA	WINCH	BIDDY
PRICE	SMOCK	THICK	WITCH	BINDI
PRICK	SNACK	TINCT	WRACK	BINDS
PRICY	SNECK	TITCH	WRECK	BIRDS
PSYCH	SNICK	TORCH	WRICK	BLADE
PUNCH	SNUCK	TOUCH	YUCCA	BONDS
QUACK	SPACE	TRACE	ZILCH	BRIDE
QUICK	SPACY	TRACH	ZINCO	BUDDY
RANCH	SPECK	TRACK	ZINCS	CADDY
RATCH	SPECS	TRACT	ZINCY	CANDY
REACH	SPICA	TRICE	ABIDE	CARDI
REACT	SPICE	TRICK	ABODE	CARDS
RECCE	SPICY	TRUCE	ACIDS	CHADS
RETCH	STACK	TRUCK	ACIDY	CHIDE
ROACH	STICK	TWICE	AMIDE	CHODE
SAUCE	STOCK	TWICT	ANODE	CLADE
SAUCY	STUCK	VETCH	ASIDE	CLODS
SECCO	SYNCH	VOICE	AZIDE	COEDS
SHACK	SYNCS	VOUCH	BALDY	COLDS
SHOCK	TALCS	WATCH	BANDO	CONDO
SHUCK	TALCY	WENCH	BANDY	CORDS
SINCE	TEACH	WHACK	BAWDY	CORDY
SLACK	TELCO	WHICH	BEADS	CREDO
SLICE	TENCH	WICCA	BEADY	CREDS

CRUDE	EXUDE	HOWDY	MONDO	RANDS
CRUDS	FADDY	KENDO	MOODS	RANDY
CRUDY	FEEDS	KIDDO	MOODY	READS
CUDDY	FINDS	KINDE	MUDDY	READY
CURDS	FOLDS	KINDS	NEDDY	REDDS
CURDY	FOODS	KINDY	NEEDS	REDDY
DADDY	FUNDI	LADDU	NEEDY	REEDE
DANDY	FUNDS	LANDS	NERDO	REEDS
DEADS	GAUDY	LARDY	NERDS	REEDY
DEEDE	GEODE	LEADS	NERDY	RINDS
DEEDS	GIDDY	LENDS	NODDY	RINDY
DIDDY	GLADE	LOADS	OUTDO	ROADS
DILDO	GLIDE	LORDY	OXIDE	ROIDS
DIODE	GOODS	MAIDE	PADDY	RONDE
DOWDS	GOODY	MAIDS	PAEDO	RONDO
DOWDY	GRADE	MARDY	PANDA	ROODS
DYADS	GUIDE	MEADS	PERDU	ROWDY
EJIDO	HANDS	MENDS	PONDS	RUDDY
ELIDE	HANDY	MERDE	PONDY	SANDO
ELUDE	HARDS	MIDDY	POODS	SANDS
EPODE	HARDY	MILDS	PRADS	SANDY
ERODE	HEADS	MINDE	PREDS	SCADS
ETUDE	HEADY	MINDS	PRIDE	SCUDO
EVADE	HOLDS	MOLDS	PRUDE	SEEDE
EXODE	HORDE	MOLDY	RAIDS	SEEDS

SEEDY	THUDS	ACHED	AIRES	ASHER
SENDS	TILDE	ACHES	ALDER	ASHES
SHADE	TOADS	ACMES	ALIEN	ASKED
SHADS	TOADY	ACNED	ALLEY	ASKER
SHADY	TODDY	ACNES	ALOED	ASKES
SHEDS	TONDO	ACRED	ALOES	ASKEW
SKIDS	TRADE	ACRES	ALTER	ASPEN
SLEDS	TRODE	ACTED	AMBER	ASPER
SLIDE	TRODS	ACTER	AMPED	ASSES
SNIDE	WADDY	ADDED	ANDED	ASSET
SODDY	WEEDS	ADDER	ANGEL	ASTER
SOLDO	WEEDY	ADIEU	ANGER	AUGER
SONDE	WILDS	AEGER	ANNEX	AWNED
SPADE	WINDS	AFTER	ANTED	AWNER
STADE	WINDY	AGLET	ANTES	AXLED
STUDS	WOODS	AGREE	APNEA	AXLES
STUDY	WOODY	AGUED	APPEL	AXMEN
SUEDE	WORDS	AGUES	APTER	BABEL
SURDS	WORDY	AIDED	ARCED	BAGEL
SWEDE	YARDS	AIDER	ARMED	BAKED
TARDY	ABBEY	AIDES	ARSED	BAKER
TEADE	ABLED	AILED	ARSES	BARED
TEDDY	ABLER	AIMED	ARTEL	BASED
TENDS	ABLES	AIMER	ASHED	BASES
TENDU	ACCEL	AIRED	ASHEN	BEDEW

BEGET	BUYER	CATES	COKER	COXES
BERET	CABER	CAVER	COKES	COYER
BESET	CADET	CAVES	COLES	COZEN
BEVEL	CAFES	CEDED	COMER	CREED
BIDET	CAGED	CEDER	COMES	CREEK
BIKER	CAGES	CELEB	COMET	CREEL
BITES	CAGEY	CHEEK	CONED	CREEP
BLEED	CAKED	CHEEP	CONES	CRIED
BLEEP	CAKES	CHEER	CONEY	CRIER
BLUES	CAKEY	CHEEZ	COOED	CRIES
BOGEY	CAMEL	CHIEF	COOER	CRUEL
BOKEH	CAMEO	CIDER	COPED	CRUES
BONER	CAMES	CITED	COPES	CRUET
BONES	CANED	CITER	CORER	CRYER
BONEY	CANES	CITES	CORES	CUBEB
BORED	CAPED	CIVET	COREY	CUBED
BOWED	CAPER	CLEEK	COTES	CUBER
BOWEL	CAPES	CLUES	COVEN	CUBES
BOWER	CARED	CLUEY	COVER	CULEX
BOXED	CARER	CODEC	COVES	CUPEL
BOXER	CARES	CODED	COVET	CURED
BOXES	CARET	CODER	COVEY	CURER
BREED	CASED	CODES	COWED	CURES
BRIEF	CASES	CODEX	COWER	CURET
BRIER	CATER	COKED	COXED	CUTER

CUTES	DIMER	DRIES	EBBED	ESPER
CYBER	DIMES	DRYER	EDGED	ESSES
DALES	DINER	DUCES	EDGER	ESTER
DAMES	DIVER	DUDES	EDGES	ETHER
DARED	DIVES	DUKES	EELED	EXCEL
DARER	DOGES	DUNES	EELER	EXPEL
DARES	DOMED	DUPED	EGGED	FACED
DATED	DOMES	DUPER	EGRET	FACES
DATER	DONEE	DUPES	EIDER	FACET
DATES	DOPED	DUVET	ELDER	FADED
DAYER	DOPER	DUXES	ELKES	FADES
DAZED	DOPES	DWEEB	ELMEN	FAKED
DAZES	DOPEY	DYKES	ELVER	FAKER
DEFER	DOSES	DYKEY	ELVES	FAMED
DEKES	DOTER	DYNES	EMBED	FARED
DENEB	DOTES	EAGER	EMBER	FARES
DENES	DOVES	EARED	EMCEE	FATED
DESEX	DOWEL	EASED	EMEER	FATES
DETER	DOWER	EASEL	EMMER	FAZED
DEVEL	DOYEN	EASER	EMMET	FECES
DICER	DOZEN	EASES	ENDED	FEVER
DICES	DOZER	EATED	ENTER	FEWER
DICEY	DOZES	EATEN	ERNES	FIBER
DIKER	DRIED	EATER	ERRED	FILED
DIKES	DRIER	EAVES	ESKER	FILES

FILET	GAPER	HATES	HYPED	JAWED
FINED	GAVEL	HAVEN	HYPER	JEWED
FINER	GAZED	HAVES	IDLER	JEWEL
FINES	GAZES	HAZED	IMBED	JIBED
FIRED	GENES	HAZEL	IMPEL	JIBES
FIREE	GILET	HIDER	IMPEX	JIVED
FIXED	GIVEN	HIDES	INCEL	JIVER
FIXER	GIVER	HIKER	INDEX	JIVES
FIXES	GIVES	HIRED	INFER	JIVEY
FLEEK	GLUED	HIVES	INLET	JOKED
FLEER	GLUEY	HOKEY	INNER	JOKER
FLEET	GOFER	HOLER	INSET	JOKES
FLIER	GOLEM	HOLES	INTEL	JOKEY
FLIES	GONER	HOLEY	INTER	JONES
FLYER	GOOEY	HOMES	IRKED	JOYED
FOGEY	GREED	HOMEY	ISLET	JUKED
FOYER	GREEK	HONED	JADED	JUKES
FREED	GREEN	HONEY	JADES	JULEP
FREER	GREET	HOOEY	JAGER	KALES
FRIED	GRIEF	HOPED	JAKES	KAMES
FUMES	GRUEL	HOPES	JALEO	KEYED
FUSED	HADES	HOTEL	JANES	KEYER
GAMER	HAREM	HOVEL	JAPED	KIKES
GAMES	HATED	HOVER	JAPER	KIPED
GAPED	HATER	HYMEN	JAPES	KIPES

KITED	LINER	MARES	MINES	MORES
KITES	LINES	MASER	MIRED	MOSEY
KNEED	LIVED	MATED	MIREX	MOTED
KNEEL	LIVEN	MATER	MISER	MOTEL
KNEES	LIVER	MATES	MISES	MOTES
LABEL	LIVES	MATEY	MITER	MOTET
LACED	LONER	MAVEN	MITES	MOVED
LADEN	LOSEL	MAWED	MIXED	MOVER
LAGER	LOSER	MAZER	MIXER	MOVES
LASER	LOSES	MAZES	MIXES	MOWER
LATER	LOVED	MELEE	MOBES	MULES
LATEX	LOVER	MEMES	MODEL	MULEY
LAYER	LOVES	MERES	MODEM	MUREX
LEPER	LOWER	METER	MODES	MUSED
LEVEE	LUBED	METES	MOHEL	MUSER
LEVEL	LURED	MIKED	MOKES	MUSES
LEVER	LURER	MIKES	MOLES	MUSET
LIBEL	LURES	MILER	MONES	MUTED
LIFER	MACES	MILES	MONEY	MUTER
LIKED	MAGES	MIMED	MOOER	MUTES
LIKEN	MAKER	MIMEO	MOPED	NABES
LIKES	MAKES	MIMER	MOPER	NAKED
LIMEY	MALES	MIMES	MOPES	NAKER
LINED	MANED	MINED	MOPEY	NAMED
LINEN	MANES	MINER	MOREL	NAMER

NAMES	NOSER	OFFER	OUTED	PAREU
NARES	NOSES	OFTEN	OUTER	PASEO
NATES	NOSEY	OFTER	OUZEL	PATED
NAVEL	NOTED	OGLED	OWLER	PATEN
NAVES	NOTER	OGLER	OWLET	PATER
NAZES	NOTES	OGLES	OWNED	PATES
NEVER	NOVEL	OGRES	OWNER	PAVED
NEVES	NOWED	OILED	OXTER	PAVER
NEWEL	NUDER	OILER	PACED	PAWED
NEWER	NUDES	OLDEN	PACER	PAWER
NEWES	NUKER	OLDER	PACES	PAYED
NGWEE	NUKES	ONCER	PACEY	PAYEE
NICER	NUMEN	ONCET	PAGED	PAYER
NINES	OAKED	ONSET	PAGER	PENES
NISEI	OAKEN	OOZED	PAGES	PETER
NITES	OARED	OOZES	PALEA	PEWEE
NIXED	OASES	OPTED	PALED	PIKED
NIXES	OATER	OPTER	PALES	PIKER
NODED	OAVES	ORBED	PANED	PIKES
NODES	OBOES	ORDER	PANEL	PILED
NOMEN	OCHER	ORIEL	PANES	PILER
NOMES	OCREA	ORMER	PAPER	PILES
NONES	OCTET	OSIER	PARED	PINES
NONET	ODDER	OTHER	PAREN	PINEY
NOSED	OFFED	OTTER	PARER	PIPER

PIPES	PRYER	RAMEN	RENEW	RIVEL
PIPET	PUBES	RANEE	REPEL	RIVEN
PIXEL	PUCES	RAPED	RESES	RIVER
PLIER	PUKER	RAPER	RESET	RIVES
PLIES	PUKES	RAPES	REVEL	RIVET
PLYER	PULER	RARER	REVER	ROBED
POGEY	PULES	RASES	RICER	ROBES
POKED	PURED	RATED	RICES	RODEO
POKER	PUREE	RATEL	RIDER	RODES
POKES	PURER	RATER	RIDES	ROGER
POKEY	PYRES	RATES	RIFER	ROKES
POLES	QUEEF	RAVEL	RILED	ROLES
POPES	QUEEN	RAVEN	RILEY	ROMEO
PORED	QUEER	RAVER	RIMED	ROPER
PORER	QUIET	RAVES	RIMER	ROPES
PORES	RACED	RAWER	RIMES	ROSEN
POSED	RACER	RAYED	RINED	ROSES
POSER	RACES	RAZED	RINES	ROTES
POSES	RAGED	RAZER	RIPEN	ROVER
POWER	RAGER	REBEC	RIPER	ROWED
POXES	RAGES	REBEL	RIPES	ROWEL
PREEN	RAKED	REFER	RISEN	ROWEN
PRIED	RAKER	REGEN	RISER	ROWER
PRIER	RAKES	REKEY	RISES	RUBES
PROEM	RAMED	REMEX	RITES	RUDER

RULED	SAYER	SILEX	SOLER	TAKEN
RULER	SCREE	SINES	SOLES	TAKER
RULES	SCREW	SINEW	SONES	TAKES
RUMEN	SEDER	SIPES	SORES	TALED
RUNED	SEMEN	SIREE	SOWED	TALES
RUNES	SENES	SIREN	SOWER	TAMED
RUPEE	SERES	SIRES	SPEED	TAMER
RUSES	SEVEN	SISES	SPEEL	TAMES
SABER	SEVER	SITES	SPIED	TAPED
SADES	SEWER	SIXER	SPIEL	TAPER
SAFER	SEXER	SIXES	SPIES	TAPES
SAFES	SEXES	SIZER	SPREE	TAPET
SAGES	SHEEN	SIZES	STEED	TARED
SAKER	SHEEP	SKEET	STEEK	TARES
SAKES	SHEER	SKIER	STEEL	TASED
SALEP	SHEET	SKIES	STEEP	TASER
SALES	SHIER	SKYEY	STEER	TASES
SAMEY	SHIES	SLEEK	STIES	TATER
SAREE	SHOER	SLEEP	STOEP	TAXED
SATED	SHOES	SLEET	STREW	TAXER
SATES	SHRED	SLOES	SUPER	TAXES
SAVED	SHREW	SNEER	SWEEP	TEAED
SAVER	SHYER	SOBER	SWEET	TEHEE
SAVES	SIDES	SOKEN	TABES	TELEX
SAWER	SILES	SOKES	TAKED	TENET

TEPEE	TOMES	TRYED	UPPER	WANED
THEED	TONED	TRYER	UPSET	WARES
THEES	TONER	TUBED	URGED	WATER
THIEF	TONES	TUBER	URGES	WAVED
THREE	TOPER	TUBES	USHER	WAVER
THREW	TORES	TUNED	UTTER	WAVES
TIDED	TOTED	TUNER	VALET	WAVEY
TIDES	TOTEM	TUNES	VEXED	WAXEN
TIGER	TOTER	TUTEE	VIBES	WHEEL
TILED	TOTES	TWEED	VICES	WIDEN
TILER	TOWED	TWEEN	VIDEO	WIDER
TILES	TOWEE	TWEET	VINES	WIFEY
TIMED	TOWEL	TYPED	VIPER	WILES
TIMER	TOWER	TYPES	VIXEN	WIPED
TIMES	TOYED	TYRED	VOTED	WIPER
TINED	TOYER	TYRES	VOTER	WIPES
TINES	TREED	ULCER	VOWED	WIRED
TIRED	TREEN	UMBER	VOWEL	WISER
TIRES	TREES	UNDER	WADER	WOMEN
TITER	TRIED	UNMET	WAFER	WOOED
TOKED	TRIER	UNPEG	WAGED	WOOER
TOKEN	TRIES	UNSET	WAGER	WOVEN
TOKES	TRUED	UNSEX	WAGES	WOWED
TOLED	TRUER	UNWED	WAKEN	XEBEC
TOLES	TRUES	UPPED	WALES	XYLEM

YAMEN	CLEFT	JIFFY	SELFS	ALIGN
YARER	CLIFF	KERFS	SERFS	AMIGA
YAWED	CLIFT	KNIFE	SHAFT	AMIGO
YESES	COIFS	LEAFY	SHIFT	BADGE
YODEL	COMFY	LOOFA	SKIFF	BAGGY
YOKED	CRAFT	MIFFS	SLUFF	BANGS
YOKEL	CROFT	MUFFS	SNAFU	BARGE
YOKES	CUFFS	NAKFA	SNIFF	BEIGE
ZAXES	DAFFS	NIFFY	SNIFT	BILGE
ZONED	DAFFY	POOFS	SNUFF	BINGE
ZONER	DEIFY	POOFY	SPIFF	BINGO
ZONES	DELFT	POUFS	STAFF	BLOGS
ABAFT	DIFFS	PROFS	STIFF	BODGE
ALOFT	DRAFF	PUFFY	STUFF	BOGGY
BEEFY	DRAFT	QUAFF	SWIFT	BONGO
BLUFF	DRIFT	REEFS	TAFFY	BOUGH
BOFFO	EDIFY	REEFY	THEFT	BUDGE
BUFFO	FLUFF	REIFY	TIFFS	BUGGY
CAFFS	GAFFE	RIFFS	TUFFS	BULGE
CALFS	GOOFY	ROOFS	TURFS	CADGE
CHAFE	GRAFT	ROOFY	TURFY	CARGO
CHAFF	GRIFT	RUFFE	UNIFY	CHUGS
CHEFS	GRUFF	RUFFS	WHIFF	CIGGY
CHUFA	HUFFY	SCOFF	ADAGE	CLOGS
CHUFF	JIFFS	SCUFF	AJUGA	COIGN

CONGA	FLAGS	LARGE	MULGA	PRIGS
CORGI	FOGGY	LAUGH	MUNGO	PUDGE
COUGH	FORGE	LEDGE	NAGGY	PUDGY
CRAGS	FORGO	LIEGE	NEIGH	PURGE
DAGGA	FUDGE	LINGO	NIGGA	RAGGY
DEIGN	FUGGY	LODGE	NUDGE	RANGA
DINGE	FUNGI	LONGS	OLOGY	RANGE
DINGO	GAUGE	LOUGH	OMEGA	RANGI
DINGS	GORGE	LUNGE	OUTGO	RANGY
DINGY	GOUGE	LUNGI	PANGA	REIGN
DIRGE	GUNGE	LUNGS	PANGS	RIDGE
DODGE	GUNGY	MANGA	PARGE	RIDGY
DODGY	HANGS	MANGE	PEGGY	RINGS
DOGGE	HEDGE	MANGO	PHAGE	ROUGE
DOGGY	HINGE	MANGY	PIGGY	ROUGH
DONGS	IMAGE	MARGE	PINGO	RUNGS
DOUGH	JAGGS	MARGO	PINGS	SAGGY
DRAGS	JAGGY	MERGE	PLAGE	SARGE
DREGS	JIGGY	MIDGE	PLUGS	SEDGE
DRUGS	JINGO	MINGY	PODGE	SERGE
DUNGS	JIRGA	MOGGY	PODGY	SHAGS
ELEGY	JUDGE	MONGO	PONGS	SIEGE
FANGS	JUDGY	MONGS	PONGY	SINGE
FAUGH	KEDGE	MUDGE	PORGY	SINGS
FEIGN	KINGS	MUGGY	PREGO	SLAGS

SLOGS	THIGH	ALPHA	MACHO	RASHY
SLUGS	THUGS	ANCHO	MASHY	RATHE
SNAGS	TINGE	ARCHY	MATHS	RICHE
SNUGS	TINGS	AROHA	MECHA	RIGHT
SOGGY	TONGA	AUGHT	MESHY	RISHI
SONGS	TONGS	BATHE	MIGHT	ROCHE
SOUGH	TOUGH	BATHS	MOCHA	RUCHE
STAGE	TRIGS	BIGHT	MOCHI	RUSHY
STAGS	TWIGS	BOCHE	MOTHS	SADHU
STAGY	USAGE	BOTHY	MOTHY	SHAHS
STOGY	VENGE	BUSHY	MUCHO	SIGHS
SURGE	VERGE	CACHE	MUSHY	SIGHT
SWAGE	VIRGA	CUSHY	MYTHS	SOPHS
SWAGS	VLOGS	DACHA	MYTHY	SOPHY
SWIGS	VULGO	DISHY	NACHO	SPAHI
TAGGY	WEDGE	DUCHY	NICHE	SUSHI
TAIGA	WEDGY	ECCHI	NIGHT	TACHE
TANGA	WEIGH	EIGHT	OATHS	TACHS
TANGI	WINGS	FIGHT	OUCHE	TATHS
TANGO	WODGE	FISHY	OUGHT	TECHS
TANGS	WONGA	GUSHY	PASHA	TECHY
TANGY	YEGGS	ITCHY	PATHS	TIGHT
TENGE	ZINGS	KASHA	PITHY	TITHE
TERGA	ZINGY	LIGHT	PUSHY	WASHY
THEGN	ALOHA	LITHE	RAPHE	WIGHT

WITHY	APHID	BASIS	COBIA	DENIM
YACHT	APHIS	BATIK	COLIC	DESIS
AALII	APSIS	BEDIM	COMIC	DEVIL
ABOIL	ARGIL	BEFIT	COMIX	DIDIE
ACRID	ARMIE	BEGIN	CONIC	DIGIT
ACTIN	AROID	BELIE	COSIE	DISIR
ADMIN	ARRIS	BRAID	COVIN	DIVIS
ADMIT	ARSIS	BRAIN	COZIE	DIXIE
ADMIX	ASDIC	BROIL	CUBIC	DOGIE
AEGIS	ASPIC	BRUIT	CUBIT	DOXIE
AERIE	ASPIE	CABIN	CUMIN	DRAIL
AFFIX	ASTIR	CALIF	CUPID	DRAIN
AGAIN	ATRIA	CALIX	CURIA	DROID
AGGIE	ATTIC	CANID	CURIE	DROIT
ALCID	AUDIO	CAVIL	CURIO	DRUID
ALGID	AUDIT	CERIC	CUTIE	DUTIE
ALGIN	AURIC	CHAIN	CUTIN	EERIE
ALKIE	AUXIN	CHAIR	CUTIS	ELFIN
AMAIN	AVAIL	CHAIS	CYNIC	EMAIL
AMBIT	AVOID	CHOIR	DANIO	ENTIA
AMNIA	AWAIT	CILIA	DAVID	EOSIN
AMNIO	AZOIC	CITIE	DAVIT	EQUID
AMRIT	BASIC	CIVIC	DEBIT	EQUIP
ANTIC	BASIL	CIVIL	DEFIB	ERMIN
ANVIL	BASIN	CLAIM	DEMIT	ETHIC

EYRIE	INDIE	MAFIA	MURID	OVOID
EYRIR	INFIX	MAFIC	MUSIC	OXLIP
FAKIR	INUIT	MAGIC	MUSIT	PANIC
FETID	JUVIE	MANIA	MUTIS	PATIN
FINIS	KAFIR	MANIC	NADIR	PATIO
FLAIL	KEFIR	MANIS	NAVIE	PEDIS
FLAIR	KILIM	MARIA	NAZIS	PENIS
FLUID	KININ	MAVIN	NEWIE	PERIL
FOLIO	LABIA	MAVIS	NIHIL	PETIT
FRAIL	LAMIA	MAXIM	NITID	PILIS
FRUIT	LATIN	MAXIS	NIXIE	PIPIT
GAMIN	LEGIT	MEDIA	NORIA	PIXIE
GELID	LEXIS	MEDIC	NOTIF	PLAID
GENIC	LICIT	MERIT	NUDIE	PLAIN
GENIE	LIMIT	MESIC	OASIS	PLAIT
GRAIL	LIPID	METIC	OHMIC	PODIA
GRAIN	LIVID	MIDIS	OLDIE	POKIE
GROIN	LOGIC	MIMIC	OLLIE	POLIO
HABIT	LOGIN	MINIM	ONTIC	POLIS
HELIX	LOUIS	MIRID	OOTID	PORIN
HOMIE	LUCID	MOTIF	OPSIN	POSIT
HUMID	LUDIC	MOVIE	OPTIC	PUBIC
IBLIS	LUMIC	MOXIE	ORBIT	PUBIS
IMMIX	LURID	MUCID	ORGIC	PUNIC
INDIA	LYRIC	MUCIN	ORRIS	PUPIL

PURIS	RESIN	SHTIK	TAKIN	TWAIN
PYXIS	RESIT	SIGIL	TAMIS	TYPIC
QILIN	RICIN	SKEIN	TAPIR	UNFIT
QUAIL	RIDIC	SLAIN	TAPIS	UNFIX
QUOIN	RIGID	SMAIL	TAXIS	UNLIT
RABIC	ROBIN	SNAIL	TELIC	UNTIE
RABID	RONIN	SOLID	TEPID	UNTIL
RADII	ROSIN	SONIC	THEIR	UNZIP
RADIO	ROTIS	SPAIN	THRID	VALID
RADIX	RUNIC	SPLIT	TIBIA	VAPID
RAMIE	RUTIN	SPOIL	TIMID	VATIC
RANIS	SAHIB	SPRIG	TIYIN	VIGIL
RAPID	SAPID	SPRIT	TONIC	VISIT
RATIO	SARIN	SQUIB	TOPIC	VIVID
RAVIN	SARIS	SQUID	TORIC	VOMIT
RECIT	SATIN	STAID	TORII	XENIA
REDID	SAVIN	STAIN	TOXIC	XENIC
REFIT	SCRIM	STAIR	TOXIN	XERIC
REFIX	SCRIP	STEIN	TRAIL	XYLIC
REJIG	SEMIS	STOIC	TRAIN	YETIS
RELIC	SEPIA	STRIA	TRAIT	YOGIC
REMIT	SERIE	STRIP	TULIP	YOGIN
REMIX	SERIF	SUFIS	TUMID	YOGIS
RENIG	SERIN	SWAIN	TUNIC	YONIC
RENIN	SHEIK	TACIT	TUPIK	YONIS

ZAMIA	CASKS	DIRKS	HACKY	KINKY
ZAYIN	CHOKE	DISKS	HAIKU	KOOKY
ZOOID	CHOKY	DOCKS	HECKA	LACKS
EMOJI	COCKS	DORKS	HINKY	LANKY
GANJA	COCKY	DORKY	HOKKU	LARKY
HAJJI	CONKS	DRAKE	HOOKY	LAWKS
KANJI	CONKY	DUCKS	HULKY	LEAKY
NINJA	COOKS	DUCKY	HUNKS	LINKS
SHOJI	COOKY	DUNKS	HUNKY	LOCKS
THUJA	CORKS	DUSKS	HUSKY	LOOKS
ALIKE	CORKY	DUSKY	JACKS	LUCKY
AMOKS	CRAKE	ENOKI	JACKY	MARKE
AWAKE	DACKS	ENSKY	JERKS	MARKS
AWOKE	DANKS	EVOKE	JERKY	MASKS
BALKY	DARKE	FLAKE	JINKS	MICKS
BEAKY	DARKS	FLAKY	JOCKS	MILKO
BLOKE	DARKY	FLUKE	JOCKY	MILKS
BOOKS	DECKS	FLUKY	JUNKS	MILKY
BRAKE	DEKKO	FOLKS	JUNKY	MINKS
BROKE	DESKS	FUNKY	KECKS	MOCKS
BUCKS	DICKS	GAWKY	KEEKS	MONKS
BULKY	DICKY	GEEKY	KHAKI	MUCKY
BURKA	DINKS	GRIKE	KICKS	MURKY
BURKE	DINKY	GUNKY	KICKY	MUSKS
CALKS	DIRKE	HACKS	KINKS	MUSKY

NARKS	POLKA	SACKS	SPOKE	TRIKE
NARKY	POOKA	SARKS	STAKE	TUCKS
NECKE	PORKY	SARKY	STIKE	TUSKS
NECKS	PUCKS	SEEKS	STOKE	TUSKY
NICKS	PUKKA	SHAKA	SUCKA	VODKA
NOOKS	PUNKS	SHAKE	SUCKS	WACKE
NOOKY	PUNKY	SHAKO	SUCKY	WACKO
PACKS	QUAKE	SHAKY	SULKS	WACKY
PARKA	QUAKY	SICKO	SULKY	WALKS
PARKS	RACKS	SILKS	TACKS	WONKY
PARKY	RANKE	SILKY	TACKY	WORKS
PAWKY	RANKS	SINKS	TALKE	YAKKY
PEAKS	REEKS	SLAKE	TALKS	YANKS
PEAKY	REEKY	SLOKA	TALKY	YOLKS
PECKE	REIKI	SMOKE	TANKA	YOLKY
PECKS	RICKS	SMOKO	TANKS	YONKS
PERKS	RINKS	SMOKY	TANKY	YORKS
PERKY	RISKS	SNAKE	TASKS	YUCKS
PESKY	RISKY	SNAKY	TEAKS	YUCKY
PICKS	ROCKS	SOAKS	TICKS	YUKKY
PICKY	ROCKY	SOCKS	TICKY	ZINKY
PINKO	ROOKE	SOOKS	TIKKA	ZONKS
PINKS	ROOKS	SOOKY	TINKS	ZONKY
PINKY	ROOKY	SPIKE	TOOKE	ABELE
POCKS	RUSKS	SPIKY	TREKS	ACYLS

ADDLE	AXILE	CAULK	CYCLE	DWELL
ADULT	BADLY	CELLA	DAHLS	DWELT
AGILE	BALLS	CELLI	DAILY	EAGLE
AHOLD	BALLY	CELLO	DALLY	EARLE
AIOLI	BAULK	CELLS	DEALE	EARLS
AISLE	BELLE	CHALK	DEALS	EARLY
AMBLE	BELLS	CHELA	DEALT	EMULE
AMOLE	BELLY	CHILD	DELLS	EVILL
AMPLE	BIBLE	CHILE	DHOLE	EVILS
AMPLY	BILLS	CHILI	DIALS	EXALT
ANALS	BILLY	CHILL	DILLS	EXILE
ANELE	BOGLE	CHOLO	DILLY	EXULT
ANGLE	BOILS	CHYLE	DIMLY	FABLE
ANILE	BRILL	COALS	DOILY	FAILS
ANKLE	BUGLE	COALY	DOLLS	FALLS
ANOLE	BUILD	COILS	DOLLY	FATLY
APOLS	BUILT	COOLE	DOOLY	FAULT
APPLE	BULLS	COOLY	DOULA	FEELS
APPLY	BULLY	COULD	DRILL	FELLA
APTLY	BURLY	COWLS	DROLL	FIELD
ARILS	CABLE	COYLY	DRYLY	FILLS
ASYLA	CALLA	CULLS	DUALS	FILLY
ATILT	CALLI	CULLY	DUELS	FOLLY
ATOLL	CALLS	CURLS	DULLY	FOOLS
AXELS	CARLE	CURLY	DWALE	FRILL

FUELS	ICILY	MAILS	NOBLE	POLLY
FULLY	IDYLL	MALLS	NOBLY	POOLS
GABLE	IMPLY	MANLY	NULLS	POULT
GAILY	JAILS	MAPLE	NYALA	PRILL
GIRLS	JELLY	MARLE	OBELI	PROLE
GIRLY	JOLLY	MARLY	OCULI	PSALM
GOALS	JOULE	MAULS	ODDLY	PULLS
GODLY	JOWLS	MEALS	ONELY	PULLY
GOLLY	JOWLY	MEALY	OPALS	QUALM
GRILL	KAILS	MERLE	ORALS	QUELL
GUILD	KEELS	MEWLS	OVALS	QUILL
GUILE	KELLS	MILLS	OVOLO	QUILT
GUILT	KELLY	MOILE	OVULE	RAILE
GULLY	KIDLY	MOILS	PAILS	RAILS
HAULM	KILLS	MOLLY	PALLS	RALLY
HAULT	KNELL	MOOLA	PALLY	REALM
HEELS	KNELT	MOULD	PARLE	REALS
HELLA	KNOLL	MOULT	PEALS	REELS
HELLO	KVELL	MULLA	PEELS	RELLY
HILLS	LADLE	MULLS	PEPLA	REPLY
HILLY	LOLLY	NABLA	PHYLA	RIALS
HOLLO	LOWLY	NAILS	PILLS	RIFLE
HOLLY	MACLE	NAILY	PILLY	RILLE
HOTLY	MADLY	NELLY	POILU	RILLS
HURLY	MAILE	NEWLY	POLLS	ROILY

ROLLS	SHYLY	SPILL	TELLY	WALLS
ROLLY	SIDLE	SPILT	TESLA	WAULK
RUBLE	SILLS	STALE	THILL	WELLY
SABLE	SILLY	STALK	THOLE	WHALE
SADLY	SKALD	STALL	TILLS	WHELK
SAILE	SKILL	STELA	TILLY	WHELM
SAILS	SKILS	STELE	TITLE	WHELP
SALLY	SKULK	STILB	TOILE	WHILE
SAULT	SKULL	STILE	TOILS	WHOLE
SCALD	SLYLY	STILL	TOLLS	WIELD
SCALE	SMALL	STILT	TOOLS	WILLY
SCALP	SMELL	STOLE	TRILL	WOOLY
SCALY	SMELT	STYLE	TROLL	WORLD
SCOLD	SMILE	SULLY	TRULL	WOULD
SCULL	SMOLT	SURLY	TRULY	WRYLY
SEALS	SNELL	SWALE	TULLE	YELLS
SELLE	SOCLE	SWELL	TWILL	YIELD
SELLS	SOILE	SWILL	UGALI	YOWLS
SELLY	SOILS	SWOLE	UNCLE	ZEALE
SHALE	SOULE	TABLA	UTILE	ZEALS
SHALL	SOULS	TABLE	UVULA	AGAMA
SHELF	SPALL	TAILS	VAULT	ALAMO
SHELL	SPELL	TALLY	VILLA	ALUMN
SHILL	SPELT	TEALS	VIOLA	ALUMS
SHULS	SPILE	TELLS	VOILA	ANIMA

ANIME	CLAMP	DOOMS	GAMMY	MUMMY
ANOMY	CLAMS	DOOMY	GERMS	NEEMB
AROMA	CLIMB	DORMS	GIZMO	NEEMS
ATOMS	CLIME	DRAMA	GLOMP	NEUME
ATOMY	CLOMP	DRAMS	GNOME	NEUMS
BALMY	CLUMP	DRUMS	GRIME	NORMA
BARMY	COMMA	DUMMY	GRIMY	NORMS
BEAMS	COMMO	DUOMO	GRUMP	PALMS
BEAMY	COMMS	EDEMA	GUMMY	PALMY
BHUMI	COMMY	ELEMI	HAMMY	PELMA
BIOME	COSMO	ENEMA	HARMS	PIGMY
BLAME	CRAME	ENEMY	ITEMS	PLUMB
BLIMP	CRAMP	ETYMA	JAMMY	PLUME
BOOMY	CRAMS	EXAMS	JEMMY	PLUMP
BRUME	CREMS	FEMME	JIMMY	PLUMS
CALMS	CRIME	FILMS	KARMA	PLUMY
CALMY	CRIMP	FILMY	LLAMA	POEME
CHAMP	CRIMS	FIRMS	LOAMY	POEMS
CHAMS	CRUMB	FLAME	LOOMS	POMMY
CHEMO	CRUMP	FLUME	MAGMA	PRAME
CHIME	DEEMS	FLUMP	MALMS	PRAMS
CHOMP	DERMA	FOAMY	MAMMA	PRIME
CHUMP	DERMS	FORMS	MAMMY	PRIMO
CHUMS	DOGMA	FRAME	MOMMA	PRIMP
CHYME	DOLMA	FRUMP	MOMMY	PROMO

PROMS	SLIMS	THEME	AGEND	AXING
PYGMY	SLIMY	THUMB	AGENT	AXONE
REAME	SLUMP	THUMP	AGING	AXONS
REAMS	SLUMS	THYME	AGONE	AZINE
RHOMB	SPAMS	THYMI	AGONS	BANNS
RHUMB	SPUME	THYMY	AGONY	BEANO
RHYME	SPUMY	TRAMP	AHING	BEANS
ROOME	STAMP	TRAMS	AKENS	BEING
ROOMS	STEMS	TRIMS	ALONE	BLAND
ROOMY	STIME	TROMP	ALONG	BLANK
RUMMY	STIMY	TRUMP	AMEND	BLEND
SALMI	STOMA	TUMMY	AMENS	BLIND
SAMMY	STOMP	UMAMI	AMENT	BLING
SCAMP	STUMP	WHIMS	AMINE	BLINK
SCAMS	STUMS	WHOMP	AMINO	BLOND
SCHMO	STYMY	WHUMP	AMONG	BLUNT
SCUMS	SUMMA	WORMY	ANENT	BOING
SEAMS	SWAMI	YUMMO	APING	BONNY
SEAMY	SWAMP	YUMMY	ARENA	BOONG
SEEMS	SWIMS	ZOOMS	ASANA	BORNE
SHAME	TALMA	ZOOMY	ASYNC	BOUND
SHAMS	TAMMY	ABEND	ATONE	BRAND
SIGMA	TEAMS	ACING	AVANT	BRINE
SKIMP	TEEMS	ACINI	AVENS	BRING
SLIME	TERMS	AEONS	AWING	BRINK

BRINY	COINE	DOWNY	FIEND	GUANO
BRUNT	COINS	DRANK	FLANK	HAUNT
BUNNY	COONS	DRINK	FLING	HENNA
BURNS	CORNS	DRONE	FLINT	HORNS
BURNT	CORNU	DRUNK	FLUNG	HORNY
CANNA	CORNY	DUNNY	FLUNK	HOUND
CANNY	COUNT	DYING	FOUND	HYENA
CARNY	CRANE	EARNS	FOUNT	ICING
CHANT	CRANK	EARNT	FRANK	ICONS
CHINA	CRANS	EBONS	FROND	INANE
CHINE	CRONE	EBONY	FRONT	IRONS
CHINK	CRONY	EKING	FUNNY	IRONY
CHINO	CRUNK	ELAND	GAINS	JAUNT
CHINS	CYANS	ELANS	GAUNT	JEANS
CHUNK	DAMNS	EMEND	GIANT	JENNY
CLANG	DAUNT	EVENS	GLAND	JINNI
CLANK	DAWNS	EVENT	GLINT	JOHNS
CLANS	DEANS	EXINE	GOING	JOINS
CLINE	DERNS	EXONS	GONNA	JOINT
CLING	DIANA	EYING	GOUND	KEENE
CLINK	DIENE	FAINT	GRAND	KEENS
CLONE	DJINN	FANNE	GRANT	KHANS
CLONK	DOING	FANNY	GRIND	KIANG
CLUNG	DONNA	FAUNA	GRINS	KILNS
CLUNK	DOWNS	FEINT	GRUNT	LEANS

LIANG	NANNY	PENNY	PRANG	SCONE
LIENS	NEONS	PEONS	PRANK	SEINE
LLANO	NINNY	PEONY	PRINK	SEINS
LOANS	NOONE	PHONE	PRINT	SENNA
LOINS	NOONS	PHONO	PRONE	SHANK
LOONY	NOUNS	PHONS	PRONG	SHINE
LYING	NOUNY	PHONY	PRONS	SHINS
MAINS	OHING	PIANO	PRUNE	SHINY
MANNA	OMENS	PINNA	PUNNY	SHONE
MANNY	OPENS	PINNY	RAINS	SHUNT
MAUND	OPINE	PIONS	RAINY	SIENS
MEANS	ORANG	PLANE	REENS	SIENT
MEANT	OVENS	PLANK	REINS	SIGNA
MEANY	OVINE	PLANS	RHINO	SIGNS
MESNE	OWING	PLANT	ROUND	SKANK
MIENS	OZONE	PLINK	RUINS	SKINS
MINNY	PAINS	PLONK	RUNNY	SKINT
MOANS	PAINT	PLUNK	SAINT	SKUNK
MOANY	PANNE	POINT	SAUNA	SLANG
MOONS	PAWNS	POONS	SCANS	SLANT
MOONY	PEANS	PORNO	SCANT	SLING
MORNS	PEENS	PORNS	SCENA	SLINK
MOUND	PENNA	PORNY	SCEND	SLUNK
MOUNT	PENNE	POUND	SCENE	SONNY
MUONS	PENNI	PRANA	SCENT	SOUND

SPANG	SUNNI	TOONS	VIAND	ALCOS
SPANK	SUNNY	TOWNE	VYING	ALDOL
SPANS	SWANG	TOWNS	WANNA	ALGOR
SPEND	SWANK	TOWNY	WARNS	ALLOT
SPENT	SWANS	TRANQ	WEENY	ALLOW
SPINE	SWINE	TRANS	WHANG	ALLOY
SPINS	SWING	TRANT	WHINE	ALOOF
SPINY	SWINK	TREND	WHINY	ALTOS
SPUNK	SWUNG	TRINE	WOUND	AMBON
STAND	TAINT	TRONA	WRING	AMBOS
STANE	TARNS	TRUNK	WRONG	ANCON
STANK	TAUNT	TUNNY	WRUNG	ANION
STENO	TAWNY	TURNS	XOANA	ANNOY
STENT	TEENS	TWANG	YARNS	APRON
STING	TEENY	TWANK	YAWNS	ARBOR
STINK	TENNO	TWINE	YAWNY	ARDOR
STINT	THANE	TWINS	YOUNG	ARGON
STONE	THANK	TWINY	ABBOT	ARGOT
STONG	THING	TYING	ABHOR	ARMOR
STONK	THINK	UPEND	ACHOO	ARROW
STONY	THINS	URINE	ACTOR	ARROZ
STUNG	THONG	USING	ADIOS	ARSON
STUNT	THUNK	VAUNT	AFOOT	ASCOT
SUING	TINNY	VEINS	AFROS	ATMOS
SUNNA	TONNE	VEINY	AGLOW	AUTOS

AVION	CAPON	DEPOT	ESTOC	INGOT
AXIOM	CAROB	DETOX	ESTOP	JABOT
AXION	CAROL	DEVON	ETHOS	JACOB
BACON	CAROM	DICOT	EUROS	JUROR
BARON	CHAOS	DIDOS	EXPOS	KAPOK
BATON	CHRON	DINOS	EXTOL	KAZOO
BAYOU	COCOA	DIVOT	FAVOR	KILOS
BEFOG	COCOS	DOLOR	FELON	KUDOS
BEGOT	CODON	DONOR	FLOOD	LABOR
BELOW	COLON	DROOL	FLOOR	LEMON
BIGOT	COLOR	DROOP	FUROR	LOGON
BIJOU	COROL	ECHOS	FUTON	LOGOS
BISON	CROOK	EIDOS	GLOOM	MACON
BLOOD	CROON	ELBOW	GLOOP	MAHOE
BLOOM	CRUOR	EMBOG	GRIOT	MAJOR
BOSOM	CYTOL	ENDOW	GROOM	MANOR
BOTOX	DADOS	ENJOY	HAVOC	MASON
BROOD	DECON	ENROL	HEDON	MAYOR
BROOK	DECOR	ENVOI	HERON	MAYOS
BROOM	DECOY	ENVOY	HONOR	MELON
BUXOM	DEFOG	EPHOD	HUMOR	MEMOS
CAHOW	DEMOB	EPHOR	ICHOR	MESON
CAMOS	DEMOI	ERGON	IDIOM	MILOS
CANOE	DEMON	ERGOT	IDIOT	MINOR
CANON	DEMOS	ERROR	IGLOO	MOJOS

MORON	PROOF	SCROW	SPOOR	THROW
MOTOR	PYLON	SENOR	SPROG	TIGON
MUSOS	RACON	SEPOY	STOOD	TIROS
NABOB	RADON	SEROW	STOOK	TOPOS
NINON	RAYON	SHOOK	STOOL	TOYON
NYLON	RAZOR	SHOON	STOOP	TRIOS
ONION	RECON	SHOOP	STROP	TROOP
OSMOL	REDOS	SHOOT	SUDOR	TUMOR
OXBOW	REDOX	SILOS	SWOON	TUTOR
PAEON	REPOS	SIMON	SWOOP	TYPOS
PAROL	REPOT	SLOOP	SYNOD	TYROS
PAYOR	RIGOR	SNOOD	SYSOP	UNBOX
PEKOE	ROBOT	SNOOK	TABOO	UNCOS
PESOS	ROTOR	SNOOP	TABOR	UNION
PHLOX	RUMOR	SNOOT	TACOS	VALOR
PICOT	SABOT	SOKOL	TALON	VAPOR
PILOT	SALON	SOLON	TAROT	VENOM
PINOT	SAPOR	SOLOS	TAXON	VIGOR
PITON	SAROD	SOPOR	TAXOR	VISOR
PIVOT	SAVOR	SOROR	TELOS	WAGON
POGOS	SAVOY	SPLOT	TENON	WAHOO
POLOS	SCION	SPOOF	TENOR	WHOOP
POTOO	SCOOP	SPOOK	THIOL	WIDOW
PRION	SCOOT	SPOOL	THROB	XENON
PRIOR	SCROD	SPOON	THROE	XEROX

XYLOL	CLIPS	DRIPS	JUMPS	PEEPS
YAHOO	COAPT	DROPS	JUMPY	PEPPY
YAKOW	COMPO	DRUPE	KAPPA	PERPS
ZEROS	COMPS	DUMPS	KEEPE	PIMPS
ADAPT	COOPS	DUMPY	KEEPS	PIPPY
ADEPT	COOPT	DUPPY	KEMPT	POMPS
ADOPT	CORPS	ELOPE	KNAPS	POOPS
AGAPE	COUPE	ERUPT	LEAPT	POPPA
ALEPH	COUPS	FLAPS	LOOPY	POPPY
AREPA	COYPU	GASPS	LUMPY	PROPS
ATOPY	CRAPS	GIMPY	LYMPH	PULPS
BUMPS	CREPE	GLYPH	MOPPY	PULPY
BUMPY	CREPT	GRAPE	MORPH	PUMPS
CAMPI	CREPY	GRAPH	MUMPS	PUPPY
CAMPO	CRIPS	GRIPE	MYOPE	QUIPS
CAMPS	CROPS	GROPE	MYOPY	RAMPS
CAMPY	CRYPT	HAPPY	NAPPE	RAPPA
CARPI	CUPPA	HARPY	NAPPY	RASPS
CARPS	CUPPY	HEAPS	NIPPY	RASPY
CHAPE	CUSPS	HELPS	NYMPH	ROMPS
CHAPS	DEEPS	HIPPO	OKAPI	RUMPS
CHIPS	DERPY	HIPPY	OOMPH	SAMPS
CHOPS	DIMPS	INAPT	PAMPA	SAPPY
CLAPS	DIPPY	INEPT	PAPPY	SCAPE
CLEPE	DRAPE	JEEPS	PEEPE	SCAPI

SCOPA	STOPE	TUMPS	ADORN	AZURE
SCOPE	STOPS	TURPS	AFIRE	AZURN
SEEPS	STUPA	UNAPT	AFORE	AZURY
SHAPE	STUPE	WASPY	AGARS	BAIRN
SHIPS	SUMPS	WEEPY	AGERS	BEARD
SHOPS	SWAPE	WIMPY	AGGRO	BEARS
SIMPS	SWAPS	WISPY	AGORA	BERRY
SIPPY	SWEPT	WRAPS	ALARM	BLARE
SKIPS	SWIPE	YAPPS	ALARY	BLURB
SLAPS	SWOPS	YAPPY	ALERT	BLURT
SLEPT	SYLPH	YAWPS	AMBRY	BOARD
SLIPS	TAMPS	YELPS	ANDRO	BOURG
SLOPE	TARPS	YIPPY	ANGRY	BOURN
SLOPS	TAUPE	YUPPY	ANTRA	BURRO
SLYPE	TEMPI	ZAPPY	ANTRE	BURRY
SNAPS	TEMPO	ZIPPO	ANURY	CADRE
SNIPE	TEMPS	ZIPPY	APART	CAIRN
SNIPS	TEMPT	PEROS	APERS	CARRS
SOAPS	TIPPY	ABORD	APERY	CARRY
SOAPY	TOPPY	ABORE	AVERS	CHARD
SOPPY	TRAPS	ABORN	AVERT	CHARE
SOUPS	TRAPT	ABORT	AWARD	CHARM
SOUPY	TRIPE	ACERB	AWARE	CHARS
STEPS	TRIPS	ACORN	AWARN	CHART
STIPE	TROPE	ADORE	AWORK	CHARY

CHERT	DEERE	FAIRY	HOURS	MACRO
CHIRO	DEERS	FEARS	HURRY	MAIRE
CHIRP	DIARY	FERRY	HYDRA	MARRY
CHIRR	DOBRA	FIBRE	HYDRO	MERRY
CHORD	DOBRO	FIERY	INERT	METRE
CHORE	DOERS	FJORD	INTRA	METRO
CHURL	DOORS	FLARE	INTRO	MICRO
CHURN	DOWRY	FLIRT	INURE	MITRE
CHURR	DURRA	FLORA	INURN	MOIRE
CLARO	DWARF	FURRY	IVORY	MOORS
CLARY	DYERS	GENRE	JEERS	MOORY
CLERK	EAGRE	GLARE	JERRY	MOURN
COBRA	EMERG	GLORY	JEWRY	MUCRO
COPRA	EMERY	GOURD	JOURS	MUDRA
COURS	EMIRS	GUARD	KARRI	MURRE
COURT	ENORM	HAIRY	KAURI	MYRRH
CRORE	ENTRE	HARRY	KERRY	NACRE
CRURA	ENTRY	HEARD	KNURL	NAIRA
CURRY	EVERE	HEARS	LAIRD	NEARE
CZARS	EVERT	HEART	LEARN	NEARS
DAIRY	EVERY	HEIRS	LEERY	NECRO
DEARN	EXERT	HETRO	LIARS	NEGRO
DEARS	EXTRA	HIJRA	LIBRA	NEURO
DEARY	EXURB	HOARD	LORRY	NITRO
DECRY	EYERS	HOARY	LUCRE	OCHRE

ODORS	POORE	SEERS	SNORT	STORY
OMBRE	PURRS	SHARD	SOARS	SUCRE
ONERS	PURRY	SHARE	SORRY	SUERS
ONERY	QUERY	SHARK	SOURS	SUTRA
OPERA	QUIRK	SHARP	SPARE	SWARD
OPERS	REARM	SHART	SPARK	SWARM
OUTRE	REARS	SHERO	SPARS	SWART
OVARY	REORG	SHIRE	SPERM	SWIRL
OVERS	REPRO	SHIRK	SPIRE	SWORD
OVERT	RETRO	SHIRT	SPORE	SWORE
PADRE	RETRY	SHORE	SPORK	SWORN
PAGRI	ROARS	SHORT	SPORT	TARRE
PAIRE	SABRA	SKARN	SPURN	TARRY
PAIRS	SABRE	SKIRR	SPURS	TAYRA
PARRY	SACRA	SKIRT	SPURT	TEARE
PEARE	SAURY	SLURP	STARE	TEARS
PEARL	SCARD	SLURS	STARK	TEARY
PEARS	SCARE	SMARM	STARS	TERRA
PEART	SCARF	SMART	START	TERRY
PEARY	SCARP	SMIRK	STERN	TETRA
PEERS	SCARS	SMURF	STIRK	THERE
PERRY	SCARY	SNARE	STIRS	THERM
PHARM	SCORE	SNARK	STORE	THIRD
PHARO	SCORN	SNARL	STORK	THORN
PIERS	SCURF	SNORE	STORM	THORO

THORP	WORRY	AVAST	CHESS	CURSE
TIARA	YEARE	AVISO	CHEST	CURST
TIERS	YEARN	AWASH	CHOSE	DAISY
TIGRE	YEARS	BEAST	CISSY	DEISM
TOURS	YOURS	BIRSE	CLASH	DEIST
TOWRE	ZAIRE	BITSY	CLASP	DENSE
TSARS	ZEBRA	BLAST	CLASS	DIPSO
TWERK	ABASE	BLESS	CLAST	DITSY
TWERP	ABASH	BLEST	CLOSE	DORSA
TWIRL	ABASK	BLISS	COAST	DOUSE
ULTRA	ABUSE	BLUSH	CONST	DOWSE
UMBRA	ABYSM	BOAST	COPSE	DRESS
USERS	ABYSS	BOOST	COPSY	DROSS
USURP	ADUST	BOSSY	CORSE	DULSE
USURY	AGIST	BRASH	CRASH	EGEST
WEARS	AMASS	BRASS	CRASS	ERASE
WEARY	AMISS	BRISK	CRESC	EROSE
WEIRD	AMUSE	BRUSH	CRESS	EXIST
WHARF	ANGST	BURST	CREST	FALSE
WHERE	ANISE	CAUSE	CRISE	FARSI
WHIRL	ANTSY	CEASE	CRISP	FEAST
WHIRR	APISH	CENSE	CROSS	FEIST
WHORE	ARISE	CHASE	CRUSE	FIRST
WHORL	AROSE	CHASM	CRUSH	FLASH
WIRRA	ARTSY	CHAST	CRUST	FLASK

FLESH	HARSH	MASSA	ONEST	PRISM
FLOSS	HEIST	MASSY	OWEST	PROSE
FLUSH	HISSY	MENSA	PAISA	PROSS
FOIST	HOIST	MENSE	PALSY	PROSY
FOSSE	HORSE	MESSY	PANSY	PULSE
FRESH	HORSY	MIASM	PARSE	PURSE
FRISK	HOUSE	MIDST	PASSE	PURSY
FROST	HURST	MISSY	PATSY	PUSSY
FUSSY	HUSSY	MOIST	PAUSE	QUASH
GASSY	JOIST	MOMSY	PEASE	QUASI
GEESE	JOUST	MOOSE	PERSE	QUEST
GHOST	KARST	MOSSY	PHASE	RAISE
GLASS	KIOSK	MOUSE	PHISH	REUSE
GLOSS	KISSY	MOUSY	PISSY	RINSE
GNASH	LAPSE	MUMSY	PLASH	ROAST
GOOSE	LASSO	MUSSY	PLASM	ROOST
GORSE	LEASE	NEWSY	PLUSH	ROUSE
GRASP	LEASH	NISSE	POESY	ROUST
GRASS	LEAST	NOISE	POISE	SALSA
GROSS	LOOSE	NOISY	POPSY	SASSE
GUESS	LOUSE	NOOSE	POSSE	SASSY
GUEST	LOUSY	NURSE	PRASE	SEISM
GUISE	MAIST	NUTSY	PRESS	SENSE
GUTSY	MANSE	OBESE	PREST	SHUSH
GYPSY	MARSH	ODIST	PRISE	SISSY

SKOSH	TORSO	YOUSE	BOOTH	CHITS
SLASH	TOSSY	AARTI	BOOTS	CHUTE
SLOSH	TOUSY	ABATE	BOOTY	CLOTH
SLUSH	TRASH	ABETS	BOTTY	CLOTS
SMASH	TRASS	ABUTS	BOUTS	COATE
SOUSE	TRESS	ABUTT	BROTH	COATI
SPASM	TRUSS	ACUTE	BRUTE	COATS
STASH	TRUST	AGATE	BUSTY	COLTS
SUDSY	TRYST	AGITA	BUTTE	CONTE
SWASH	TWIST	AKITA	BUTTY	COOTS
SWISH	UKASE	ALATE	CACTI	COOTY
SWISS	UNUSE	AMITY	CANTO	COSTA
TANSY	VERSE	AORTA	CANTS	COSTS
TARSI	VERSO	ARETE	CANTY	COTTA
TAWSE	WAIST	AUNTS	CARTE	COUTH
TEASE	WELSH	AUNTY	CARTS	CRATE
TENSE	WHISH	BASTE	CASTE	CRWTH
TERSE	WHISK	BATTY	CASTS	CULTS
THESE	WHOSE	BEATS	CATTY	CULTY
THESP	WORSE	BERTH	CELTS	CUNTS
TIPSY	WORST	BETTY	CENTO	CYSTS
TOAST	WREST	BIOTA	CENTS	DARTS
TORSE	WRIST	BIRTH	CERTS	DEATH
TORSI	WURST	BITTY	CESTA	DEBTS
TORSK	YEAST	BLITZ	CHATS	DEETS

DEITY	ELUTE	GLITZ	JUNTO	MEATS
DELTA	EMITS	GOTTA	JUSTS	MEATY
DENTS	EMOTE	GRATE	JUTTY	MEETS
DEPTH	EMPTY	GRITH	KARTS	MELTY
DEPTS	ENATE	GRITS	KENTE	METTS
DHOTI	EXITS	GUSTO	KILTS	MINTS
DICTA	FACTS	GUSTY	KNITS	MINTY
DICTY	FAITH	GUTTY	KNOTS	MIRTH
DIETS	FATTY	HALTS	LAITY	MISTS
DINTS	FEATS	HASTE	LASTS	MISTY
DIRTY	FIFTH	HASTY	LATTE	MITTS
DITTO	FIFTY	HAUTE	LEFTY	MOATS
DITTY	FILTH	HEATH	LIFTS	MOLTS
DOLTS	FIRTH	HEFTY	LISTS	MONTE
DOTTY	FLUTE	HERTZ	LOATH	MONTH
DUCTS	FORTE	HINTS	LOFTY	MOOTS
DUETS	FORTH	HOSTS	LUSTY	MORTS
DUETT	FORTY	HURTS	MALTA	MOSTS
DUSTS	FRITZ	IRATE	MALTS	MOTTE
DUSTY	FROTH	JESTS	MALTY	MOTTO
EARTH	FUSTY	JETTY	MANTA	MOUTH
EASTS	GENTS	JILTS	MARTS	MUFTI
EDITS	GESTE	JOLTS	MASTS	MULTI
ELATE	GIFTS	JOLTY	MATTE	MUSTS
ELITE	GIRTH	JUNTA	MATTY	MUSTY

NASTY	PARTY	PLUTE	RASTA	SCOTS
NATTY	PASTA	POETE	RATTY	SCUTA
NEATH	PASTE	POETS	REATA	SCUTE
NEATO	PASTS	POOTS	RECTA	SEATS
NEATS	PASTY	PORTA	RECTO	SECTS
NERTS	PATTY	PORTS	RENTS	SEITY
NESTS	PEATS	POSTS	RESTS	SENTE
NETTS	PEATY	POTTO	RIATA	SENTI
NETTY	PENTS	POTTY	RIFTS	SENTS
NEWTS	PESTO	POUTS	RIOTS	SEPTA
NIFTY	PESTS	POUTY	ROOTS	SEPTS
NINTH	PESTY	PRATE	ROOTY	SETTS
NORTH	PETTY	PROTO	ROUTE	SHETH
NUTTY	PHOTO	PUNTS	ROUTS	SHITE
OASTS	PICTS	PUNTY	RUNTS	SHITS
OBITS	PIETS	PUTTO	RUNTY	SHOTS
OMITS	PIETY	PUTTS	RUSTS	SHUTS
ORATE	PINTO	PUTTY	RUSTY	SISTA
OUSTS	PINTS	QUITE	RUTTY	SIXTH
OVATE	PISTE	QUITS	SALTS	SIXTY
PACTS	PITTA	QUOTA	SALTY	SKATE
PANTO	PLATE	QUOTE	SANTO	SKATS
PANTS	PLATS	RAFTS	SAUTE	SKITE
PANTY	PLATT	RAITA	SCATH	SKITS
PARTS	PLOTS	RANTS	SCATT	SLATE

SLATS	SPOTS	TESTY	UNITY	ZLOTY
SLATY	STATE	TEXTS	VASTY	ZOOTY
SLITE	STATS	THATS	VISTA	ABOUT
SLITS	STOTE	THETA	WAITS	ACCUS
SLOTH	SUETY	TILTH	WALTZ	AFOUL
SLOTS	SUITE	TILTS	WANTS	ALBUM
SLUTS	SUITS	TINTS	WARTY	ALOUD
SMITE	SWATH	TITTY	WASTE	AMOUR
SMITH	SWATS	TOOTH	WHITE	AMPUL
SMUTS	SWOTS	TOOTS	WHITY	ANNUL
SNOTS	TACTS	TORTE	WIDTH	ARGUE
SOFTA	TANTO	TORTS	WITTY	ASCUS
SOFTS	TARTS	TOUTS	WORTH	AUGUR
SOFTY	TARTY	TRETS	WRATH	AWFUL
SOOTH	TASTE	TRITE	WRITE	BEAUT
SOOTY	TASTY	TROTH	WROTE	BEGUN
SORTA	TATTS	TROTS	WROTH	BOGUS
SORTE	TATTY	TRUTH	XYSTI	BONUS
SORTS	TEATS	TUFTS	XYSTS	CAJUN
SOUTH	TECTA	TUFTY	YENTA	CAPUT
SPATE	TEETH	TUTTI	YETTS	CARUS
SPATS	TENTH	TWITE	YOUTH	CECUM
SPITE	TENTS	TWITS	ZESTS	CLOUD
SPITS	TESTA	UNITE	ZESTY	CLOUT
SPITZ	TESTS	UNITS	ZITTY	CROUP

CUTUP	HOKUM	MOGUL	PSEUD	SHOUT
DATUM	HUMUS	MUCUS	QUEUE	SHRUB
DEBUG	IMBUE	MURUS	RAMUS	SHRUG
DEBUT	INCUR	NEGUS	REBUS	SHTUP
DEGUT	INCUS	NEVUS	REBUT	SIMUL
DEMUR	INPUT	NEXUM	RECUR	SINUS
DONUT	ISSUE	NEXUS	REDUX	SITUS
DURUM	JANUS	NIDUS	REFUT	SNOUT
EMBUS	JESUS	NODUS	RERUN	SOLUS
ENDUE	JORUM	NOTUM	REVUE	SORUS
ENNUI	KAPUT	NOVUM	RHEUM	SPOUT
ENSUE	KAPUT	OAKUM	ROGUE	SPRUE
FETUS	KHOUM	OCCUR	ROGUY	STOUP
FLOUR	KNOUT	ODEUM	ROQUE	STOUT
FLOUT	LETUP	ODIUM	SAGUM	STRUM
FOCUS	LOCUM	ODOUR	SCAUP	STRUT
FORUM	LOCUS	OLEUM	SCOUR	SULUS
FRAUD	LOTUS	OMBUD	SCOUT	SUNUP
FUGUE	MAGUS	OPIUM	SCRUB	SUSUS
GAMUT	MANUS	PICUL	SCRUM	SYRUP
GENUS	MENUS	PILUS	SEBUM	TABUN
GETUP	MIAUL	PINUP	SEDUM	TALUS
GHOUL	MINUS	PIOUS	SEGUE	TENUE
GROUP	MIXUP	PIQUE	SERUM	THOUS
GROUT	MODUS	PROUD	SETUP	THRUM

TOFUS	CHIVY	LARVA	SHIVA	BLOWY
TONUS	CIVVY	LEAVE	SHIVE	BRAWL
TOQUE	CLAVE	MAUVE	SHIVS	BRAWN
TORUS	CLEVE	NAIVE	SHOVE	BROWN
TROUT	CLOVE	NAVVY	SIEVE	CHEWS
TUQUE	CORVE	NERVE	SILVA	CHEWY
UNCUT	CRAVE	NERVY	SKIVE	CHOWS
UNDUE	CURVE	NIEVE	SLAVE	CLAWS
UNFUN	CURVY	OGIVE	SLIVE	CLEWS
VAGUE	DELVE	OLIVE	SOLVE	CLOWN
VALUE	DIVVY	PEAVY	SPIVS	CRAWL
VELUM	DRIVE	PEEVE	STAVE	CREWS
VENUE	DROVE	PERVE	STIVE	CROWD
VENUS	GLOVE	PERVS	STOVE	CROWN
VIRUS	GRAVE	PERVY	SUAVE	CROWS
VOGUE	GRAVY	PRIVY	TRAVE	DRAWL
XERUS	GROVE	PROVE	TROVE	DRAWN
ABOVE	GUAVA	REEVE	VALVE	DRAWS
AGAVE	HALVE	SALVE	VERVE	DROWN
ALIVE	HEAVE	SALVO	VULVA	FLAWS
BEVVY	HEAVY	SAVVY	WAIVE	FLOWS
BRAVE	HELVE	SELVA	WEAVE	FLOWY
BRAVO	HOOVE	SERVE	AVOWS	FROWN
CARVE	KEEVE	SERVO	BLOWN	GROWL
CHIVE	KNIVE	SHAVE	BLOWS	GROWN

GROWS	THAWY	JOEYS	CRAZE	PRIZE
KNOWE	THEWS	OBEYS	CRAZY	PZAZZ
KNOWN	THEWY	OKAYS	CROZE	RITZY
KNOWS	TRAWL	OXEYE	DITZY	SCUZZ
MEOWS	TREWS	PLAYA	DIZZY	SEIZE
PLOWS	TROWS	PLAYS	DOOZY	SMAZE
PRAWN	VIEWS	PLOYS	FIZZY	SPAZZ
PROWL	ATAXY	POLYP	FRIZZ	SWIZZ
PROWS	EPOXY	SATYR	FROZE	TAZZA
SCHWA	MINXY	SHAYS	FURZE	TAZZE
SCOWL	PREXY	SIBYL	FUZZY	TIZZY
SCOWS	PROXY	SLEYS	GAUZE	WHIZZ
SHAWL	ABAYA	STAYS	GAUZY	WINZE
SHAWM	ALKYD	SWAYS	GLAZE	WOOZY
SHOWN	ALKYL	TRAYS	GONZO	XYZZY
SHOWS	ALLYL	TREYS	GRAZE	
SHOWY	BERYL	VINYL	GYOZA	
SLOWS	CALYX	XENYL	JAZZY	
SMEWS	CHAYS	XYLYL	MAIZE	
SNOWS	CLAYS	ABUZZ	MATZO	
SNOWY	CRAYS	AMAZE	MEZZO	
SPAWN	DRAYS	BLAZE	MUZZY	
SPAWS	DREYS	BOOZE	PIZZA	
STEWS	ENZYM	BOOZY	PIZZE	
THAWS	ETHYL	BUZZY	PLAZA	

ABACA	BUBBA	DAGGA	GUAVA	MAMMA
ABAYA	BURKA	DELTA	GYOZA	MANGA
AGAMA	CALLA	DERMA	HECKA	MANIA
AGITA	CANNA	DIANA	HELLA	MANNA
AGORA	CEIBA	DICTA	HENNA	MANTA
AJUGA	CELLA	DOBRA	HIJRA	MARIA
AKITA	CESTA	DOGMA	HYDRA	MASSA
ALOHA	CHELA	DOLMA	HYENA	MECCA
ALPHA	CHICA	DONNA	INDIA	MECHA
AMEBA	CHINA	DORSA	INTRA	MEDIA
AMIGA	CHUFA	DOULA	JIRGA	MENSA
AMNIA	CILIA	DRAMA	JUNTA	MOCHA
ANIMA	CIRCA	DURRA	KAPPA	MOMMA
ANTRA	COBIA	EDEMA	KARMA	MOOLA
AORTA	COBRA	ENEMA	KASHA	MUDRA
APNEA	COCOA	ENTIA	LABIA	MULGA
ARECA	COMMA	ERICA	LAMIA	MULLA
ARENA	CONGA	ETYMA	LARVA	NABLA
AREPA	COPRA	EXTRA	LIBRA	NAIRA
AROHA	COSTA	FAUNA	LLAMA	NAKFA
AROMA	COTTA	FELLA	LOOFA	NIGGA
ASANA	CRURA	FLORA	MAFIA	NINJA
ASYLA	CUPPA	GANJA	MAGMA	NORIA
ATRIA	CURIA	GONNA	MALTA	NORMA
BIOTA	DACHA	GOTTA	MAMBA	NYALA

OCREA	PORTA	SEPTA	TAYRA	VULVA
OMEGA	PRANA	SHAKA	TAZZA	WANNA
OPERA	PUKKA	SHIVA	TECTA	WICCA
PAISA	QUOTA	SIGMA	TERGA	WIRRA
PALEA	RAITA	SIGNA	TERRA	WONGA
PAMPA	RANGA	SILVA	TESLA	XENIA
PANDA	RAPPA	SIMBA	TESTA	XOANA
PANGA	RASTA	SISTA	TETRA	YENTA
PARKA	REATA	SLOKA	THECA	YUCCA
PASHA	RECTA	SOFTA	THETA	ZAMIA
PASTA	RIATA	SORTA	THUJA	ZEBRA
PELMA	RUMBA	SPICA	TIARA	ACERB
PENNA	SABRA	STELA	TIBIA	BLURB
PEPLA	SACRA	STOMA	TIKKA	CAROB
PHYLA	SALSA	STRIA	TONGA	CELEB
PINNA	SAMBA	STUPA	TRONA	CLIMB
PITTA	SAUNA	SUCKA	ULTRA	COHAB
PIZZA	SCENA	SUMMA	UMBRA	CRUMB
PLAYA	SCHWA	SUNNA	UVULA	CUBEB
PLAZA	SCOPA	SUTRA	VILLA	DEFIB
PLICA	SCUBA	TABLA	VIOLA	DEMOB
PODIA	SCUTA	TAIGA	VIRGA	DENEB
POLKA	SELVA	TALMA	VISTA	DWEEB
POOKA	SENNA	TANGA	VODKA	EXURB
POPPA	SEPIA	TANKA	VOILA	HIJAB

JACOB	BASIC	MIMIC	VATIC	ALGID
KEBAB	CERIC	MUSIC	XEBEC	ALKYD
NABOB	CIVIC	OHMIC	XENIC	ALOED
NAWAB	CODEC	ONTIC	XERIC	ALOUD
NEEMB	COLIC	OPTIC	XYLIC	AMEND
NIQAB	COMIC	ORGIC	YOGIC	AMPED
PLUMB	CONIC	PANIC	YONIC	ANDED
REHAB	CRESC	PUBIC	ABEND	ANTED
RHOMB	CUBIC	PUNIC	ABLED	APHID
RHUMB	CYNIC	RABIC	ABORD	ARCED
SAHIB	ESTOC	REBEC	ACHED	ARMED
SCRUB	ETHIC	RELIC	ACNED	AROID
SHRUB	GENIC	RIDIC	ACRED	ARSED
SQUAB	HAVOC	RUNIC	ACRID	ASHED
SQUIB	LILAC	SERAC	ACTED	ASKED
STILB	LOGIC	SONIC	ADDED	AVOID
THROB	LUDIC	STOIC	AGEND	AWARD
THUMB	LUMIC	SUMAC	AGUED	AWNED
ANTIC	LYRIC	TELIC	AHEAD	AXLED
ASDIC	MAFIC	TONIC	AHOLD	BAKED
ASPIC	MAGIC	TOPIC	AIDED	BARED
ASYNC	MANIC	TORIC	AILED	BASED
ATTIC	MEDIC	TOXIC	AIMED	BEARD
AURIC	MESIC	TUNIC	AIRED	BLAND
AZOIC	METIC	TYPIC	ALCID	BLEED

BLEND	CHILD	DOMED	FAMED	GONAD
BLIND	CHORD	DOPED	FARED	GOUND
BLOND	CITED	DREAD	FATED	GOURD
BLOOD	CLOUD	DRIED	FAZED	GRAND
BOARD	CODED	DROID	FETID	GREED
BORED	COKED	DRUID	FIELD	GRIND
BOUND	CONED	DRYAD	FIEND	GUARD
BOWED	COOED	DUPED	FILED	GUILD
BOXED	COPED	EARED	FINED	HATED
BRAID	COULD	EASED	FIRED	HAZED
BRAND	COWED	EATED	FIXED	HEARD
BREAD	COXED	EBBED	FJORD	HEXAD
BREED	CREED	EDGED	FLOOD	HIRED
BROAD	CRIED	EELED	FLUID	HOARD
BROOD	CROWD	EGGED	FOUND	HONED
BUILD	CUBED	ELAND	FRAUD	HOPED
CAGED	CUPID	EMBED	FREED	HOUND
CAKED	CURED	EMEND	FRIED	HUMID
CANED	CYCAD	ENDED	FROND	HYPED
CANID	DARED	EPHOD	FUSED	IMBED
CAPED	DATED	EQUID	GAPED	IRKED
CARED	DAVID	ERRED	GAZED	JADED
CASED	DAZED	FACED	GELID	JAPED
CEDED	DECAD	FADED	GLAND	JAWED
CHARD	DISAD	FAKED	GLUED	JEWED

JIBED	MAUND	NOMAD	PATED	RAZED
JIHAD	MAWED	NONAD	PAVED	REDID
JIVED	MIKED	NOSED	PAWED	RIGID
JOKED	MIMED	NOTED	PAYED	RILED
JOYED	MINED	NOWED	PIKED	RIMED
JUKED	MIRED	OAKED	PILED	RINED
KEYED	MIRID	OARED	PLAID	ROBED
KIPED	MIXED	OCTAD	PLEAD	ROUND
KITED	MONAD	OFFED	POKED	ROWED
KNEAD	MOPED	OGLED	PORED	RULED
KNEED	MOTED	OILED	POSED	RUNED
LACED	MOULD	OMBUD	POUND	SALAD
LAIRD	MOUND	OOTID	PRIED	SAPID
LIKED	MOVED	OOZED	PROUD	SAROD
LINED	MUCID	OPTED	PSEUD	SATED
LIPID	MURID	ORBED	PURED	SAVED
LIVED	MUSED	OREAD	RABID	SCALD
LIVID	MUTED	OUTED	RACED	SCARD
LOVED	NAIAD	OVOID	RAGED	SCEND
LUBED	NAKED	OWNED	RAKED	SCOLD
LUCID	NAMED	PACED	RAMED	SCROD
LURED	NICAD	PAGED	RAPED	SHARD
LURID	NITID	PALED	RAPID	SHRED
MANED	NIXED	PANED	RATED	SKALD
MATED	NODED	PARED	RAYED	SNOOD

SOLID	THEED	TWEED	WOWED	AGGIE
SOUND	THIRD	TYPED	YAWED	AGILE
SOWED	THRID	TYRED	YIELD	AGONE
SPEED	TIDED	UNWED	YOKED	AGREE
SPEND	TILED	UPEND	ZONED	AISLE
SPIED	TIMED	UPPED	ZOOID	ALATE
SQUAD	TIMID	URGED	ABASE	ALGAE
SQUID	TINED	VALID	ABATE	ALIKE
STAID	TIRED	VAPID	ABELE	ALIVE
STAND	TOKED	VEXED	ABIDE	ALKIE
STEAD	TOLED	VIAND	ABODE	ALONE
STEED	TONED	VIVID	ABORE	AMAZE
STOOD	TOTED	VOTED	ABOVE	AMBLE
SWARD	TOWED	VOWED	ABUSE	AMICE
SWORD	TOYED	WAGED	ACUTE	AMIDE
SYNOD	TREAD	WANED	ADAGE	AMINE
TAKED	TREED	WAVED	ADDLE	AMOLE
TALED	TREND	WEIRD	ADOBE	AMPLE
TAMED	TRIAD	WIELD	ADORE	AMUSE
TAPED	TRIED	WIPED	AERIE	ANELE
TARED	TRUED	WIRED	AFIRE	ANGLE
TASED	TRYED	WOOED	AFORE	ANILE
TAXED	TUBED	WORLD	AGAPE	ANIME
TEAED	TUMID	WOULD	AGATE	ANISE
TEPID	TUNED	WOUND	AGAVE	ANKLE

ANODE	BASTE	BRIDE	CHASE	COMAE
ANOLE	BATHE	BRINE	CHIDE	COMBE
ANTRE	BEIGE	BROKE	CHILE	CONTE
APACE	BELIE	BRUME	CHIME	COOLE
APPLE	BELLE	BRUTE	CHINE	COPSE
AQUAE	BIBLE	BUDGE	CHIVE	CORSE
ARETE	BILGE	BUGLE	CHODE	CORVE
ARGUE	BINGE	BULGE	CHOKE	COSIE
ARISE	BIOME	BURKE	CHORE	COUPE
ARMIE	BIRSE	BUTTE	CHOSE	COXAE
AROSE	BLADE	CABLE	CHUTE	COZIE
ASIDE	BLAME	CACHE	CHYLE	CRAKE
ASPIE	BLARE	CADGE	CHYME	CRAME
ATONE	BLAZE	CADRE	CITIE	CRANE
AURAE	BLOKE	CANOE	CLADE	CRATE
AWAKE	BOCHE	CARLE	CLAVE	CRAVE
AWARE	BODGE	CARTE	CLEPE	CRAZE
AWOKE	BOGLE	CARVE	CLEVE	CREPE
AXILE	BONCE	CASTE	CLIME	CRIME
AXONE	BOOZE	CAUSE	CLINE	CRISE
AZIDE	BORNE	CEASE	CLONE	CRONE
AZINE	BRACE	CENSE	CLOSE	CRORE
AZURE	BRAKE	CHAFE	CLOVE	CROZE
BADGE	BRAVE	CHAPE	COATE	CRUDE
BARGE	BRIBE	CHARE	COINE	CRUSE

CURIE	DOGIE	ELUTE	FEMME	GENRE
CURSE	DONEE	EMCEE	FENCE	GEODE
CURVE	DOUSE	EMOTE	FIBRE	GESTE
CUTIE	DOWSE	EMULE	FIREE	GLADE
CYCLE	DOXIE	ENATE	FLAKE	GLARE
DANCE	DRAKE	ENDUE	FLAME	GLAZE
DARKE	DRAPE	ENSUE	FLARE	GLIDE
DAUBE	DRIVE	ENTRE	FLUKE	GLOBE
DEALE	DRONE	EPODE	FLUME	GLOVE
DEEDE	DROVE	ERASE	FLUTE	GNOME
DEERE	DRUPE	ERODE	FORCE	GOOSE
DEICE	DULSE	EROSE	FORGE	GORGE
DELVE	DUNCE	ETUDE	FORTE	GORSE
DENSE	DUTIE	EVADE	FOSSE	GOUGE
DEUCE	DWALE	EVERE	FRAME	GRACE
DHOLE	EAGLE	EVOKE	FROZE	GRADE
DIDIE	EAGRE	EXILE	FUDGE	GRAPE
DIENE	EARLE	EXINE	FUGUE	GRATE
DINGE	EDUCE	EXODE	FURZE	GRAVE
DIODE	EERIE	EXUDE	GABLE	GRAZE
DIRGE	ELATE	EYRIE	GAFFE	GRIKE
DIRKE	ELIDE	FABLE	GAUGE	GRIME
DIXIE	ELITE	FALSE	GAUZE	GRIPE
DODGE	ELOPE	FANNE	GEESE	GROPE
DOGGE	ELUDE	FARCE	GENIE	GROVE

GUIDE	JUDGE	LOUSE	MIDGE	NICHE
GUILE	JUICE	LUCRE	MINCE	NIECE
GUISE	JUVIE	LUNGE	MINDE	NIEVE
GUNGE	KEDGE	MACLE	MITRE	NISSE
HALVE	KEENE	MAHOE	MOILE	NIXIE
HASTE	KEEPE	MAIDE	MOIRE	NOBLE
HAUTE	KEEVE	MAILE	MONTE	NOICE
HEAVE	KENTE	MAIRE	MOOSE	NOISE
HEDGE	KINDE	MAIZE	MOTTE	NONCE
HELVE	KNIFE	MANGE	MOUSE	NOONE
HENCE	KNIVE	MANSE	MOVIE	NOOSE
HINGE	KNOWE	MAPLE	MOXIE	NOVAE
HOMIE	LADLE	MARGE	MUDGE	NUDGE
HOOVE	LANCE	MARKE	MURRE	NUDIE
HORDE	LAPSE	MARLE	MYOPE	NURSE
HORSE	LARGE	MATTE	NACRE	OBESE
HOUSE	LATTE	MAUVE	NAIVE	OCHRE
IMAGE	LEASE	MAYBE	NAPPE	OGIVE
IMBUE	LEAVE	MELEE	NAVIE	OLDIE
INANE	LEDGE	MENSE	NEARE	OLIVE
INDIE	LEVEE	MERDE	NECKE	OLLIE
INURE	LIEGE	MERGE	NERVE	OMBRE
IRATE	LITHE	MERLE	NEUME	OPINE
ISSUE	LODGE	MESNE	NEWIE	ORATE
JOULE	LOOSE	METRE	NGWEE	OUCHE

OUNCE	PEKOE	POKIE	QUAKE	ROCHE
OUTRE	PENCE	PONCE	QUEUE	ROGUE
OVATE	PENNE	POORE	QUITE	RONDE
OVINE	PERSE	POSSE	QUOTE	ROOKE
OVULE	PERVE	PRAME	RAILE	ROOME
OXEYE	PEWEE	PRASE	RAISE	ROQUE
OXIDE	PHAGE	PRATE	RAMIE	ROUGE
OZONE	PHASE	PRICE	RANEE	ROUSE
PADRE	PHONE	PRIDE	RANGE	ROUTE
PAIRE	PIECE	PRIME	RANKE	RUBLE
PANNE	PIQUE	PRISE	RAPHE	RUCHE
PARGE	PISTE	PRIZE	RATHE	RUFFE
PARLE	PIXIE	PROBE	REAME	RUPEE
PARSE	PIZZE	PROLE	REBBE	SABLE
PASSE	PLACE	PRONE	RECCE	SABRE
PASTE	PLAGE	PROSE	REEDE	SAILE
PAUCE	PLANE	PROVE	REEVE	SALVE
PAUSE	PLATE	PRUDE	REUSE	SAREE
PAYEE	PLEBE	PRUNE	REVUE	SARGE
PEACE	PLUME	PUDGE	RHYME	SASSE
PEARE	PLUTE	PULSE	RICHE	SAUCE
PEASE	PODGE	PUPAE	RIDGE	SAUTE
PECKE	POEME	PUREE	RIFLE	SCALE
PEEPE	POETE	PURGE	RILLE	SCAPE
PEEVE	POISE	PURSE	RINSE	SCARE

SCENE	SHINE	SLYPE	SPIRE	STORE
SCONE	SHIRE	SMAZE	SPITE	STOTE
SCOPE	SHITE	SMILE	SPOKE	STOVE
SCORE	SHIVE	SMITE	SPORE	STUPE
SCREE	SHONE	SMOKE	SPREE	STYLE
SCUTE	SHORE	SNAKE	SPRUE	SUAVE
SEDGE	SHOVE	SNARE	SPUME	SUCRE
SEEDE	SIDLE	SNIDE	STADE	SUEDE
SEGUE	SIEGE	SNIPE	STAGE	SUITE
SEINE	SIEVE	SNORE	STAKE	SURGE
SEIZE	SINCE	SOCLE	STALE	SWAGE
SELLE	SINGE	SOILE	STANE	SWALE
SENSE	SIREE	SOLVE	STARE	SWAPE
SENTE	SKATE	SONDE	STATE	SWEDE
SERGE	SKITE	SORTE	STAVE	SWINE
SERIE	SKIVE	SOULE	STELE	SWIPE
SERVE	SLAKE	SOUSE	STIKE	SWOLE
SETAE	SLATE	SPACE	STILE	SWORE
SHADE	SLAVE	SPADE	STIME	TABLE
SHAKE	SLICE	SPARE	STIPE	TACHE
SHALE	SLIDE	SPATE	STIVE	TALKE
SHAME	SLIME	SPICE	STOKE	TARRE
SHAPE	SLITE	SPIKE	STOLE	TASTE
SHARE	SLIVE	SPILE	STONE	TAUPE
SHAVE	SLOPE	SPINE	STOPE	TAWSE

TAZZE	TOGAE	TUTEE	WASTE	CHAFF
TEADE	TOILE	TWICE	WEAVE	CHIEF
TEARE	TONNE	TWINE	WEDGE	CHUFF
TEASE	TOOKE	TWITE	WHALE	CLIFF
TEHEE	TOQUE	UKASE	WHERE	DECAF
TENGE	TORSE	UNCLE	WHILE	DRAFF
TENSE	TORTE	UNDUE	WHINE	DWARF
TENUE	TOWEE	UNITE	WHITE	FLUFF
TEPEE	TOWNE	UNTIE	WHOLE	GRIEF
TERCE	TOWRE	UNUSE	WHORE	GRUFF
TERSE	TRACE	URINE	WHOSE	KENAF
THANE	TRADE	USAGE	WINCE	MOTIF
THEBE	TRAVE	UTILE	WINZE	NOTIF
THEME	TRIBE	VAGUE	WODGE	PILAF
THERE	TRICE	VALUE	WORSE	PROOF
THESE	TRIKE	VALVE	WRITE	QUAFF
THOLE	TRINE	VENGE	WROTE	QUEEF
THREE	TRIPE	VENUE	YEARE	SCARF
THROE	TRITE	VERGE	YOUSE	SCOFF
THYME	TRODE	VERSE	ZAIRE	SCUFF
TIGRE	TROPE	VERVE	ZEALE	SCURF
TILDE	TROVE	VOGUE	ALOOF	SERIF
TINGE	TRUCE	VOICE	BLUFF	SHEAF
TITHE	TULLE	WACKE	BRIEF	SHELF
TITLE	TUQUE	WAIVE	CALIF	SKIFF

SLUFF	BOURG	REJIG	WHANG	BRASH
SMURF	BRING	RENIG	WRING	BROTH
SNIFF	CLANG	REORG	WRONG	BRUSH
SNUFF	CLING	SCRAG	WRUNG	BUNCH
SPIFF	CLUNG	SHRUG	YOUNG	BUTCH
SPOOF	DEBUG	SLANG	ABASH	CATCH
STAFF	DEFOG	SLING	AITCH	CINCH
STIFF	DOING	SPANG	ALEPH	CLASH
STUFF	DYING	SPRAG	APISH	CLOTH
THIEF	EKING	SPRIG	AWASH	COACH
WHARF	EMBOG	SPROG	BATCH	CONCH
WHIFF	EMERG	STING	BEACH	COUCH
ACING	EYING	STONG	BEECH	COUGH
AGING	FLING	STUNG	BELCH	COUTH
AHING	FLUNG	SUING	BENCH	CRASH
ALONG	GOING	SWANG	BERTH	CRUSH
AMONG	ICING	SWING	BIRCH	CRWTH
APING	KIANG	SWUNG	BIRTH	DEATH
AWING	LIANG	THING	BITCH	DEPTH
AXING	LYING	THONG	BLECH	DITCH
BEFOG	OHING	TWANG	BLUSH	DOUGH
BEING	ORANG	TYING	BOKEH	DUTCH
BLING	OWING	UNPEG	BOOTH	EARTH
BOING	PRANG	USING	BOTCH	EPHAH
BOONG	PRONG	VYING	BOUGH	EPOCH

FAITH	HITCH	MITCH	PLASH	SLOTH
FAUGH	HOOCH	MONTH	PLUSH	SLUSH
FETCH	HUNCH	MOOCH	POACH	SMASH
FIFTH	HUTCH	MORPH	POOCH	SMITH
FILCH	JONAH	MOUTH	PORCH	SOOTH
FILTH	JUDAH	MULCH	POTCH	SOUGH
FIRTH	KETCH	MUNCH	POUCH	SOUTH
FLASH	LATCH	MYNAH	PSYCH	STASH
FLESH	LAUGH	MYRRH	PUNCH	SURAH
FLUSH	LEACH	NATCH	QUASH	SWASH
FORTH	LEASH	NEATH	RAJAH	SWATH
FRESH	LEECH	NEIGH	RANCH	SWISH
FROTH	LETCH	NINTH	RATCH	SYLPH
GALAH	LOATH	NORTH	REACH	SYNCH
GIRTH	LOUGH	NOTCH	RETCH	SYRAH
GLYPH	LUNCH	NYMPH	ROACH	TEACH
GNASH	LURCH	OBEAH	ROUGH	TEETH
GOOCH	LYMPH	OOMPH	SARAH	TENCH
GRAPH	LYNCH	PARCH	SCATH	TENTH
GRITH	MARCH	PATCH	SHETH	THIGH
GULCH	MARSH	PEACH	SHUSH	TILTH
HARSH	MATCH	PERCH	SIXTH	TITCH
HATCH	MERCH	PHISH	SKOSH	TOOTH
HEATH	MILCH	PINCH	SLASH	TORCH
HENCH	MIRTH	PITCH	SLOSH	TOUCH

TOUGH	AIOLI	ENVOI	RADII	ABACK
TRACH	ALIBI	FARSI	RANGI	ABASK
TRASH	AMICI	FUNDI	REIKI	ALACK
TROTH	ASSAI	FUNGI	RISHI	AMUCK
TRUTH	BHUMI	HAJJI	SALMI	AWORK
VETCH	BINDI	JINNI	SCAPI	BATIK
VOUCH	CACTI	KANJI	SENTI	BAULK
WATCH	CALLI	KARRI	SERAI	BLACK
WEIGH	CAMPI	KAURI	SHOJI	BLANK
WELSH	CARDI	KHAKI	SPAHI	BLEAK
WENCH	CARPI	LANAI	SUNNI	BLINK
WHICH	CELLI	LUNGI	SUSHI	BLOCK
WHISH	CHIBI	MALAI	SWAMI	BREAK
WIDTH	CHILI	MOCHI	TANGI	BRICK
WINCH	COATI	MUFTI	TARSI	BRINK
WITCH	COCCI	MULTI	TEMPI	BRISK
WORTH	CORGI	NISEI	TERAI	BROOK
WRATH	DEMOI	OBELI	THYMI	CAULK
WROTH	DHOBI	OCULI	TORII	CHALK
YOUTH	DHOTI	OKAPI	TORSI	CHECK
ZILCH	ECCHI	ORIBI	TUTTI	CHEEK
AALII	ELEMI	PAGRI	UGALI	CHICK
AARTI	EMOJI	PENNI	UMAMI	CHINK
ABACI	ENNUI	QUASI	XYSTI	CHOCK
ACINI	ENOKI	RABBI	ZOMBI	CHUCK

CHUNK	DRUNK	PLUNK	SMIRK	STOCK
CLACK	EPICK	PRANK	SMOCK	STONK
CLANK	FLANK	PRICK	SNACK	STOOK
CLEEK	FLASK	PRINK	SNARK	STORK
CLERK	FLECK	QUACK	SNEAK	STUCK
CLICK	FLEEK	QUICK	SNECK	SWANK
CLINK	FLICK	QUIRK	SNICK	SWINK
CLOAK	FLOCK	SHACK	SNOOK	THANK
CLOCK	FLUNK	SHANK	SNUCK	THICK
CLONK	FRANK	SHARK	SPANK	THINK
CLUCK	FREAK	SHEIK	SPARK	THUNK
CLUNK	FRICK	SHIRK	SPEAK	TORSK
CRACK	FRISK	SHOCK	SPECK	TRACK
CRANK	FROCK	SHOOK	SPOOK	TRICK
CREAK	GREEK	SHTIK	SPORK	TRUCK
CREEK	HOICK	SHUCK	SPUNK	TRUNK
CRICK	KAPOK	SKANK	STACK	TUPIK
CROAK	KAYAK	SKULK	STALK	TWANK
CROCK	KIOSK	SKUNK	STANK	TWEAK
CROOK	KNACK	SLACK	STARK	TWERK
CRUCK	KNOCK	SLEEK	STEAK	WAULK
CRUNK	PLANK	SLICK	STEEK	WHACK
DRANK	PLINK	SLINK	STICK	WHELK
DRECK	PLONK	SLUNK	STINK	WHISK
DRINK	PLUCK	SMACK	STIRK	WRACK

WREAK	BABEL	CRAWL	EXTOL	JEWEL
WRECK	BAGEL	CREEL	FATAL	JOUAL
WRICK	BANAL	CRUEL	FERAL	JURAL
ABOIL	BASAL	CUPEL	FETAL	KAMAL
ACCEL	BASIL	CYTOL	FINAL	KNEEL
AFOUL	BERYL	DECAL	FLAIL	KNELL
ALDOL	BEVEL	DEVEL	FOCAL	KNOLL
ALGAL	BOWEL	DEVIL	FRAIL	KNURL
ALKYL	BRAWL	DOWEL	FRILL	KVELL
ALLYL	BRILL	DRAIL	GAVEL	LABEL
AMPUL	BROIL	DRAWL	GHOUL	LEGAL
ANGEL	CABAL	DRILL	GRAIL	LEVEL
ANNAL	CAMEL	DROLL	GRILL	LIBEL
ANNUL	CANAL	DROOL	GROWL	LOCAL
ANVIL	CAROL	DURAL	GRUEL	LOSEL
APPAL	CAVIL	DWAAL	HALAL	LOYAL
APPEL	CECAL	DWELL	HAZEL	MAHAL
AREAL	CHILL	EASEL	HOTEL	MEDAL
ARGIL	CHURL	EMAIL	HOVEL	METAL
ARTEL	CITAL	ENROL	IDEAL	MIAUL
ATOLL	CIVIL	EQUAL	IDYLL	MODAL
AURAL	COPAL	ETHYL	IMPEL	MODEL
AVAIL	CORAL	EVILL	INCEL	MOGUL
AWFUL	COROL	EXCEL	INTEL	MOHEL
AXIAL	COXAL	EXPEL	JACAL	MOLAL

MORAL	PENAL	ROWEL	SOKOL	TRAWL
MOREL	PERIL	ROYAL	SPALL	TRIAL
MOTEL	PETAL	RURAL	SPEEL	TRILL
MUCAL	PHIAL	SALAL	SPELL	TROLL
MURAL	PICUL	SCOWL	SPIEL	TRULL
NASAL	PIXEL	SCULL	SPILL	TUBAL
NATAL	PRIAL	SEPAL	SPOIL	TWILL
NAVAL	PRILL	SHALL	SPOOL	TWIRL
NAVEL	PROWL	SHAWL	SPYAL	UNTIL
NEWEL	PUPAL	SHELL	STALL	USUAL
NIHIL	PUPIL	SHILL	STEAL	VENAL
NIVAL	PYRAL	SHOAL	STEEL	VIGIL
NODAL	QUAIL	SIBYL	STILL	VINYL
NOPAL	QUELL	SIGIL	STOOL	VIRAL
NOVEL	QUILL	SIMUL	SWELL	VITAL
OCTAL	RATEL	SISAL	SWILL	VOCAL
OFFAL	RAVEL	SKILL	SWIRL	VOWEL
ORIEL	REBEL	SKOAL	TEPAL	WHEAL
OSMOL	REGAL	SKULL	THILL	WHEEL
OUZEL	RENAL	SMAIL	THIOL	WHIRL
PANEL	REPEL	SMALL	TIDAL	WHORL
PAPAL	REVEL	SMELL	TONAL	XENYL
PAROL	RIVAL	SNAIL	TOTAL	XYLOL
PEARL	RIVEL	SNARL	TOWEL	XYLYL
PEDAL	RIYAL	SNELL	TRAIL	YODEL

YOKEL	ENZYM	OAKUM	SPASM	AMBON
ZONAL	FORUM	ODEUM	SPERM	ANCON
ABEAM	GLEAM	ODIUM	STEAM	ANION
ABYSM	GLOOM	OGHAM	STORM	APIAN
ALARM	GOLEM	OLEUM	STRUM	APRON
ALBUM	GROOM	OPIUM	SWARM	ARGON
AXIOM	HARAM	PHARM	THERM	ARSON
BEDIM	HAREM	PLASM	THRUM	ASHEN
BLOOM	HAULM	PRISM	TOTEM	ASPEN
BOSOM	HOKUM	PROEM	VELUM	ATMAN
BROOM	IDIOM	PSALM	VENOM	AUXIN
BUXOM	ISLAM	QUALM	WHELM	AVIAN
CAROM	JORUM	REALM	XYLEM	AVION
CECUM	KHOUM	REARM	ABORN	AWARN
CHARM	KILIM	RHEUM	ACORN	AXION
CHASM	LOCUM	SAGUM	ACTIN	AXMAN
CLAIM	MADAM	SCRAM	ADMAN	AXMEN
CREAM	MAXIM	SCRIM	ADMIN	AZURN
DATUM	MIASM	SCRUM	ADORN	BACON
DEISM	MINIM	SEBUM	AGAIN	BAIRN
DENIM	MODEM	SEDUM	ALGIN	BARON
DREAM	NEXUM	SEISM	ALIEN	BASIN
DUNAM	NOTAM	SERUM	ALIGN	BATON
DURUM	NOTUM	SHAWM	ALUMN	BEGAN
ENORM	NOVUM	SMARM	AMAIN	BEGIN

BEGUN	CROWN	FUTON	LIVEN	PAEAN
BISON	CUMIN	GAMIN	LOGAN	PAEON
BLOWN	CUTIN	GIVEN	LOGIN	PAGAN
BOGAN	DEARN	GLEAN	LOGON	PAREN
BOURN	DECON	GRAIN	MACON	PATEN
BRAIN	DEIGN	GREEN	MASON	PATIN
BRAWN	DEMON	GROAN	MAVEN	PECAN
BROWN	DEVON	GROIN	MAVIN	PITON
CABIN	DEWAN	GROWN	MELON	PLAIN
CAIRN	DIVAN	HAVEN	MESON	PORIN
CAJUN	DJINN	HEDON	MORON	PRAWN
CANON	DOYEN	HERON	MOURN	PREEN
CAPON	DOZEN	HUMAN	MUCIN	PRION
CHAIN	DRAIN	HYMEN	NINON	PYLON
CHRON	DRAWN	INURN	NOMAN	QILIN
CHURN	DROWN	JAPAN	NOMEN	QUEAN
CLEAN	EATEN	KININ	NUMEN	QUEEN
CLOWN	ELFIN	KNOWN	NYLON	QUOIN
CODON	ELMEN	LADEN	OAKEN	RACON
COIGN	EOSIN	LATIN	OCEAN	RADON
COLON	ERGON	LEARN	OFTEN	RAMEN
COVEN	ERMIN	LEMAN	OLDEN	RAVEN
COVIN	FEIGN	LEMON	ONION	RAVIN
COZEN	FELON	LIKEN	OPSIN	RAYON
CROON	FROWN	LINEN	ORGAN	RECON

REDAN	SCORN	STEIN	UNBAN	AMINO
REGEN	SCRAN	STERN	UNFUN	AMNIO
REIGN	SEDAN	SWAIN	UNION	ANCHO
RENIN	SEMEN	SWOON	UNMAN	ANDRO
RERUN	SERIN	SWORN	URBAN	AUDIO
RESIN	SEVEN	TABUN	VEGAN	AVISO
RICIN	SHEEN	TAKEN	VIXEN	BANDO
RIPEN	SHOON	TAKIN	WAGON	BEANO
RISEN	SHOWN	TALON	WAKEN	BIMBO
RIVEN	SIMON	TAXON	WAXEN	BINGO
ROBIN	SIREN	TENON	WIDEN	BOFFO
ROMAN	SKARN	THEGN	WOMAN	BONGO
RONIN	SKEAN	THORN	WOMEN	BRAVO
ROSEN	SKEIN	TIGON	WOVEN	BUFFO
ROSIN	SLAIN	TITAN	XENON	BUNCO
ROWAN	SOKEN	TIYIN	XYLAN	BURRO
ROWEN	SOLAN	TOKEN	YAMEN	CACAO
RUMEN	SOLON	TORAN	YEARN	CAMEO
RUTIN	SOMAN	TOXIN	YOGIN	CAMPO
SALON	SPAIN	TOYON	ZAYIN	CANTO
SARIN	SPAWN	TRAIN	ACHOO	CARGO
SATAN	SPOON	TREEN	ADOBO	CELLO
SATIN	SPURN	TWAIN	AGGRO	CENTO
SAVIN	STAIN	TWEEN	ALAMO	CHEMO
SCION	STEAN	TYRAN	AMIGO	CHINO

CHIRO	GIZMO	MACRO	OUTGO	RATIO
CHOLO	GONZO	MAMBO	OVOLO	RECTO
CISCO	GUANO	MANGO	PAEDO	REPRO
CLARO	GUMBO	MARGO	PANTO	RETRO
COMBO	GUSTO	MATZO	PASEO	RHINO
COMMO	HELLO	METRO	PATIO	RODEO
COMPO	HETRO	MEZZO	PESTO	ROMEO
CONDO	HIPPO	MICRO	PHARO	RONDO
COSMO	HOLLO	MILKO	PHONO	SALVO
CREDO	HYDRO	MIMEO	PHOTO	SAMBO
CURIO	IGLOO	MONDO	PIANO	SANDO
DANIO	INTRO	MONGO	PINGO	SANTO
DEKKO	JALEO	MOTTO	PINKO	SCHMO
DILDO	JINGO	MUCHO	PINTO	SCUDO
DINGO	JUMBO	MUCRO	PISCO	SECCO
DIPSO	JUNCO	MUNGO	POLIO	SERVO
DISCO	JUNTO	NACHO	PORNO	SHAKO
DITTO	KAZOO	NARCO	POTOO	SHERO
DOBRO	KENDO	NEATO	POTTO	SICKO
DUMBO	KIDDO	NECRO	PREGO	SMOKO
DUOMO	LASSO	NEGRO	PRIMO	SOLDO
EJIDO	LIMBO	NERDO	PROMO	STENO
FOLIO	LINGO	NEURO	PROTO	TABOO
FORGO	LLANO	NITRO	PUTTO	TANGO
GARBO	MACHO	OUTDO	RADIO	TANTO

TELCO	CLAMP	MIXUP	SNOOP	TWERP
TEMPO	CLASP	OXLIP	STAMP	UNZIP
TENNO	CLOMP	PINUP	STEEP	USURP
THORO	CLUMP	PLUMP	STOEP	WHELP
TONDO	CRAMP	POLYP	STOMP	WHOMP
TORSO	CREEP	PRIMP	STOOP	WHOOP
TURBO	CRIMP	RECAP	STOUP	WHUMP
VERSO	CRISP	SALEP	STRAP	TRANQ
VIDEO	CROUP	SCALP	STRIP	ABEAR
VULGO	CRUMP	SCAMP	STROP	ABHOR
WACKO	CUTUP	SCARP	STUMP	ABLER
WAHOO	DROOP	SCAUP	SUNUP	ACTER
YAHOO	EQUIP	SCOOP	SWAMP	ACTOR
YOBBO	ESTOP	SCRAP	SWEEP	ADDER
YUMMO	FLUMP	SCRIP	SWOOP	AEGER
ZINCO	FRUMP	SETUP	SYRUP	AFTER
ZIPPO	GETUP	SHARP	SYSOP	AIDER
BLEEP	GLOMP	SHEEP	THESP	AIMER
BLIMP	GLOOP	SHOOP	THORP	ALDER
CHAMP	GRASP	SHTUP	THUMP	ALGOR
CHEAP	GROUP	SKIMP	TRAMP	ALTAR
CHEEP	GRUMP	SLEEP	TROMP	ALTER
CHIRP	JALAP	SLOOP	TROOP	AMBER
CHOMP	JULEP	SLUMP	TRUMP	AMOUR
CHUMP	LETUP	SLURP	TULIP	ANGER

APPAR	CARER	CRYER	DOPER	ESTER
APTER	CATER	CUBER	DOTER	ETHER
ARBOR	CAVER	CURER	DOWER	EYRIR
ARDOR	CEDAR	CUTER	DOZER	FAKER
ARMOR	CEDER	CYBER	DREAR	FAKIR
ASHER	CHAIR	DAMAR	DRIER	FAVOR
ASKER	CHEER	DARER	DRYER	FEVER
ASPER	CHIRR	DATER	DUPER	FEWER
ASTER	CHOIR	DAYER	EAGER	FIBER
ASTIR	CHURR	DEBAR	EASER	FINER
ATTAR	CIDER	DECOR	EATER	FIXER
AUGER	CIGAR	DEFER	EDGER	FLAIR
AUGUR	CITER	DEMUR	EELER	FLEER
AWNER	CLEAR	DENAR	EGGAR	FLIER
BAKER	CODER	DETER	EIDER	FLOOR
BIKER	COKER	DEWAR	ELDER	FLOUR
BLEAR	COLOR	DICER	ELVER	FLYER
BONER	COMER	DIKER	EMBER	FOYER
BOWER	COOER	DIMER	EMEER	FREER
BOXER	CORER	DINAR	EMMER	FRIAR
BOYAR	COVER	DINER	ENTER	FUBAR
BRIER	COWER	DISIR	EPHOR	FUROR
BUYER	COYER	DIVER	ERROR	GAMER
CABER	CRIER	DOLOR	ESKER	GAPER
CAPER	CRUOR	DONOR	ESPER	GIVER

GOFER	LAGER	MILER	NUDER	PAPER
GONER	LAHAR	MIMER	NUKER	PARER
HATER	LASER	MINER	OATER	PATER
HIDER	LATER	MINOR	OCCUR	PAVER
HIKER	LAYER	MISER	OCHER	PAWER
HOLER	LEPER	MITER	ODDER	PAYER
HONOR	LEVER	MIXER	ODOUR	PAYOR
HOVER	LIFER	MOLAR	OFFER	PETER
HUMOR	LINER	MOOER	OFTER	PIKER
HYPER	LIVER	MOPER	OGLER	PILER
ICHOR	LONER	MOTOR	OILER	PIPER
IDLER	LOSER	MOVER	OLDER	PLIER
INCUR	LOVER	MOWER	ONCER	PLYER
INFER	LOWER	MUDAR	OPTER	POKER
INNER	LUNAR	MUSER	ORDER	POLAR
INTER	LURER	MUTER	ORMER	PORER
JAGER	MAJOR	MYLAR	OSIER	POSER
JAPER	MAKER	NADIR	OTHER	POWER
JIVER	MALAR	NAKER	OTTER	PRIER
JOKER	MANOR	NAMER	OUTER	PRIOR
JUROR	MASER	NEVER	OWLER	PRYER
KAFIR	MATER	NEWER	OWNER	PUKER
KEFIR	MAYOR	NICER	OXTER	PULER
KEYER	MAZER	NOSER	PACER	PURER
LABOR	METER	NOTER	PAGER	QUEER

RACER	ROTOR	SHOER	TABOR	TUMOR
RADAR	ROVER	SHYER	TAKER	TUNER
RAGER	ROWER	SITAR	TAMER	TUTOR
RAKER	RUDER	SIXER	TAPER	ULCER
RAPER	RULER	SIZER	TAPIR	UMBER
RARER	RUMOR	SKIER	TASER	UNDER
RATER	SABER	SKIRR	TATER	UPPER
RAVER	SAFER	SMEAR	TAXER	USHER
RAWER	SAGAR	SNEER	TAXOR	UTTER
RAZER	SAKER	SOBER	TENOR	VALOR
RAZOR	SAPOR	SOFAR	THEIR	VAPOR
REBAR	SATYR	SOLAR	TIGER	VICAR
RECUR	SAVER	SOLER	TILER	VIGOR
REFER	SAVOR	SONAR	TIMER	VIPER
REVER	SAWER	SOPOR	TITER	VISOR
RICER	SAYER	SOROR	TOLAR	VOLAR
RIDER	SCOUR	SOWER	TONER	VOTER
RIFER	SEDER	SPEAR	TOPER	WADER
RIGOR	SENOR	SPOOR	TOTER	WAFER
RIMER	SEVER	STAIR	TOWER	WAGER
RIPER	SEWER	STEER	TOYER	WATER
RISER	SEXER	SUDOR	TRIER	WAVER
RIVER	SHEAR	SUGAR	TRUER	WHIRR
ROGER	SHEER	SUPER	TRYER	WIDER
ROPER	SHIER	SWEAR	TUBER	WIPER

WISER	AKENS	ARSIS	BEADS	BRASS
WOOER	ALCOS	ASCUS	BEAMS	BUCKS
YARER	ALIAS	ASHES	BEANS	BULLS
ZONER	ALOES	ASKES	BEARS	BUMPS
ABETS	ALTOS	ASSES	BEATS	BURNS
ABLES	ALUMS	ATLAS	BELLS	CACAS
ABUTS	AMASS	ATMOS	BILLS	CAFES
ABYSS	AMBOS	ATOMS	BINDS	CAFFS
ACCUS	AMENS	AUNTS	BIRDS	CAGES
ACHES	AMISS	AURAS	BITES	CAKES
ACIDS	AMOKS	AUTOS	BLESS	CALFS
ACMES	ANALS	AVENS	BLISS	CALKS
ACNES	ANNAS	AVERS	BLOGS	CALLS
ACRES	ANTES	AVGAS	BLOWS	CALMS
ACYLS	APERS	AVOWS	BLUES	CAMAS
ADIOS	APHIS	AXELS	BOGUS	CAMES
AEGIS	APOLS	AXLES	BOILS	CAMOS
AEONS	APSIS	AXONS	BONDS	CAMPS
AFROS	AQUAS	BALLS	BONES	CANES
AGARS	AREAS	BANGS	BONUS	CANTS
AGERS	ARIAS	BANNS	BOOBS	CAPES
AGONS	ARILS	BARBS	BOOKS	CARDS
AGUES	ARRAS	BASES	BOOTS	CARES
AIDES	ARRIS	BASIS	BOUTS	CARPS
AIRES	ARSES	BATHS	BOXES	CARRS

CARTS	CHIPS	COBBS	COOTS	CRIBS
CARUS	CHITS	COCAS	COPES	CRIES
CASAS	CHOCS	COCKS	CORDS	CRIMS
CASES	CHOPS	COCOS	CORES	CRIPS
CASKS	CHOWS	CODAS	CORKS	CROPS
CASTS	CHUBS	CODES	CORNS	CROSS
CATES	CHUGS	COEDS	CORPS	CROWS
CAVES	CHUMS	COIFS	COSTS	CRUDS
CELLS	CIRCS	COILS	COTES	CRUES
CELTS	CITES	COINS	COUPS	CUBES
CENTS	CLAMS	COKES	COURS	CUFFS
CERTS	CLANS	COLAS	COVES	CULLS
CHADS	CLAPS	COLDS	COWLS	CULTS
CHAIS	CLASS	COLES	COXES	CUNTS
CHAMS	CLAWS	COLTS	CRABS	CURBS
CHAOS	CLAYS	COMAS	CRAGS	CURDS
CHAPS	CLEWS	COMBS	CRAMS	CURES
CHARS	CLIPS	COMES	CRANS	CURLS
CHATS	CLODS	COMMS	CRAPS	CUSPS
CHAYS	CLOGS	COMPS	CRASS	CUTES
CHEFS	CLOTS	CONES	CRAYS	CUTIS
CHESS	CLUBS	CONKS	CREDS	CYANS
CHEWS	CLUES	COOKS	CREMS	CYSTS
CHICS	COALS	COONS	CRESS	CZARS
CHINS	COATS	COOPS	CREWS	DACKS

DADAS	DEETS	DINTS	DOZES	DUNGS
DADOS	DEKES	DIRKS	DRABS	DUNKS
DAFFS	DELLS	DISCS	DRAGS	DUPES
DAHLS	DEMOS	DISKS	DRAMS	DUSKS
DALES	DENES	DIVAS	DRAWS	DUSTS
DAMES	DENTS	DIVES	DRAYS	DUXES
DAMNS	DEPTS	DIVIS	DREGS	DYADS
DANKS	DERMS	DOCKS	DRESS	DYERS
DARES	DERNS	DOERS	DREYS	DYKES
DARKS	DESIS	DOGES	DRIES	DYNES
DARTS	DESKS	DOLLS	DRIPS	EARLS
DATES	DEVAS	DOLTS	DROPS	EARNS
DAUBS	DIALS	DOMES	DROSS	EASES
DAWNS	DICES	DONGS	DRUGS	EASTS
DAZES	DICKS	DOOMS	DRUMS	EAVES
DEADS	DIDOS	DOORS	DUALS	EBONS
DEALS	DIETS	DOPES	DUCES	ECHOS
DEANS	DIFFS	DORKS	DUCKS	EDGES
DEARS	DIKES	DORMS	DUCTS	EDITS
DEBTS	DILLS	DOSAS	DUDES	EIDOS
DECKS	DIMES	DOSES	DUELS	ELANS
DEEDS	DIMPS	DOTES	DUETS	ELKES
DEEMS	DINGS	DOVES	DUKES	ELVES
DEEPS	DINKS	DOWDS	DUMPS	EMBUS
DEERS	DINOS	DOWNS	DUNES	EMIRS

EMITS	FEEDS	FUNDS	HALTS	HUMUS
EPICS	FEELS	GAINS	HANDS	HUNKS
ERNES	FETUS	GAMES	HANGS	HURTS
ESSES	FILES	GASPS	HARDS	IBLIS
ETHOS	FILLS	GAZES	HARMS	ICONS
EUROS	FILMS	GENES	HATES	IDEAS
EVENS	FINDS	GENTS	HAVES	INCUS
EVILS	FINES	GENUS	HEADS	IRONS
EXAMS	FINIS	GERMS	HEAPS	ITEMS
EXECS	FIRMS	GIFTS	HEARS	JACKS
EXITS	FIXES	GIRLS	HEELS	JADES
EXONS	FLAGS	GIVES	HEIRS	JAGGS
EXPOS	FLAPS	GLASS	HELPS	JAILS
EYERS	FLAWS	GLOSS	HERBS	JAKES
FACES	FLIES	GOALS	HIDES	JAMBS
FACTS	FLOSS	GOODS	HILLS	JANES
FADES	FLOWS	GRABS	HINTS	JANUS
FAILS	FOCUS	GRASS	HIVES	JAPES
FALLS	FOLDS	GRINS	HOLDS	JEANS
FANGS	FOLKS	GRITS	HOLES	JEEPS
FARES	FOODS	GROSS	HOMES	JEERS
FATES	FOOLS	GROWS	HOPES	JERKS
FEARS	FORMS	GUESS	HORNS	JESTS
FEATS	FUELS	HACKS	HOSTS	JESUS
FECES	FUMES	HADES	HOURS	JIBBS

JIBES	KEEKS	LANDS	LOSES	MASKS
JIFFS	KEELS	LASTS	LOTUS	MASTS
JILTS	KEENS	LAWKS	LOUIS	MATES
JINKS	KEEPS	LEADS	LOVES	MATHS
JIVES	KELLS	LEANS	LUNGS	MAULS
JOCKS	KERFS	LENDS	LURES	MAVIS
JOEYS	KHANS	LEXIS	MACES	MAXIS
JOHNS	KICKS	LIARS	MAGES	MAYOS
JOINS	KIKES	LIENS	MAGUS	MAZES
JOKES	KILLS	LIFTS	MAIDS	MEADS
JOLTS	KILNS	LIKES	MAILS	MEALS
JONES	KILOS	LIMBS	MAINS	MEANS
JOURS	KILTS	LINES	MAKES	MEATS
JOWLS	KINDS	LINKS	MALES	MEETS
JUKES	KINGS	LISTS	MALLS	MEMES
JUMPS	KINKS	LIVES	MALMS	MEMOS
JUNKS	KIPES	LOADS	MALTS	MENDS
JUSTS	KITES	LOANS	MAMAS	MENUS
KAILS	KNAPS	LOCKS	MANES	MEOWS
KAKAS	KNEES	LOCUS	MANIS	MERCS
KALES	KNITS	LOGOS	MANUS	MERES
KAMES	KNOTS	LOINS	MARCS	MESAS
KANAS	KNOWS	LONGS	MARES	METES
KARTS	KUDOS	LOOKS	MARKS	METTS
KECKS	LACKS	LOOMS	MARTS	MEWLS

MICAS	MOCKS	MUFFS	NEATS	NOOBS
MICKS	MODES	MULES	NECKS	NOOKS
MIDIS	MODUS	MULLS	NEEDS	NOONS
MIENS	MOILS	MUMPS	NEEMS	NORMS
MIFFS	MOJOS	MUONS	NEGUS	NOSES
MIKES	MOKES	MURUS	NEONS	NOTES
MILDS	MOLDS	MUSES	NERDS	NOUNS
MILES	MOLES	MUSKS	NERTS	NOVAS
MILKS	MOLTS	MUSOS	NESTS	NUDES
MILLS	MONES	MUSTS	NETTS	NUKES
MILOS	MONGS	MUTES	NEUMS	NULLS
MIMES	MONKS	MUTIS	NEVES	OASES
MINDS	MOODS	MYTHS	NEVUS	OASIS
MINES	MOONS	NABES	NEWES	OASTS
MINKS	MOORS	NAGAS	NEWTS	OATHS
MINTS	MOOTS	NAILS	NEXUS	OAVES
MINUS	MOPES	NAMES	NICKS	OBEYS
MISES	MORES	NANAS	NIDUS	OBITS
MISTS	MORNS	NARES	NINES	OBOES
MITES	MORTS	NARKS	NITES	ODORS
MITTS	MOSTS	NATES	NIXES	OGLES
MIXES	MOTES	NAVES	NODES	OGRES
MOANS	MOTHS	NAZES	NODUS	OKAYS
MOATS	MOVES	NAZIS	NOMES	OKRAS
MOBES	MUCUS	NEARS	NONES	OMENS

OMITS	PAPAS	PERVS	PLEBS	POPES
ONERS	PARKS	PESOS	PLIES	PORES
OOZES	PARTS	PESTS	PLOTS	PORNS
OPALS	PASTS	PHONS	PLOWS	PORTS
OPENS	PATES	PICKS	PLOYS	POSES
OPERS	PATHS	PICTS	PLUGS	POSTS
ORALS	PAWNS	PIERS	PLUMS	POUFS
ORRIS	PEAKS	PIETS	POCKS	POUTS
OUSTS	PEALS	PIKES	POEMS	POXES
OVALS	PEANS	PILES	POETS	PRADS
OVENS	PEARS	PILIS	POGOS	PRAMS
OVERS	PEATS	PILLS	POKES	PREDS
PACES	PECKS	PILUS	POLES	PRESS
PACKS	PEDIS	PIMPS	POLIS	PRIGS
PACTS	PEELS	PINES	POLLS	PROBS
PAGES	PEENS	PINGS	POLOS	PROFS
PAILS	PEEPS	PINKS	POMPS	PROMS
PAINS	PEERS	PINTS	PONDS	PRONS
PAIRS	PENES	PIONS	PONGS	PROPS
PALES	PENIS	PIOUS	POODS	PROSS
PALLS	PENTS	PIPES	POOFS	PROWS
PALMS	PEONS	PLANS	POOLS	PUBES
PANES	PERKS	PLATS	POONS	PUBIS
PANGS	PERPS	PLAYS	POOPS	PUCES
PANTS	PERQS	PLEAS	POOTS	PUCKS

PUKES	RAMPS	REPOS	RODES	RUSES
PULES	RAMUS	RESES	ROIDS	RUSKS
PULLS	RANDS	RESTS	ROKES	RUSTS
PULPS	RANIS	RIALS	ROLES	SACKS
PUMAS	RANKS	RICES	ROLLS	SADES
PUMPS	RANTS	RICKS	ROMPS	SAFES
PUNKS	RAPES	RIDES	ROODS	SAGAS
PUNTS	RASES	RIFFS	ROOFS	SAGES
PUPAS	RASPS	RIFTS	ROOKS	SAILS
PURIS	RATES	RILLS	ROOMS	SAKES
PURRS	RAVES	RIMES	ROOTS	SALES
PUTTS	READS	RINDS	ROPES	SALTS
PYRES	REALS	RINES	ROSES	SAMPS
PYXIS	REAMS	RINGS	ROTAS	SANDS
QUIPS	REARS	RINKS	ROTES	SARIS
QUITS	REBUS	RIOTS	ROTIS	SARKS
RACES	REDDS	RIPES	ROUTS	SATES
RACKS	REDOS	RISES	RUBES	SAVES
RAFTS	REEDS	RISKS	RUFFS	SCABS
RAGES	REEFS	RITES	RUINS	SCADS
RAIDS	REEKS	RIVES	RULES	SCAMS
RAILS	REELS	ROADS	RUMPS	SCANS
RAINS	REENS	ROARS	RUNES	SCARS
RAJAS	REINS	ROBES	RUNGS	SCOBS
RAKES	RENTS	ROCKS	RUNTS	SCOTS

SCOWS	SHAHS	SINES	SLIPS	SOCKS
SCUMS	SHAMS	SINGS	SLITS	SODAS
SEALS	SHAYS	SINKS	SLOBS	SOFAS
SEAMS	SHEDS	SINUS	SLOES	SOFTS
SEATS	SHIES	SIPES	SLOGS	SOILS
SECTS	SHINS	SIRES	SLOPS	SOKES
SEEDS	SHIPS	SISES	SLOTS	SOLES
SEEKS	SHITS	SITES	SLOWS	SOLOS
SEEMS	SHIVS	SITUS	SLUGS	SOLUS
SEEPS	SHOES	SIXES	SLUMS	SOMAS
SEERS	SHOPS	SIZES	SLURS	SONES
SEINS	SHOTS	SKATS	SLUTS	SONGS
SELFS	SHOWS	SKIDS	SMEWS	SOOKS
SELLS	SHULS	SKIES	SMUTS	SOPHS
SEMIS	SHUTS	SKILS	SNAGS	SORBS
SENDS	SIDES	SKINS	SNAPS	SORES
SENES	SIENS	SKIPS	SNIPS	SORTS
SENTS	SIGHS	SKITS	SNOBS	SORUS
SEPTS	SIGNS	SLABS	SNOTS	SOULS
SERES	SILES	SLAGS	SNOWS	SOUPS
SERFS	SILKS	SLAPS	SNUBS	SOURS
SETTS	SILLS	SLATS	SNUGS	SPAMS
SEXES	SILOS	SLEDS	SOAKS	SPANS
SHADS	SIMAS	SLEYS	SOAPS	SPARS
SHAGS	SIMPS	SLIMS	SOARS	SPATS

SPAWS	SUITS	TAKES	TEAMS	TIERS
SPECS	SULKS	TALCS	TEARS	TIFFS
SPIES	SULUS	TALES	TEATS	TILES
SPINS	SUMPS	TALKS	TECHS	TILLS
SPITS	SURAS	TALUS	TEEMS	TILTS
SPIVS	SURDS	TAMAS	TEENS	TIMES
SPOTS	SUSUS	TAMES	TELLS	TINES
SPURS	SWABS	TAMIS	TELOS	TINGS
STABS	SWAGS	TAMPS	TEMPS	TINKS
STAGS	SWANS	TANGS	TENDS	TINTS
STARS	SWAPS	TANKS	TENTS	TIRES
STATS	SWATS	TAPES	TERMS	TIROS
STAYS	SWAYS	TAPIS	TESTS	TOADS
STEMS	SWIGS	TARES	TEXAS	TOFUS
STEPS	SWIMS	TARNS	TEXTS	TOGAS
STEWS	SWISS	TARPS	THATS	TOILS
STIES	SWOPS	TARTS	THAWS	TOKES
STIRS	SWOTS	TASES	THEES	TOLES
STOPS	SYNCS	TASKS	THEWS	TOLLS
STUBS	TABES	TATHS	THINS	TOMBS
STUDS	TACHS	TATTS	THOUS	TOMES
STUMS	TACKS	TAXES	THUDS	TONES
SUCKS	TACOS	TAXIS	THUGS	TONGS
SUERS	TACTS	TEAKS	TICKS	TONUS
SUFIS	TAILS	TEALS	TIDES	TOOLS

TOONS	TRIPS	TYRES	WEEDS	YETTS
TOOTS	TRODS	TYROS	WHIMS	YOGAS
TOPOS	TROTS	UNCOS	WILDS	YOGIS
TORES	TROWS	UNITS	WILES	YOKES
TORTS	TRUES	URGES	WINDS	YOLKS
TORUS	TRUSS	USERS	WINGS	YONIS
TOTES	TSARS	VEINS	WIPES	YONKS
TOURS	TUBAS	VENUS	WOODS	YORKS
TOUTS	TUBES	VERBS	WORDS	YOURS
TOWNS	TUCKS	VIBES	WORKS	YOWLS
TRAMS	TUFAS	VICES	WRAPS	YUCKS
TRANS	TUFFS	VIEWS	XERUS	ZAXES
TRAPS	TUFTS	VINES	XYSTS	ZEALS
TRASS	TUMPS	VIRUS	YANKS	ZEROS
TRAYS	TUNAS	VLOGS	YAPPS	ZESTS
TREES	TUNES	WAGES	YARDS	ZINCS
TREKS	TURFS	WAITS	YARNS	ZINGS
TRESS	TURNS	WALES	YAWNS	ZONES
TRETS	TURPS	WALKS	YAWPS	ZONKS
TREWS	TUSKS	WALLS	YEARS	ZOOMS
TREYS	TWIGS	WANTS	YEGGS	ABAFT
TRIES	TWINS	WARES	YELLS	ABBAT
TRIGS	TWITS	WARNS	YELPS	ABBOT
TRIMS	TYPES	WAVES	YESES	ABORT
TRIOS	TYPOS	WEARS	YETIS	ABOUT

ABUTT	AUDIT	BRUNT	COUNT	DIGIT
ADAPT	AUGHT	BUILT	COURT	DIVOT
ADEPT	AVANT	BURNT	COVET	DONUT
ADMIT	AVAST	BURST	CRAFT	DOUBT
ADOPT	AVERT	CADET	CREAT	DRAFT
ADULT	AWAIT	CAPUT	CREPT	DRIFT
ADUST	BEAST	CARAT	CREST	DROIT
AFOOT	BEAUT	CARET	CROFT	DUCAT
AGENT	BEFIT	CHANT	CRUET	DUETT
AGIST	BEGET	CHART	CRUST	DUVET
AGLET	BEGOT	CHAST	CRYPT	DWELT
ALERT	BERET	CHEAT	CUBIT	EARNT
ALLOT	BESET	CHERT	CURET	EDICT
ALOFT	BIDET	CHEST	CURST	EDUCT
AMBIT	BIGHT	CIVET	DAUNT	EGEST
AMENT	BIGOT	CLAST	DAVIT	EGRET
AMRIT	BLAST	CLEAT	DEALT	EIGHT
ANENT	BLEAT	CLEFT	DEBIT	EJECT
ANGST	BLEST	CLIFT	DEBUT	ELECT
APART	BLOAT	CLOUT	DEGUT	EMMET
ARGOT	BLUNT	COAPT	DEIST	ENACT
ARHAT	BLURT	COAST	DELFT	EPACT
ASCOT	BOAST	COMET	DEMIT	ERECT
ASSET	BOOST	CONST	DEPOT	ERGOT
ATILT	BRUIT	COOPT	DICOT	ERUCT

ERUPT	FOUNT	HEIST	KNOUT	ONEST
EVENT	FRONT	HOIST	LEAPT	ONSET
EVERT	FROST	HURST	LEAST	ORBIT
EVICT	FRUIT	IDIOT	LEGIT	OUGHT
EXACT	GAMUT	INAPT	LICIT	OVERT
EXALT	GAUNT	INEPT	LIGHT	OWEST
EXERT	GHOST	INERT	LIMIT	OWLET
EXIST	GIANT	INGOT	MAIST	PAINT
EXPAT	GILET	INLET	MANAT	PEART
EXULT	GLINT	INPUT	MEANT	PETIT
FACET	GLOAT	INSET	MERIT	PICOT
FAINT	GRAFT	INUIT	MIDST	PILOT
FAULT	GRANT	ISLET	MIGHT	PINOT
FEAST	GREAT	JABOT	MOIST	PIPET
FEINT	GREET	JAUNT	MOTET	PIPIT
FEIST	GRIFT	JOINT	MOULT	PIVOT
FIGHT	GRIOT	JOIST	MOUNT	PLAIT
FILET	GROUT	JOUST	MULCT	PLANT
FIRST	GRUNT	JURAT	MUSET	PLATT
FLEET	GUEST	KAPUT	MUSIT	PLEAT
FLINT	GUILT	KAPUT	NIGHT	POINT
FLIRT	HABIT	KARAT	NONET	POSIT
FLOAT	HAULT	KARST	OCTET	POULT
FLOUT	HAUNT	KEMPT	ODIST	PREST
FOIST	HEART	KNELT	ONCET	PRINT

QANAT	SCENT	SNOOT	SWEET	UNAPT
QUEST	SCOOT	SNORT	SWEPT	UNCUT
QUIET	SCOUT	SNOUT	SWIFT	UNFIT
QUILT	SHAFT	SPELT	TACIT	UNLIT
REACT	SHART	SPENT	TAINT	UNMET
REBUT	SHEET	SPILT	TAPET	UNSET
RECIT	SHIFT	SPLAT	TAROT	UPSET
REFIT	SHIRT	SPLIT	TAUNT	VALET
REFUT	SHOAT	SPLOT	TEMPT	VAULT
REMIT	SHOOT	SPORT	TENET	VAUNT
REPOT	SHORT	SPOUT	THEFT	VISIT
RESET	SHOUT	SPRAT	TIGHT	VOMIT
RESIT	SHUNT	SPRIT	TINCT	WAIST
RIGHT	SIENT	SPURT	TOAST	WHEAT
RIVET	SIGHT	SQUAT	TRACT	WIGHT
ROAST	SKEET	START	TRAIT	WORST
ROBOT	SKINT	STENT	TRANT	WREST
ROOST	SKIRT	STILT	TRAPT	WRIST
ROUST	SLANT	STINT	TREAT	WURST
SABOT	SLEET	STOAT	TROUT	YACHT
SAINT	SLEPT	STOUT	TRUST	YEAST
SALAT	SMART	STRUT	TRYST	ZAKAT
SAULT	SMELT	STUNT	TWEET	ADIEU
SCANT	SMOLT	SWART	TWICT	BAYOU
SCATT	SNIFT	SWEAT	TWIST	BIJOU

CORNU	RENEW	DESEX	ABBEY	ATOPY
COYPU	SCREW	DETOX	ACIDY	AUNTY
HAIKU	SCROW	HELIX	AGONY	AZURY
HOKKU	SEROW	HYRAX	ALARY	BADLY
LADDU	SHREW	IMMIX	ALLAY	BAGGY
NOYAU	SINEW	IMPEX	ALLEY	BALDY
PAREU	SQUAW	INDEX	ALLOY	BALKY
PERDU	STRAW	INFIX	ALWAY	BALLY
POILU	STREW	LATEX	AMBRY	BALMY
SADHU	THREW	MIREX	AMITY	BANDY
SNAFU	THROW	MUREX	AMPLY	BARMY
TENDU	WIDOW	PHLOX	ANGRY	BATTY
AGLOW	YAKOW	RADIX	ANNOY	BAWDY
ALLOW	ADDAX	REDOX	ANOMY	BEADY
ARROW	ADMIX	REDUX	ANTSY	BEAKY
ASKEW	AFFIX	REFIX	ANURY	BEAMY
BEDEW	ANNEX	RELAX	APERY	BEEFY
BELOW	AUDAX	REMEX	APPLY	BELAY
BYLAW	BORAX	REMIX	APTLY	BELLY
CAHOW	BOTOX	SILEX	ARCHY	BENDY
ELBOW	CALIX	TELEX	ARRAY	BERRY
ENDOW	CALYX	UNBOX	ARTSY	BETTY
MACAW	CODEX	UNFIX	ASSAY	BEVVY
OXBOW	COMIX	UNSEX	ATAXY	BIDDY
PSHAW	CULEX	XEROX	ATOMY	BILBY

238

BILLY	BUSBY	CLARY	CUDDY	DERBY
BITSY	BUSHY	CLUEY	CULLY	DERPY
BITTY	BUSTY	COALY	CULTY	DIARY
BLOWY	BUTTY	COBBY	CUPPY	DICEY
BOBBY	BUZZY	COCKY	CURDY	DICKY
BOGEY	BYWAY	COMFY	CURLY	DICTY
BOGGY	CABBY	COMMY	CURRY	DIDDY
BONEY	CADDY	CONEY	CURVY	DILLY
BONNY	CAGEY	CONKY	CUSHY	DIMLY
BOOBY	CAKEY	COOKY	DADDY	DINGY
BOOMY	CALMY	COOLY	DAFFY	DINKY
BOOTY	CAMPY	COOTY	DAILY	DIPPY
BOOZY	CANDY	COPAY	DAIRY	DIRTY
BOSSY	CANNY	COPSY	DAISY	DISHY
BOTHY	CANTY	CORDY	DALLY	DITSY
BOTTY	CARNY	COREY	DANDY	DITTY
BRINY	CARRY	CORKY	DARBY	DITZY
BUDDY	CATTY	CORNY	DARKY	DIVVY
BUGGY	CHARY	COVEY	DEARY	DIZZY
BULKY	CHEWY	COYLY	DECAY	DOBBY
BULLY	CHIVY	CRAZY	DECOY	DODGY
BUMPY	CHOKY	CREPY	DECRY	DOGGY
BUNNY	CIGGY	CRONY	DEIFY	DOILY
BURLY	CISSY	CRUDY	DEITY	DOLLY
BURRY	CIVVY	CUBBY	DELAY	DOOLY

DOOMY	EMPTY	FLYBY	GIRLY	HARDY
DOOZY	ENEMY	FOAMY	GLORY	HARPY
DOPEY	ENJOY	FOGEY	GLUEY	HARRY
DORKY	ENSKY	FOGGY	GOBBY	HASTY
DOTTY	ENTRY	FOLLY	GODLY	HEADY
DOWDY	ENVOY	FORAY	GOLLY	HEAVY
DOWNY	EPOXY	FORTY	GOODY	HEFTY
DOWRY	ESSAY	FUGGY	GOOEY	HILLY
DRYLY	EVERY	FULLY	GOOFY	HINKY
DUCHY	FADDY	FUNKY	GRAVY	HIPPY
DUCKY	FAIRY	FUNNY	GRIMY	HISSY
DULLY	FANCY	FURRY	GULLY	HOARY
DUMMY	FANNY	FUSSY	GUMMY	HOBBY
DUMPY	FATLY	FUSTY	GUNGY	HOKEY
DUNNY	FATTY	FUZZY	GUNKY	HOLEY
DUPPY	FERRY	GABBY	GUSHY	HOLLY
DUSKY	FIERY	GAILY	GUSTY	HOMEY
DUSTY	FIFTY	GAMMY	GUTSY	HONEY
DYKEY	FILLY	GASSY	GUTTY	HOOEY
EARLY	FILMY	GAUDY	GYPSY	HOOKY
EBONY	FISHY	GAUZY	HACKY	HORNY
EDIFY	FIZZY	GAWKY	HAIRY	HORSY
ELEGY	FLAKY	GEEKY	HAMMY	HOTLY
EMBAY	FLOWY	GIDDY	HANDY	HOWDY
EMERY	FLUKY	GIMPY	HAPPY	HUBBY

HUFFY	JIGGY	LARKY	MANNY	MOANY
HULKY	JIMMY	LEAFY	MARDY	MOGGY
HUNKY	JIVEY	LEAKY	MARLY	MOLDY
HURLY	JOCKY	LEERY	MARRY	MOLLY
HURRY	JOKEY	LEFTY	MASHY	MOMMY
HUSKY	JOLLY	LIMEY	MASSY	MOMSY
HUSSY	JOLTY	LOAMY	MATEY	MONEY
ICILY	JOWLY	LOBBY	MATTY	MOODY
IMPLY	JUDGY	LOFTY	MEALY	MOONY
INLAY	JUICY	LOLLY	MEANY	MOORY
IRONY	JUMBY	LOOBY	MEATY	MOPEY
ITCHY	JUMPY	LOONY	MELTY	MOPPY
IVORY	JUNKY	LOOPY	MERCY	MORAY
JACKY	JUTTY	LORDY	MERRY	MOSEY
JAGGY	KELLY	LORRY	MESHY	MOSSY
JAMMY	KERRY	LOUSY	MESSY	MOTHY
JAZZY	KICKY	LOWLY	MIDDY	MOUSY
JELLY	KIDLY	LUCKY	MILKY	MUCKY
JEMMY	KINDY	LUMPY	MINCY	MUDDY
JENNY	KINKY	LUSTY	MINGY	MUGGY
JERKY	KISSY	MADLY	MINNY	MULEY
JERRY	KOOKY	MALTY	MINTY	MUMMY
JETTY	LAITY	MAMMY	MINXY	MUMSY
JEWRY	LANKY	MANGY	MISSY	MURKY
JIFFY	LARDY	MANLY	MISTY	MUSHY

MUSKY	NIFTY	PALMY	PETTY	POPPY
MUSSY	NIMBY	PALSY	PHONY	POPSY
MUSTY	NINNY	PANSY	PICCY	PORGY
MUZZY	NIPPY	PANTY	PICKY	PORKY
MYOPY	NOBBY	PAPPY	PIETY	PORNY
MYTHY	NOBLY	PARKY	PIGGY	POTTY
NAGGY	NODDY	PARRY	PIGMY	POUTY
NAILY	NOISY	PARTY	PILLY	PREXY
NANCY	NOOBY	PASTY	PINAY	PRICY
NANNY	NOOKY	PATSY	PINEY	PRIVY
NAPPY	NOSEY	PATTY	PINKY	PROSY
NARKY	NOUNY	PAWKY	PINNY	PROXY
NASTY	NOWAY	PEAKY	PIPPY	PUDGY
NATTY	NUBBY	PEARY	PISSY	PUFFY
NAVVY	NUTSY	PEATY	PITHY	PULLY
NEBBY	NUTTY	PEAVY	PLUMY	PULPY
NEDDY	ODDLY	PEGGY	PODGY	PUNKY
NEEDY	OLOGY	PENNY	POESY	PUNNY
NELLY	ONELY	PEONY	POGEY	PUNTY
NERDY	ONERY	PEPPY	POKEY	PUPPY
NERVY	ORACY	PERKY	POLLY	PURRY
NETTY	OVARY	PERRY	POMMY	PURSY
NEWLY	PACEY	PERVY	PONDY	PUSHY
NEWSY	PADDY	PESKY	PONGY	PUSSY
NIFFY	PALLY	PESTY	POOFY	PUTTY

PYGMY	RILEY	SAMEY	SIPPY	SPINY
QUAKY	RINDY	SAMMY	SISSY	SPLAY
QUERY	RISKY	SANDY	SIXTY	SPRAY
RAGGY	RITZY	SAPPY	SKYEY	SPUMY
RAINY	ROCKY	SARKY	SLATY	STAGY
RALLY	ROGUY	SASSY	SLIMY	STIMY
RANDY	ROILY	SATAY	SLYLY	STOGY
RANGY	ROLLY	SAUCY	SMOKY	STONY
RASHY	ROOFY	SAURY	SNAKY	STORY
RASPY	ROOKY	SAVOY	SNOWY	STRAY
RATTY	ROOMY	SAVVY	SOAPY	STUDY
READY	ROOTY	SCALY	SOBBY	STYMY
REDDY	ROWDY	SCARY	SODDY	SUCKY
REEDY	RUDDY	SEAMY	SOFTY	SUDSY
REEFY	RUGBY	SEEDY	SOGGY	SUETY
REEKY	RUMMY	SEITY	SONNY	SULKY
REIFY	RUNNY	SELLY	SOOKY	SULLY
REKEY	RUNTY	SEPOY	SOOTY	SUNNY
RELAY	RUSHY	SHADY	SOPHY	SURLY
RELLY	RUSTY	SHAKY	SOPPY	TABBY
REPAY	RUTTY	SHINY	SORRY	TACKY
REPLY	SADLY	SHOWY	SOUPY	TAFFY
RETRY	SAGGY	SHYLY	SPACY	TAGGY
RIBBY	SALLY	SILKY	SPICY	TALCY
RIDGY	SALTY	SILLY	SPIKY	TALKY

TALLY	TIPSY	WACKY	WORDY	ABUZZ
TAMMY	TITTY	WADDY	WORMY	ARROZ
TANGY	TIZZY	WARTY	WORRY	BLITZ
TANKY	TOADY	WASHY	WRYLY	CHEEZ
TANSY	TODAY	WASPY	XYZZY	FRITZ
TARDY	TODDY	WAVEY	YAKKY	FRIZZ
TARRY	TOPPY	WEARY	YAPPY	GLITZ
TARTY	TOSSY	WEDGY	YAWNY	HERTZ
TASTY	TOUSY	WEEDY	YIPPY	PZAZZ
TATTY	TOWNY	WEENY	YOLKY	SCUZZ
TAWNY	TRULY	WEEPY	YUCKY	SPAZZ
TEARY	TUBBY	WELLY	YUKKY	SPITZ
TECHY	TUFTY	WHINY	YUMMY	SWIZZ
TEDDY	TUMMY	WHITY	YUPPY	TOPAZ
TEENY	TUNNY	WIFEY	ZAPPY	WALTZ
TELLY	TURFY	WILLY	ZESTY	WHIZZ
TERRY	TUSKY	WIMPY	ZINCY	
TESTY	TWINY	WINDY	ZINGY	
THAWY	UNIFY	WISPY	ZINKY	
THEWY	UNITY	WITHY	ZIPPY	
THYMY	UNLAY	WITTY	ZITTY	
TICKY	UNSAY	WONKY	ZLOTY	
TILLY	USURY	WOODY	ZONKY	
TINNY	VASTY	WOOLY	ZOOMY	
TIPPY	VEINY	WOOZY	ZOOTY	

ALSO IN THE SERIES...

WORDLE ACTIVITY BOOK
Two Player Puzzle Game

- Detailed, easy to understand **instructions** on how to play and score;
- 200 **game boards** with alphabet, hints and game scores;
- 500 **commonly used five letter words**, to use for help or inspiration;
- **Templates** for keeping the scores and writing down the secret words.

BIG BOOK OF WORDLE
Over 500 Puzzles

- Over **500 Wordle puzzles;**
- **Three difficulty levels**: Easy, Medium and Expert;
- Helpful **hints and solutions** to every puzzle, at the end of the book;
- **Train your brain** and **increase your vocabulary**, while spending **time away from the screens**.

RELEASE TIME: JULY 2022

PICK UP YOUR COPIES ON AMAZON!

Dear Reader,

I hope you enjoyed playing "Wordle" with this reference book.

The idea for this book came about when I realised that people search for a reference book online, but the offerings can be improved.

Have you found this book helpful?

I would love to know, so please share your feedback with me on Amazon. I look forward to reading every review!

Kind Regards,
Adelaide Reed

Made in United States
Orlando, FL
04 October 2022

23008449R00135